American Indian Autobiography

American Indian Autobiography

H. DAVID BRUMBLE III

UNIVERSITY OF CALIFORNIA PRESS
Berkeley   Los Angeles   London

Some portions of this book have appeared elsewhere. Chapter 4 is a revision of "*Sun Chief* and Gregorio's 'Life Story': Social Scientists and American Indian Autobiographers," *The Journal of American Studies*, vol. 20 (1986); chapter 5 appeared as "Sam Blowsnake's Confessions: *Crashing Thunder* and the History of American Indian Autobiography," *The Canadian Review of American Studies*, vol. 16 (1985), reprinted in Brian Swann and Arnold Krupat, *Recovering the Word: Essays on Native American Literature* (Berkeley, Los Angeles, London: Univ. of California Press, 1987); chapter 6 is a revision of "The Two Albert Hensley Autobiographies and the History of American Indian Autobiography," *American Quarterly*, vol. 37 (1985); some pages of chapters 1 and 8 appeared in "*The Way to Rainy Mountain* and the History of American Indian Autobiography," in Kenneth Roemer, *Approaches to Teaching N. Scott Momaday's The Way to Rainy Mountain* (New York: MLA Press, 1988); some entries in the Bibliography first appeared in "A Supplement to *An Annotated Bibliography of American Indian and Eskimo Autobiographies*," *Western American Literature*, vol. 17 (1982). I am grateful to all my editors for their help and their kind permission to reprint this material.

University of California Press
Berkeley and Los Angeles, California

University of California Press, Ltd.
London, England

Library of Congress Cataloging-in-Publication Data

Brumble, H. David
American Indian autobiography.

Bibliography: p.
Includes index.
1. Indians of North America—Biography—History and
criticism.   2. Autobiography.   I. Title.
E89.5B78   1988   970.004'97   88–14425
ISBN 0–520–06245–0 (alk. paper)

Printed in the United States of America

1 2 3 4 5 6 7 8 9

For David,
my son and friend

Contents

Preface

Names are always a problem in dealing with American Indians. In the first place, should we refer to Indians or Native Americans or Amerindians? I have chosen "Indians"; this is how most of the Indians I have met refer to themselves. The names of tribes differ, too, and more widely. "Navaho" was the generally accepted spelling during the 1940s; now the preferred spelling is "Navajo." Sometimes Arikaras were called Rees. The northern Athabaskan language that used to be known as Kutchin is now Gwich'in. George Horse Capture (1980:11) says that his own people ought really to be called White Clay People, *A'aninin*, not Gros Ventres. Sarah Winnemucca's people had the name Paiute (Winnemucca prefers the spelling, Piute) bestowed on them by whites, along with such other names as Pi-Utah and Paviosto. They knew themselves as the Numa, the people. But they were also known as Snake Indians in Oregon—and they were unrelated to the Southern Paiutes, who spoke a very different language (Canfield, 1983:3). And the Ojibwas are the Chippewas; Eskimos are the Inuit. In general, I try—except, of course, when quoting—to use the tribal name that is now most widely accepted.

And then there is the Babel of names for individuals. The confusion is partly a result of the widespread Indian custom of taking several names during a lifetime; partly it is because many Indians had and have Anglo names as well as Indian-language names. Hakadah became Ohiyesa; Ohiyesa became Charles Alexander Eastman. Many Indians are best known by the English translation of their names: Black Elk, Two Leggings, White Bull, Yellow Wolf. Others are better known by their names in the original language. In this case we often have widely varied spellings because one anthropologist's phoneticization may differ from another's attempt. Sometimes even a single anthropologist may try different versions of the same name. One of Edward Sapir's informant-autobiographers is Tom Saayaachapis in some publications; elsewhere he is Tom Sayach'apis or just Tom. One must also remember that many of the Indian autobiographers are known to us only by their pseudonyms—and sometimes more than one pseudonym. Alexander and Dorothea Leighton, for example, took down a life story from a Navajo hand-trembler. In one book he is *Gregorio, the Hand-Trembler;* in another he is Jaime. In general, rather than attempt to work out what might have been the "real" name, I have used that name which is given most prominence in the autobiography. With this warning, then, the Indian autobiographies are listed in a separate bibliography, each under the Indian's name. The listings include the autobiographers' birth dates and tribal affiliations.

I have limited myself here, as I did in *An Annotated Bibliography of American Indian and Eskimo Autobiographies* (1981), to Native American autobiography north of the Mexican border. I have stopped at the border because a stopping point was necessary; there are Latin American Indian autobiographies that are well worth reading. Elizabeth Burgos-Debray, for example, has recently edited the autobiography of Rigoberta Menchu, a Mayan Indian: *I . . . Rigoberta Menchu* (1984). Menchu tells the altogether harrowing story of Mayan life in Guatemala, where the burghers, government, police, and army still—in the 1980s—feel free to rape, torture, rob, and kill Indians. Menchu's autobiography needs to be read in America, where there is far too little awareness of the savage treatment of Indians in more than one Latin American country.

I should also, perhaps, explain why this book about American Indian autobiography does not devote a chapter to *Black Elk Speaks*, by far the best-known American Indian autobiography. It simply seems to me that Black Elk has been unusually well served by his commentators. Robert Sayre's (1971) early discussion of the book is still very helpful. Sally McClusky (1972) was the first literary scholar to draw attention to the problem of editor-narrator relationships. In 1979 Michael Castro provided the first extended comparison of *Black Elk Speaks* and the Neihardt–Black Elk transcripts; Castro later expanded this treatment and published it as a chapter in his *Interpreting the Indian: Twentieth-Century Poets and the Native American* (1983). Raymond DeMallie's *The Sixth Grandfather* (1984) finally made available a carefully edited and fully annotated edition of the Black Elk transcripts. Paul Olson (1982) has written a learned commentary on the book's symbolic systems. Olson's work along with Clyde Holler's (1984) provides much of what we need to know to understand Black Elk's sense of ritual. When to these studies could be added those of Arnold Krupat (1985:107–136),

Kenneth Lincoln (1983:82–121), Thomas Overholt (1978), Julian Rice (1985), William Nichols (1983), and Carol Holly (1979), it did seem best to concentrate on some other autobiographies, which are less well understood.

I think that one of the best conventions of scholarly writing is the paragraph of thanks. This paragraph is certainly the most pleasant in the writing—except for the uncomfortable sense that someone might be forgotten. I think that my greatest debt is to Arnold Krupat. Arnold and I have been discussing these autobiographies with one another for seven years now. These discussions have been a real pleasure to me and a steady source of guidance. I could not have gone far with this book had I not had the help of a number of anthropologists. I am grateful, then, to Jack Roberts, William Sturtevant, William S. Simmons, Peter Nabokov, David Aberle, Rosamond Spicer, Elizabeth Colson, and Evon Vogt. Dr. Alexander Leighton has also helped me to understand the ways of those who studied the ways of the Indians. N. Scott Momaday allowed me to interview him; I am as grateful for his cordiality as for what he taught me. Paul Olson, my teacher, has helped in many ways, but most by suggesting that I look more carefully at the Indians' own contribution to the collaborative autobiographies. Michael West has helped me a great deal with this book, reading and rereading these chapters over a period of several years. Roy Harvey Pearce and Robert Sayre read the manuscript; I am grateful for their astute suggestions. Bill Pfisterer, Ronald Scollon, and Ray Barnhardt took the time to explain to me their work with recent Alaskan autobiographies. Roger Acord helped me with the history of the social sciences. I am grateful to Hazel Hertzberg and to my colleagues Bob Gale, Walt Evert, and Ed Marrs for their careful reading of my manuscript. Mary Briscoe has helped me with her wide awareness of American autobiography. She has also helped me in all the ways that a good department chair can. I am grateful for all that my editor, Susan Gallick, has done for my book. My research was substantially aided by grants from the Vira I. Heinz Fund and the University of Pittsburgh's Central Research Development Fund. Families usually come last in these paragraphs of thanks, not usually, I think, because their contribution is least. My own family, Harriet, Lizzie, and David, have provided understanding that is more basic than the kind which can be acknowledged in a footnote.

Introduction

I first read *Sun Chief,* the autobiography of Don Talayesva, some ten years ago. The book begins in this way:

> When we were within our mother's womb, we happened to hurt her. She has told me how she went to a medicine man in her pain. He worked on her, felt her breasts and belly, and told her that we were twins. She was surprised and afraid. She said, "but I only want one baby." "Then I will put them together," replied the doctor. He took some corn meal outside the door and sprinkled it to the sun. Then he spun some black and white threads into a string, and tied it around my mother's left wrist. It is a powerful way to unite babies. We twins began, likewise, to twist ourselves into one child. My mother also helped to bring us together by her strong wish for only one baby. (25)

This passage startled me, and it still has that power now, after many readings. There is something wonderful here. Talayesva seems so confident that the world is as the Hopis know it to be. He speaks so confidently about this time when he was twins. He speaks with such confidence about this "powerful way to unite babies." It shakes my sense that the world is as *I* know it to be. The Indian autobiographies are full of such moments. Red Crow, a Blood Indian, proudly recalls his part in the massacre and scalping of nearly a hundred Cree women. Afterward, he assures us, there was "great jubilation" (131). But he does not seem to us to be an evil man. Isaac Tens, a Gitksan shaman, tells about the decline of his powers after he began using church prayers in his healing. Crows Heart, a Mandan, tells about his self-torture in the eagle-trapping—his "suffering for the birds." Leather thongs were tied to skewers, the skewers pushed through the flesh on his chest, the thongs tied to stakes pounded into the ground at the edge of a bluff, and then Crows Heart dropped himself off the bluff. This was to prepare him, spiritually, to sit motionless in a pit, beneath a tethered, struggling rabbit, waiting for an eagle to dive a thousand feet to strike the rabbit. Then, just as the eagle hit, Crows Heart

1

would lunge for the legs, to pull the screaming bird down into the darkness of the pit.

Such stories are at once easy to understand and difficult to comprehend. Don Talayesva, for another example, tells us a good deal about his mother. She was his "dear mother" (346). "The greatest sorrow of my life," he says, "was the death of my mother. It was harder to bear than the loss of my children or my long sickness and years of impotence" (325). Here we feel at home with Talayesva; these are feelings we can sympathize with quite immediately. We begin to bask in the warmth of a comfortable sense of shared humanity. Then we read that she died when "an evil person shot rattlesnake poison" into a small cut she had sustained. This "caused her foot to swell badly to her knee." This is a bit outside our practical experience; but witches—or Two-Hearts, as Talayesva calls them—are at least a part of our imaginative experience. Then we read:

> My mother's system also was full of bad thoughts, and I think these were harder to overcome than the poison. While she was sick, I asked her about myself: "Have I scolded you thoughtlessly, or filled your heart with sorrow in any other way?"

Here we must remember what we learned in Introductory Anthropology about the importance of harmonious social relations among the pueblo tribes. My Pittsburgh neighbor might ask his dying mother such a question in order to win her forgiveness in her last moments, in order that he might make his peace, settle his accounts, as it were. Talayesva's motivations are quite different. He wants to be certain that he is himself not responsible, literally, for her illness.

> "No," she replied. "You talked crossly when you were a child, but you never scold me now . . . but your sisters talk back to me badly, and this has made me very sad. I think that I had better die and go take care of our dear ones." Dropping my head in grief, I begged her to put aside such evil thoughts. . . . "I have thought of passing away for a long time," she replied. That remark made me angry, for it showed that she was killing herself. But I tried not to scold her.

Now we are even farther from what we expect of a Pittsburgh deathbed scene. Talayesva restrains himself, controls his anger, not out of a sentimental regard for her feelings in this dark hour, but rather because to scold her would be to make himself partly responsible, literally, for her death. And he is angry with her precisely because he feels that she is, by her bad thoughts, willfully killing herself.

> When she admitted that she was seeing dead relatives in her dreams and talking to them, I gave up hope and wondered if she was a Two-Heart herself. (325)

We have been carried quite away from our own experience and habits of mind. We can comprehend that a loving son might be angry that his mother is not "trying hard enough" to live. But here the loving son is looking down at his dying mother with the dawning assumption that she may well be a witch. This woman he had loved dearly he now considers to have been quite possibly a Two-Heart. He is full of fond memories of his mother: "My mother was the smartest and kindest person I ever knew and spent her life keeping us well and happy." And at the same time he wonders if she was a Two-Heart. She raised doubts even after her death:

> I kept seeing my mother at night in my dreams and greatly feared she would touch me, for then I would have to go with her. It seemed that she would not stay with our dear ones, but kept returning. So I finally took some sacred corn meal and pahos out to the northwest ledge, sacrificed, scolded her and told her to leave us alone and go back and stay where she belonged. And I wondered again if she were a Two-Heart. (326–27)

This is the very stuff of culture shock. In reading the autobiographies especially of those Indians who grew up in tribes without literacy, we often feel what Vincent Crapanzano has called "epistemological vertigo" (1980). Just as we seem to be establishing a comfortable relationship with one of these autobiographers, we are brought up sharp; we are forced again to wonder how high may be the walls between cultures, and how deep are sunk the foundations of those walls, how close to human bedrock?

The autobiographies also offer subtler surprises: the preliterate autobiographies especially put before us conceptions of the self that are foreign to modern, individualistic societies. In fact, the early autobiographies may be regarded as a kind of testing ground for the ideas of scholars who have tried to explain what individuality means and how conceptions of the self and identity differ from one culture to another.[1] White Bull, born in 1850, defines himself by describing his deeds and his family and the history of the Teton Sioux. Two Leggings tells about his life in such a way as to win him glory. We cannot doubt his fiercely individual pride in his accomplishment, and yet it must be clear to us how completely he was shaped by his tribe's expectations of a man and a warrior. In the phrase of the anthropologist Clifford Geertz (1984:129), it is Two Leggings's sense of his social roles which make up for him the "substance of the self." And it must be clear to us how little awareness Two Leggings has of other selves he might have been. Talayesva, prompted (as we shall see in chapter 4) by his sociologist amanuensis, struggles with two distinct ideas of the self: a traditional, tribal, Hopi sense of self and a modern, Western, individualistic sense of self.

Karl Weintraub (1975, 1978) and Georg Misch (1951) have written their histories of Western autobiography as the history of the rise of the idea of the individual in the West. Weintraub takes us back to the Greeks; Misch takes us back four millennia, to the Egyptians. A thousand years before Moses persuaded Pharaoh to let his people go, anxious Egyptian functionaries were arranging that their tombs might be graven with the records of their deeds and honors. And yet there is a sense in which Indian autobiography can take us even farther back in time. On the one hand, for the Egyptians, and the other ancients who wrote down their deeds, we cannot penetrate past the boundaries of literacy. We may *assume* that there was oral autobiographical storytelling among the ancients, but such traditions as there may have been are lost to all but inference. On the other hand, we may read hundreds of oral autobiographical tales taken down from American Indians.[2]

The historian of American Indian autobiography, then, can go back beyond the first glimmering of literacy. Thanks to the many anthropologists, poets, psychiatrists, and amateur historians who collected life stories from Indians, we can read autobiographical narratives by nonliterate Indians. It would never have occurred to these people to sit down and tell the story of their lives whole. And yet we may read their "autobiographies."

The history of American Indian autobiography, then, takes us back to further reaches of human time than Misch could achieve. And Indian autobiographers can be as modern as those Weintraub discusses late in his book:

> The growth of an individuality is possible only in this coexistence with a world. An individuality forms itself only by the active process of making the continuous encounter with the world an individualized experience. Only by continuously accepting and forming one's world can one be forming oneself. (1978:376)

Weintraub here has Goethe in mind, but he could as well have been writing about N. Scott Momaday or Leslie Silko, both of whom are highly educated, university-affiliated novelists and autobiographers. Momaday's whole conception of autobiography has precisely to do with the forming and the reforming of the self, with the ways in which our own experiences become stories, images, and so are added to all the other stories and images the mind stores up for the use of the imagination in its continuing creation of the self. Like Weintraub's history of Western autobiography, this historical treatment of Indian autobiography, then, ends with autobiographers who are thoroughly modern in their sense of what it means to tell the story of one's life. They intend in their autobiographies to explain just how it was that they came to be as they are, just *who* they are, and how they stand in relation to the forces that shaped them.

The history of American Indian autobiography, as we shall see, parallels the history of Western autobiography in many ways (Brumble, 1981:3–5). The history of Western autobiography spans some 4500 years, but with Indian autobiography there is a marvelous compression of time. N. Scott Momaday is just two generations removed from nonliterate storytellers. Two Leggings died just a few years before Momaday was born. Momaday was sixteen when Black Elk died. Several of the autobiographers grew up in traditional, tribal ways but were abruptly transplanted into the white world. And so we have autobiographies written by men like Charles Eastman, Luther Standing Bear, and Joseph Griffis, men who were trained for war and for the hunt but who were snatched away to the white man's schools, where they learned to write, and so came

to write autobiographies. We have an autobiography by Sarah Winnemucca, who was born in a brush nobee, who was taught to gather
roots and pine nuts in season. She managed to learn to read and to
write at a time when this was something of a miracle among the
Paiutes. And then there is White Bull, who drew entirely traditional
pictographs of his coups and then wrote down those same coups in
the Sioux syllabary that he had learned the year after his surrender.
As we study American Indian autobiography, then, we see again
and again taking place in single lifetime developments that took
millennia in the history of Western autobiography.

But if there are rewards in this literature, there are problems as
well. Some of the best-known Indian autobiographies, for example,
are by such Indians as Black Hawk, Plenty-coups, Geronimo, and
Black Elk. These are compelling narratives, narratives in which
much that is commonplace for the teller is exotic for the reader.
These are the narratives that make us feel "epistemological vertigo"
most keenly, that make us feel as though we are seeing the world
from a cultural perspective far from our own. This is a heady
feeling—so heady that we are inclined to forget all that the Anglo
editor had to do to make it seem that way. Indeed, it may well be
taken as evidence of these editors' skills that even scholars have
written about these autobiographies in ways which assume that the
narratives were published, crisply pure, just as they flowed from
the mouths of the Indians.

Some, like William F. Smith (1975), write as though the editors
of Indian autobiographies played no role at all. Smith compares
the structure of S. M. Barrett's edition of Geronimo's autobiography and Kinney Griffith's *The First Hundred Years of Nino Cochise*,
for example, without even mentioning that both are as-told-to autobiographies. In spite of what he might have learned from Sally
McClusky (1972) about Neihardt's contributions to *Black Elk
Speaks*, Smith still writes as though the "structure" of the book were
all Black Elk's own, as though Black Elk told Neihardt where Part I
ended and where Part II was to begin. And Jeffrey Hanson, in his
introduction to the welcome reprint of *Waheenee: An Indian Girl's
Story, Told by Herself to Gilbert L. Wilson*, has not a word to say about
the composition of the book, and so does nothing to correct the
erroneous impression left by its subtitle.

The case of Lévi-Strauss and the sorcerer is also instructive.
Midway through his *Structural Anthropology* (1963) Lévi-Strauss in-

cludes a chapter on "The Sorcerer and His Magic." The chapter is important, for in it Lévi-Strauss will demonstrate that even in such a seemingly irrational endeavor as sorcery the primitive mind is essentially like the mind of modern man. As he puts it, "we must see magical behavior as the response to a situation that is revealed to the mind through emotional manifestations, but whose essence is intellectual" (1963:184). Along his way to this conclusion Lévi-Strauss's most important evidence is "a fragment of the autobiography of a Kwakiutl Indian . . . obtained by Franz Boas" (1963: 175). Lévi-Strauss summarizes the details of this fascinating narrative as they relate to his argument. Quesalid, the Kwakiutl sorcerer, at first was skeptical of the sorcerers. "Driven by curiosity about their tricks and by the desire to expose them, he began to associate with the shamans until one of them offered to make him a member of their group" (175). Quesalid seized upon this opportunity, and so was introduced to all the shamans' trade secrets: pantomime, the simulation of fainting, the sacred songs, the technique for inducing vomiting, auscultation, obstetrics, how to fake the sucking out of foreign bodies from patients, and the use of spies ("dreamers") who would listen to private conversations and then convey to the shamans bits of information that shamans could then use to pretend prescience.

Lévi-Strauss continues his summary: "His worst suspicions confirmed, Quesalid wanted to continue his inquiry. But he was no longer free" (175). For his apprenticeship began to be known among the people, and soon he was being sought out for cures. These he accomplished, but "he did not lose his critical faculties. He interpreted his success in psychological terms" (176). He was successful, now quoting Quesalid himself, "because he [the sick person] believed strongly in his dream about me" (13). Later Quesalid visited another tribe, where he saw another shaman at work. Quoting Lévi-Strauss again:

> And here our hero vacillates for the first time. Though he had few illusions about his own technique, he has now found one which is more false, more mystifying, and more dishonest than his own. For he at least gives his clients something. . . . Quesalid's method gets results, while the other is futile. Thus our hero grapples with a problem which perhaps has its parallel in the development of modern science. Two systems which we know to be inadequate present (with respect to each other) a differential validity. (176)

Lévi-Strauss resumes his summary: after a number of other experiences, Quesalid's "original attitude has changed considerably" (178). Finally, Quesalid comes to take pride in his own achievements, and he carries on his craft conscientiously. "*The radical negativism of the free thinker,*" says Lévi-Strauss, "*has given way to more moderate feelings*" (178).[3] And thus Lévi-Strauss is able to conclude that the "essence" of sorcery is "intellectual."

This is a compelling argument, but, alas, Quesalid's narrative is not quite what Lévi-Strauss would have us believe. In the first place, Lévi-Strauss makes use of Quesalid's "fragment" without acknowledging just how far the autobiographer was from being a typical, nonliterate Kwakiutl. Although his mother tongue was Kwakiutl, although he was raised among the Kwakiutl, Quesalid's father was Scots, his mother Tlingit. More importantly, Boas had worked with Quesalid for years: Boas taught him to write Kwakiutl and worked with him extensively to refine his ear and his orthography. Boas trained him sufficiently well in field methods that Quesalid himself was able to collect a great mass of culture data from other Kwakiutl informants; Boas even had Quesalid help him in setting up Kwakiutl museum displays. As we shall see in the case of the Hopi Don Talayesva, this kind of training could affect Indian informants profoundly (chapter 4).

To claim, then, as Lévi-Strauss does without qualification, that this narrative puts the primitive mind pulsing there before us upon the page, is at best naive. Indeed, it is disingenuous of Lévi-Strauss to refer to this man at all by his Indian name, for when, in another book, he wants to cite Quesalid as an authority on Kwakiutl kinship systems, he refers to him by his Anglo name, George Hunt. And he stresses how carefully Hunt was trained by Boas: "A model investigator, Hunt collected through the years thousands of pages of information about Kwakiutl culture" (1982:166). Indeed, as Lévi-Strauss notes, some of Hunt's work had forced Boas to reformulate his theories about Kwakiutl kinship.

The second problem is apparent when Lévi-Strauss refers to Hunt's narrative as a "fragment of autobiography." It is a fragment only if we come to the narrative with the specifications of Western autobiography in mind. In fact, we may recognize the narrative as a peculiarly elongated example of a Shaman's Life, a narrative of How-I-Came-by-My-Shamanic-Powers (see chapter 1). We may be fairly certain that Hunt's narrative differs from the typical, oral Shaman's Life: first, because of Hunt's literacy, and, second, because of Hunt's ethnographic training. Boas trained Hunt to provide detail in cornucopic abundance.

Lévi-Strauss could easily have compared Hunt's narrative with a more nearly typical oral Shaman's Life, for Boas published Hunt's narrative alongside another Shaman's Life. It seems that Hunt collected an autobiographical narrative from his Kwakiutl teacher, Fool, the man who taught him the ways of the shamans. It begins in this way:

> I am . . . a hunter of all kinds of animals, I always go paddling about, for this is what I desire, seals. . . . I always get many hair seals; and so I am never poor. I was the principal one who does not believe in the shamans, when they speak about taking out sickness from sick people, and when they say that they see the souls of men; and formerly I did not believe in shamans, for I used to tell them aloud that they were lying when they were curing the sick; for I would sit down among them when they were beating time for the shamans when curing those who were very sick, and therefore I was really hated by the shamans. . . . I just wish to talk about this first. (41)

The first thing to notice about this narrative is that it begins as Hunt's does, with what Lévi-Strauss would call "the radical negativism of the free thinker." But now that we have seen it twice, now that we have seen that the apprentice begins his story in the same way as does his teacher, we may be skeptical that this has much to do with free thinking. It has more the look of a convention, an assertion of how profound has been the effect of the helping spirit upon the shaman, for he began as "the principal one who does not believe in the shamans." We should remember that Indians west of the Rockies typically did not tell stories about *seeking* powers; their stories have the powers coming to them unbidden. Fool is like Paul, stricken upon the road to Damascus. His story is the more remarkable—and we must assume his powers the larger—for his having persecuted the shamans as Paul persecuted the Christians. When we consider how often Hunt would have heard Fool's story, we can hardly be surprised that he began his narrative in the same way.

Those who wish to read Fool's narrative in its entirety will find it in the Appendix, below; but it is not difficult to see why Lévi-

Strauss chose to base his argument on Hunt's narrative rather than on Fool's more "authentically primitive" narrative. One does not sense in Fool's narrative anything like the "radical negativism of the free thinker." Disinterested readers would be little likely to assume that the "essence" of Fool's sorcery is "intellectual." Lévi-Strauss finds in Hunt more free thinking, more that is "intellectual," on the one hand because he fails to recognize one of the conventions of an oral autobiographical form, and on the other hand because of Hunt's Boasian education. It does not occur to Lévi-Strauss that Hunt/Quesalid's narrative may be influenced by preliterate autobiographical traditions; it does not occur to him that Hunt may be creating a fiction of the self—indeed, even a fiction of the self that was in some ways conventional among the Kwakiutl. For Lévi-Strauss the text is transparent, available to interpretation according to the assumptions we bring to Western autobiography.

Boas instructed Quesalid/Hunt in Western habits of mind. Geronimo, Black Elk, Plenty-coups, and Black Hawk speak to us without benefit of such education, but they do speak to us through their editors—after many hours of storytelling and questions, all slowed by interpreters. Usually the editor/amanuensis asks the kinds of questions that his literate, Western audience will expect autobiography to answer. Usually he will try to elicit stories about his subject's childhood, because his literate, Western audience expects autobiography to treat of "the formative years." And, of course, topics that ought to be taboo for the autobiographer are almost by definition going to be of great interest to the ethnographer and his Anglo audience. Then there are the hours of transcription and the editing: the ordering, cutting, and sometimes the rephrasing and the additions.

In all of this the collectors, editors, and amanuenses labored to allow us to come to know real, living, individual Indians. As Clyde Kluckhohn put it in his 1945 survey of the use of life histories in anthropology, the anthropologist very often found himself near the completion of his study of the Navajos, all of his data collected, all the kinship terminology carefully transcribed, all the subsistence patterns noted, all the rituals described and amply illustrated— with still a nagging sense that, somehow, the essence of this fascinating culture has eluded the charts, descriptions, and tables. And so he collects an autobiography. Paul Radin, for example, wrote in the introduction to his edition of Sam Blowsnake's *Autobiography of a Winnebago Indian* that such

> personal reminiscences and impressions, inadequate as they are, are likely to throw more light on the workings of the mind and emotions of primitive man than any amount of speculation from a sophisticated ethnologist. (2)

The anthropologists did collect hundreds and hundreds of auto-biographical narratives, many more than have been published. In general, the editors of these narratives want their readers to see with a Kiowa's eyes what it meant to be a Kiowa in the last years before the reservation period. *Two Leggings* is designed to allow us to see through the eyes of one Crow warrior what it meant to be a Crow warrior. Gilbert Wilson wanted to provide us with a sense of what farming meant to one Hidatsa farmer; and so he gives us Maxidiwiac's gentle, deeply moving remembrances of her life in her fields and the songs she sang over her plants. Boas published Hunt's and Fool's narratives so that we might understand Kwakiutl shamanism.[4] In the anthropological idiom, they were hoping to put before us, immediately, the emic perspective.

And yet these books must distort the selves they portray. There is a sense, of course, in which every autobiography is a fiction of the self;[5] no autobiography is a "true" representation of the self in any absolute sense. But self-written autobiography is at least the subject's *own* fiction, the subject's own conception of the self, and so it must always be authentic in this sense at least. With the as-told-to autobiographies of the nonliterate Indians, on the other hand, it is the Anglo editor, who decides, finally, what is to be the shape of his subject's "autobiography." Editors routinely cut repetitious passages, for example. Repetition grates upon the modern ear. Repetition grates upon the modern ear. But in many tribes repetition was a rhetorical feature in oral narrative. For another example, the editors almost always order their material chronologically, even though this sometimes distorts the sense of time implicit in some narratives.

It behooves us, then, to read the as-told-to narratives with considerable humility. Such autobiographies usually are, in an important sense, bicultural documents, texts in which the assumptions of Indian autobiographers *and* Anglo editors are at work. All of this considerably complicates Roy Pascal's claim that autobiographies in general "offer an unparalleled insight into the consciousness of other men. Even if what they tell us is not true, or only partly true, it is always evidence of their personality" (1960:1). The as-told-to Indian autobiographies are evidence of *two* personalities and two cultures. In such narratives we often find two different sets of narrative assumptions at work, two different sets of aims, and two very different senses of what it means to tell the story of one's life.

Worries about editor/Indian relationships have led some scholars to erase the distinction between autobiography and biography in this literature. "The 'as-told-to' autobiographies," writes Lynn O'Brien, "could with equal justice be called biographies, since the interests of the recorder often direct the narrative." And so she chose "to ignore the distinction between biography and autobiography."[6] But O'Brien is giving up, perhaps, a bit too easily. We can certainly recognize degrees of editorial interference, for example. And in the case of many of these narratives, it is possible to learn enough about the nature of the collaboration, enough about the Indian's motivations and culture, enough about the Anglo collaborator's motivations and culture, to allow some pretty good guesses about where the Indian leaves off and the Anglo begins. Arnold Krupat (1985:54–74), for example, has demonstrated this in the case of Barrett's work with Geronimo and John B. Patterson's with Black Hawk. Raymond DeMallie's meticulous edition of the Black Elk transcripts allows us to make rather fine distinctions between Neihardt and Black Elk.[7] Some of this kind of work will be attempted in these chapters as well.

It might be well to remember, too, that those who are interested in autobiography as a genre are much less concerned with "truth" than they were thirty years ago. James Olney has described this change:

> Prior to the refocusing from *bios* to *autos* there had been a rather naive threefold assumption about the writing of autobiography: first that the *bios* of autobiography could only signify "the course of a lifetime" . . . ; second that the autobiographer could narrate his life in a manner at least approaching the objective historical account . . . ; and third, that there was nothing problematical about the *autos*, no agonizing questions of identity, self-definition, or self-deception—at least none the reader need attend to—and therefore the fact that the individual was himself

> narrating the story of himself had no troubling philosophical, psychological, or historical implications. (1980:20)

Insofar as the study of autobiography is at all theoretically interesting, insofar as we look to autobiography for something other than facts about a life or facts about a historical period, it is not the study of *lives* but the study of *autobiography* (e.g., Pascal, 1960:2). It is the study of the *ways* in which human beings have *told* about their lives. It might make sense for the historian or the anthropologist to look to these narratives for the odd bit of data that might not be available elsewhere. But for those whose interest is literary or psychological, it makes no sense to blur the distinction between Indian autobiography and biography.

Of course, some would argue that many of the narratives that this history will discuss are not literature at all. There are three sources of autobiographical narratives by Maxidiwiac, for example. The most interesting of these has come down to us with the ungainly title *Agriculture of the Hidatsa Culture: An Indian Interpretation.* This was published in *Minnesota Studies in the Social Sciences.* Eagle-ribs's accounts of his war deeds were published as illustrative quotations in Pliny Earle Goddard's "Notes on the Sun Dance of the Sarsi," published in the *Anthropological Papers of the American Museum of Natural History.* A. L. Kroeber published "Black-Wolf's Narrative" as a part of his *Ethnology of the Gros Ventre.* He did so not because he was interested in autobiography, but rather to describe Gros Ventre warfare from the Indian's perspective.

Gretchen Bataille and Kathleen Sands, in their book (1984) on American Indian women's autobiography, try to distinguish systematically between such "ethnographic" autobiographies and what they call "literary" Indian autobiographies. In their view *Papago Woman,* the autobiography of Maria Chona, is literary, for example, while "The Autobiography of a Fox Indian Woman," elicited and edited by Truman Michelson, is not. In general, Bataille and Sands make their classifications according to a checklist of the features of literary autobiographies. The *literary* autobiographies, they assert, will "often employ literary techniques such as dialogue, exploration of inner emotions and responses to events, a first-person omniscient viewpoint, latitude in handling time and sequence of events, and an awareness of audience." The literary autobiographies will also "use informal, conversational language for stylistic effect." Another hallmark of the literary autobiography is that the narrator will have been "chosen because of narrative skill as well as valuable information [sic]." And the literary autobiography will be "longer" and "more comprehensive" than the ethnographic (1984:11).

There are many problems here. We are left to wonder just what a "first-person omniscient viewpoint" might be. Did Henry Adams claim to know it all? I remember that Franklin was farsighted, but not, I think, omniscient. But more importantly, the whole checklist begs the question. In those autobiographies that Bataille and Sands recognize as literary, informal, conversational language will be used "for stylistic effect." But how are we to distinguish such language from the informal, conversational language that is *not* used for stylistic effect? Will it be less literary? This is circular. And those narrators who produced literary autobiographies will have been chosen because they evinced "narrative skill"? This is, one must assume, very like "*literary* skill." Again, circular.

There is as well a more fundamental problem: can we really decide what is literature and what is not with reference to a checklist at all? Would Bataille and Sands really read through a newly published autobiography, find that the book evinced very little "latitude in handling time and sequence of events," and so decide that, no, much as they liked it, the book just could not be literature? And how are we to decide when a narrative is long enough—100 pages? 150?—or comprehensive enough to count as literature? How much could Franklin have left out of his autobiography before Bataille and Sands would feel compelled to strike it from their list? Such a checklist seems usable only so long as it is left vague. As soon as we push for specifics, each criterion becomes implausible.[8]

Another problem with their checklist is that it assumes a Western aesthetic and Western literary conventions. This might make some sense if Bataille and Sands were trying to describe the differences between oral and literate autobiography, but they are not. Many of the autobiographies that they discuss as "literary" were delivered orally. One must assume, then, that for Bataille and Sands "literary" is simply an honorific term. One of the first things that strikes us as we begin reading (relatively) unedited autobiographical tales by nonliterate Indians is that the tales tend to be brief. Surely we would be surprised were this not the case. We would not expect Pretty-shield to hold her audience there around the campfire, night after night, until she had delivered the oral equivalent of 400 pages of connected autobiography. And yet Bataille and Sands insist that a *literary* autobiography must be long—and "comprehensive." This rules out by definition virtually *all* the oral autobiographical narratives that have been published in anything like their original form. Again, remember that Bataille and Sands are trying to distinguish between ethnographic and literary autobiography, not oral and literate. One wonders how Bataille and Sands would categorize the two volumes of Left Handed's autobiography. Walter and Ruth Dyk edited this material into two volumes. The second volume—579 pages dense with ethnographic and psychological detail—covers just three years in Left Handed's life.

Bataille and Sands are typical, then, of those who want their Indian literature to come to them in Western clothing. As we have already seen in the case of Lévi-Strauss, such habits of mind lead to misunderstanding. Bataille and Sands provide many instances of just such misunderstanding. They assume, for example, that if Michelson had collected the Fox woman's story "when [she] was older we might have expected to see a turning point in her life or a climactic moment" (39). In fact, this is precisely what we should *not* expect from an autobiographer in a preliterate culture. As I hope to demonstrate, the preliterate Indians were like the ancient Egyptians, Greeks, and Romans in conceiving of their lives as the sum total of their adult deeds. Bataille and Sands are thinking not of the preliterate Fox Indians, but rather of what is characteristic of modern autobiography.[9] We do find turning points and climactic moments in the autobiographies of Rousseau, Adams, Franklin, and St. Augustine. When Eagle-ribs and White Bull tell tales of their war deeds, we do not find turning points; the stories do not work in connected fashion toward a climactic moment.[10]

This assumption that the early Indian autobiographies may be understood in the terms appropriate to discussions of modern Western autobiography accounts for much of the difficulty some critics have in keeping Indians and editors separate. At one point, for example, Bataille and Sands quote from Gilbert Wilson's preface to *Agriculture of the Hidatsa Indians*, the Maxidiwiac narratives: "The writer claims no credit beyond arranging the material and putting the interpreter's Indian-English into proper idiom." Then, just eight lines later, they say that Maxidiwiac's "account is appropriately literary, for she begins with the Hidatsa creation myth" (43). But, of course, it was not Maxidiwiac who began with the myth. Wilson decided what to keep and what to cut. And Wilson arranged the material. The editors of life-history materials almost always arrange things in chronological order (whatever may have been the sense of time implicit in the autobiographical tales themselves), and so what could come before the creation myth? We can have no idea at what point in his work with Maxidiwiac he collected this myth, nor can we know whether she told the myth spontaneously or in response to a request from Wilson. To speak, then, of *Maxidiwiac* beginning her narrative in a certain way *at all*—let alone in an "appropriately literary" way—is to make a modern autobiographer of this woman who worked her fields with a bone hoe.

This is a tendency difficult to overcome. Even when, like Bataille and Sands, we know better, we do tend to forget the editors, the collectors.[11] And we begin to read these narratives as though our own literary conventions were sufficient to see us through. I can offer an instructive—albeit embarrassing—example from my own experience. My systematic study of American Indian autobiography began with N. Scott Momaday. I had read *Black Elk Speaks*, that wonderful book, and *Sun Chief*. Then I came across Momaday's *Way to Rainy Mountain*. I was intrigued by the way he told about his life—a two-hundred-word story on one page, an even briefer story on the next, snippets of James Mooney's (1979 [1898]) work on the Kiowas scattered here and there, a bit of Kiowa history on this page, a bit of family history on the next. I decided that I wanted to find out why he wrote in this way, and so I decided to read all the published autobiographies by other Indians.

I found that reading the Indian autobiographies was not a task for a three-day weekend. Eventually, I had read more than six hundred of these narratives; but long before this I was reading them for their own sake—quite apart from my interest in Momaday.

But eventually I did return to Momaday; I thought that I had worked up a pretty fair sense of why Momaday wrote as he did. I reasoned that, since Momaday had, after all, established the Native American Studies Program at Stanford, he must have read a wide range of the Indian autobiographies.[12] I was convinced that I could explain Momaday's autobiographical method in terms of the influence of the earlier, published Indian autobiographies.

Then I had a talk with Momaday. I found that I was right and I was wrong. I was right in assuming that reading Indian autobiographies had prepared me to understand Momaday. I was wrong in assuming that Momaday had read them. This came to me as a comic revelation. I realized in that moment how book-bound I had been; I realized how much more vital oral traditions could be than I had given them credit for. The autobiographical narratives of Black Hawk, Geronimo, White Bull, Crows Heart, and Maxidiwiac had helped me to understand Momaday but not at all because Momaday had read their narratives; rather, all of them had been participants in closely related oral traditions.

In the pages that follow, then, I try to shed light upon this wonderfully diverse material by suggesting relationships between the published autobiographies and oral autobiographical traditions. This approach has led me to define autobiography broadly. For the purposes of this study, autobiography is first-person narrative that seriously purports to describe the narrator's life or episodes in that life. I am including, then, as-told-to narratives as well as self-written narratives, and brief as well as book-length narratives.[13] To confine ourselves to written autobiography—if I may be allowed a useful redundancy—would encourage us in a false sense of just how the literate Indian autobiographers came to write as they did.

Of course, many of these narratives became as-told-to autobiographies rather than biographies simply because of an editor's decision to cast his material in one form rather than another. But, again, this should not lead us to ignore the distinction between biography and autobiography. Point of view and form are essential. Even the most heavily edited autobiography at least pretends to be told from the Indian's point of view and in the Indian's own way. Biography makes no such generic promise. Gae Whitney Canfield's (1983) fine biography of Sarah Winnemucca offers an interesting case in point. Canfield's book stresses connections, relationships between one "stage" of Winnemucca's life and another. An early chapter entitled "Growing up Proud" helps us to understand just how it was that Winnemucca could have grown up to accomplish so much with so little formal education. There is a "Turning Point" chapter, a chapter on "Disillusionment." All this makes eminently good sense of the wide range of evidence that Canfield was able to collect. But Canfield's point of view is not Winnemucca's. As I will argue in chapter 2, Winnemucca herself did not conceive of her life in terms of "stages" and "turning points." Her own account of her life is much more episodic than Canfield's. And these differences are important, I will argue, for they seem to tell us something about differences between the Indian's traditional conception of the self and modern, individualistic conceptions of the self.

The present study will return to such problems again and again. I have tried to keep oral traditions and tribal habits of mind to the fore in the pages that follow. I have selected for discussion autobiographies that seem most insistently to suggest something about what is involved in moving from the tribal to the modern, individualistic world—or autobiographies that demonstrate some of the problems that face editors who try to preserve oral or tribal qualities in the narratives they edit. It is important, then, that we work to understand how the Indians' own narrative traditions may have influenced the shape of particular narratives even as they moved through the hands of editors and publishers. Little of this kind of work has been done,[14] mainly, I think, because so little is known about the patterns and traditions of preliterate, first-person storytelling.

Perhaps this situation has contributed to the striking lack of scientific analysis of these narratives, so many of which were taken down by social scientists. This must be owing at least in part to the problematic nature of the published texts, embodying as they do the conflicting motivations and autobiographical assumptions of both the Indians and their Anglo collaborators. Responsible analysis, then, must largely wait upon descriptions of the assumptions and narrative conventions native to both the Indians and their editors. I hope that this book will serve as encouragement and aid to scholars in analyzing particular autobiographical narratives in the light of particular tribal and historical contexts.

This brings up a final point and a warning about the limitations of the present study. My growing awareness of the importance of oral traditions has led me to revise my idea of this book. I worked for some years on what I imagined was a history of American Indian autobiography, but I did, finally, realize that one would have to know a good deal more than I do about individual tribes and languages and the peculiarities of particular tribal oral traditions in order to write anything like a real history of Indian autobiography. What I offer here, then, is no more than an essay toward such a history. But I am convinced that this book is headed in a fruitful direction. I am convinced that we must learn what we can about the Indians *and* the editors in order to understand the early, oral autobiographical narratives; and I am convinced that we need to understand the early, oral autobiographical narratives in order fully to appreciate the autobiographies of the later, literate Indians.

1
PRELITERATE TRADITIONS OF AMERICAN INDIAN AUTOBIOGRAPHY

The work of literary scholars on the ways in which editors have shaped Indian autobiographies has not been universally appreciated. The first such studies, for example, focussed on Neihardt's role in the making of *Black Elk Speaks*. This work readily granted that Neihardt managed to convey the spirit of Black Elk's concerns. But Sally McClusky (1972), Michael Castro (1979, 1983), and Raymond DeMallie (1984) pointed to some important differences as well. It seems, for instance, that Black Elk did not consider himself to be quite the tragic figure we find in *Black Elk Speaks*. And now we know that the oft-quoted passage at the end of the book about the death of a people's dream is Neihardt's own invention— what Black Elk "would have said if he had been able," as Neihardt put it late in his life (in McClusky, 1972:238).

As early as 1979 Vine Deloria expressed concern about the effects of such "debates . . . on the question of Neihardt's literary intrusions into Black Elk's system of beliefs." Deloria goes on to conclude that it does not matter "if we are talking with Black Elk or John Neihardt." It is easy to understand Deloria's concern; he is speaking as a *believer*, as one for whom Black Elk's words "now bid fair to become the canon or at least the theological core of a North American Indian theological canon" (1979:xiv). To speak with specificity of Neihardt's contribution to *Black Elk Speaks* might seem to diminish what is Indian in the book.

One can imagine that the work of the scholars might well be misunderstood; there is some danger that, just as these fascinating narratives have begun to reach a wide audience, just as they are beginning to appear as required reading in a wide range of college courses, they may be dismissed as something other than "authentic." And as some of the best known of the Indian autobiographies are shown to reflect the concerns of Anglo poets, historians, and anthropologists, Indians might well fear that the narratives seem to become less a part of an Apache or Navajo or Lakota heritage— more like artifacts, really, of the dominant culture.

It is important, then, to begin this historical study by concentrating on the Indians' own contribution to these autobiographies. For long before they knew anything of the written word, the Indians were delivering themselves of a wide variety of oral, autobiographical narratives. They told stories about their personal experiences quite without the aid and encouragement of Anglo amanuenses. These early Indians did not, of course, compose such autobiographies as Rousseau, Franklin, Henry Adams, Gertrude Stein, and other moderns have taught us to expect. For the most part the oral autobiographical narratives were brief and episodic. And none tells the story of a whole life, really. But if we look closely at all that has been published, we can still discern certain preliterate autobiographical traditions at work.

A historical understanding of American Indian autobiography, then, requires first what is essentially archeological spade work. And so I have dug through the published autobiographical narratives. I am aware that there are certain philological problems inherent in such an enterprise. We are, we must remember, working with translations, with sometimes heavily edited, published versions of what were originally oral narratives and interview responses. I should say, then, that in the case of the present chapter, I am making use only of narratives published by editors whose methods, as I have been able to determine them, seem to warrant at least such rough spade work as I propose here.[1] In general I have tried to look past the overall structure of the narratives, because in the book-length narratives this is largely the editor's invention. I have tried to look past the overall structure to the anecdotes, tales, and episodes that are much more likely to retain the shape (if not the phrasing) of the original telling.

Close attention to the whole range of these narratives does reveal six fairly distinct kinds of preliterate autobiographical narratives. These might be called, (1) the coup tales, (2) the less formal and usually more detailed tales of warfare and hunting, (3) the self-examinations, (4) the self-vindications, (5) the educational narratives, and (6) the tales of the acquisition of powers.

In describing these as "traditions," I am not claiming that in all tribes the same six kinds of autobiographical tales were told in the same ways. Neither am I claiming, nor, I hope, falling into the trap of assuming, that Indians were ever and always the same[2]—that if we can understand "The Indian" we will be able to understand all we need to know about Ojibwas, Kwakiutls, Apaches, Cherokees, and Black Elk, White Bull, Maxidiwiac, Albert Yava, Don Talayesva, Mountain Wolf Woman, and Belle Herbert. But one can, for example, talk meaningfully about the Plains Sun Dance while recognizing that there were important variations from tribe to tribe, that the Sun Dance was in no tribe exactly like the Sun Dance in another. It is useful to talk about *the* Peyote Cult, as long as we remember that it differed from tribe to tribe and from one period to another. By the same token, close attention to the autobiographical literature reveals that there is common ground sufficient to allow us to speak of oral autobiographical traditions among the preliterate American Indians. And an awareness of these traditions will allow us to recognize something that is ancient even in the autobiographies of such very literate moderns as N. Scott Momaday and Leslie Silko. Let us begin with the coup tales.

THE COUP TALES

To "count coup" was, literally, to strike a blow, coming from the French for "blow," a term the Indians took over from the old French trappers and traders. In a wide range of tribes, an Indian could best win honor by striking an enemy. Other feats of bravery could also be counted as coups: shooting the enemy, stealing their horses, and scalping.[3] But none of these was thought to require so much bravery as the actual striking of an enemy. Among such tribes as the Cheyenne and the Pawnee, warriors would sometimes try to rush up and strike the enemy before even attempting to kill him, so highly was the coup prized.[4] Sometimes the intent of the blow was to kill, sometimes only to humiliate. Honor could even be won by being among the first to strike a dead enemy.

In many tribes warriors were expected to advertise their coups. This was usually done orally, but sometimes the coups were acted out as well, and sometimes they were blazoned forth in pictographs (see chapter 2 for a discussion of White Bull's pictographic auto-biography). Fortunately, a fair number of these coup tales have been preserved; but we must look for them in out-of-the-way places. The anthropologist Pliny Earle Goddard, for example, included three tales by Eagle-ribs in his monograph on the Sarsi Sun Dance (1919*a*). Goddard tells us that he published these tales just as Eagle-ribs dictated them (through an interpreter) "probably in the form in which he was accustomed to recite them in the Sun Dance lodge." Here follow two of the three. The speaker was perhaps the most honored Sarsi warrior of his day:[5]

> The two tribes, Blackfoot and Sarsi, went to fight the Cree who had built and were occupying a fort. During the fight a Cree was seen lying (dead). Then I with a Blackfoot old man caught hold of the body. I tore one side of his scalp and stabbed him in the back many times, while I was stabbing him with a knife the Cree were shooting at me but they did not hit me. On this account I am called a chief.

> When I was over there, there were camps in two places. Three of us were going along in advance. I saw them coming toward us. We came back just as they were finishing putting up the lodges. I called to them: "they are coming toward us." Notwithstanding this we hurried with the setting up of a tipi and charged them. A Cree man threw his wife on a horse, but while his horse was running young men came up to her and killed her. My brothers and I killed her husband. I caught the man's scalp just as he fell and tore off one side of it. I stabbed him in the back with a knife only twice. This we did at that time. (281)

To encounter such tales here upon the printed page is to miss a good deal. Robert Jefferson, who heard Plains-Cree coup tales on a number of occasions, gives us some sense of the color and dash of these performances when the audience was large and willing. In the course of one Sun Dance, for example,

> a number of select warriors, practically naked, with bodies smeared all over with white mud, picked out in red with signs of their brave deeds, file into the arena, singing and dancing. They "dance to somebody for somebody," and their aim is to enhearten the dancers. After a while they stop dancing and one or the other tells the story of some successful raid. His oration will run as follows:—

"We were camped at such and such a place. From there a war party went out. I was one. We numbered so many. . . . Suddenly we felt the enemy. We sent out scouts. They found a large camp. . . . We brought away twenty horses. I cut loose one tied to the door of a lodge. Three days we fled. They never overtook us."

A tap or two on the drum at each sentence and a loud and long rattle at the end, show the appreciation of the audience. . . .

These accounts are usually greeted with deafening applause of drum beats. (In Goddard, 1919*b*:309)

Jefferson also witnessed acted performances of coup tales among the Cree:

The story is perhaps acted in dumb-show, if Indians of another tribe, Stoney, for example, are in camp. It is astonishing how the untutored actor can convey the required impression to the spectator. But, at least some slight knowledge of the sign language of the Plains Indians is necessary to a complete understanding of the performance. (In Goddard, 1919*b*:309)

Often, however, the dramatizations had nothing to do with crossing language barriers. Among the Sisseton Sioux, for example, the warriors who were entrusted to cut down the sacred pole for the Sun Dance lodge would tell *and act out* their coups, each before taking his blow with the ax (Skinner, 1919:383–384). Sometimes the warriors had their wives come forward and assist them in acting out their coups. (We must hope that they were as skilled in pulling their punches as they were in pantomime.)

On other occasions the delivery would be much more straightforward. But however they were delivered, the coup tales were spare. In this, Eagle-ribs's are typical of Plains coup tales. They were spare because they functioned, as it were, as the warrior's *curriculum vitae*. These tales were not primarily entertainments. Strictly speaking, a warrior could recite as coups only those feats that his tribe recognized and graded as coups. In Homer, Thirsites and Paris are archers, and their deeds are contemptible when compared with the glory Achilles and the rest win in hand-to-hand combat. And so it was, too, among the Plains Indians: in general, the grading honored close contact with the enemy. Among the Cheyenne, for example, the order was: (1) hitting with the coup stick, (2) the capture of a shield, (3) the capture of a gun, and (4) the taking of a scalp. The

Omaha also recognized a four-point scale: (1) hitting with the coup stick, (2) killing the enemy, (3) scalping, and (4) decapitating the enemy. The Ponca added the theft of horses, and they distinguished between counting coup on an unwounded enemy (the most honorable), counting coup on a wounded enemy, and counting coup on a dead enemy (M. W. Smith, 1938:428).

In the Plains tribes all of this was carefully monitored. George Bird Grinnell, who knew the Plains tribes intimately, gives us a sense of how this could work among the Pawnee. Upon a day in 1867, it seems, a band of Pawnees was pursuing six Sioux. A warrior named Baptiste wounded a Sioux with an arrow:

> Then there was a race between Baptiste and the Pawnee next behind him, to see which should count coup on the fallen man. Baptiste . . . reached him first, but just as he got to him, and was leaning over from his horse, to strike the dead man, the animal shied at the body, swerving to one side, and he failed to touch it. The horse ridden by the other Pawnee ran right over the Sioux, and his rider leaned down and touched him.

A difficult case. It was decided as follows:

> Baptiste claimed the coup . . . on the ground that he had exposed himself to all the danger, and would have hit the man if his horse had not swerved as it did from the body; but the Pawnees would not allow it, and all gave the credit of the coup to the other boy, because he actually touched the enemy. (Grinnell, 1960:247–248)

Precautions were taken to discourage fraudulent claims.[6] Warriors seldom claimed a coup without proof, either by a witness or in the form of a scalp or other war trophy. And on important occasions at least one witness would be by to corroborate what was being told. These habits of mind persisted even well into the reservation period. William Wildschut, for example, began taking down Two Leggings's life story in 1918. But still the old Crow warrior often had a friend, Bull Does Not Fall Down, in attendance, "verifying incidents" (*Two Leggings:* xiii).[7] And when Lucullus McWhorter came to take down Yellow Wolf's stories of his war deeds, he was surprised, he says,

> to see Yellow Wolf and interpreter Hart walking up from the river, accompanied by Two Moons, Roaring Eagle, and Chief David Wil-

liams. . . . These men came and sat through each day's session, mostly in silence, but there was an occasional short conference held in their own language.

Only later, McWhorter says, did he discover that "it was customary to have witnesses to what was said." These witnesses "should they detect error . . . were privileged to make corrections" (*Yellow Wolf*, 34).[8] And in times of peace, hostile tribes might meet in friendly fashion. During these meetings coup tales were often told, and so they could be checked against the memory of the sometime enemy.[9]

The coup tales, then, were the means by which a warrior established his place in his society. Kiowa warriors, for example, strove to rise up a scale of four fairly distinct ranks.[10] And warriors rose not only by doing deeds of bravery; it was necessary that these deeds be known. Christian notions of modesty and humility simply did not apply; the warrior had to publicize his deeds as soon and as often as possible. Unless his deeds were on the lips of all, he could not hope to attain the highest rank, to become the warrior whom ten other Kiowas might follow out upon the warpath (Mishkin, 1940:40).

As Eagle-ribs stands in the Sun Dance enclosure, then, he tells his coup tales: I have done this; I have done this; in the following difficult circumstances, I have done this. The tales establish and confirm who he is, what is his worth, his rank among the Sarsi. His coup tales recall the oldest autobiographical writings known to man, the inscriptions on some of the ancient Egyptian tombs, inscriptions that Herbert Butterfield has described as being "like a fantastic expansion of the driest part of an entry in *Who's Who*" (1981:49). Here, for example, is an excerpt from the inscription on the tomb of Ameni, from about 2400 B.C.:

I followed my Lord when he sailed to the South to overthrow his enemies in the four corners of Nubia. I sailed to the South as a son of a duke, as a bearer of the royal seal, as a captain to the troops of Nome of Mehetch. . . . I set the frontier of Egypt further southwards, I brought back offerings, and the praise of me reached the skies. . . . [And again] I sailed to the South to fetch gold ore for . . . Kheperkara . . . the ever living. . . . I passed [many] years as the governor of Mehetch Nome. All the works (*i.e.* the forced labor) due to the palace were performed under my direction. . . . (In Budge, 1914:135–136)

When literacy is added to Plains Indian habits of mind, the autobiographical results can be wonderfully like Ameni's list of accomplishments. Sword, an Oglala, knew no English, but he had learned to write in the Sioux syllabary. He began his autobiography but, sadly, died before he completed it. The following is an excerpt:

> I became a . . . Shaman . . . and conducted all the ceremonies of the Lakota, even the Sun Dance, which is the greatest ceremony of the Oglala. I danced the Sun Dance to become a Shaman and because of the scars on my chest no Oglala will deny my word. I was a . . . medicineman . . . and belonged to the Matopi (Bears, a cult or society of medicinemen) and the Bears have all the ceremonies of other medicinemen and much more. I was a . . . leader of war parties . . . and have fought according to Lakota customs against the enemy, both Indians and white people, so I know all the customs of war that the Oglala practiced. I was *Wakiconze* (civil magistrate) and thus know all the customs of the Oglala.

Ameni's and Sword's "autobiographies" and other ancient *res gestae* are like Eagle-ribs's coup tales because the narratives have much the same purpose. They are lists of accomplishments, each designed not to entertain, but to impress, to win regard. None of these *res gestae* provides many details. Such details as are provided serve mainly to distinguish *this* feat from other essentially similar feats that we have heard other warriors recount or that we may have read upon the lintel of some other anxious functionary's tomb. Eagle-ribs tells us, for example, that the Crees had built a fort. This might, of course, add to the danger Eagle-ribs faced in counting his coup, but it also, and perhaps most importantly, locates this particular fight in the remembrance of his audience. The calendar histories, which many of the Plains tribes kept, worked in essentially the same way: one image would be drawn to recall and to fix in time the events of a whole year.[11] Again, we must remember that for many Plains tribes there were clearly defined grades of war honors. Once a warrior has said enough to make it clear to which grade a certain deed belongs, it is time to move on to the next coup. Clearly, Ameni and Eagle-ribs aim to impress not by the careful, subtle, colorful delineation of their deeds, but rather by making clear what degree of prestige ought to be attached to each deed and by the sheer length of the list of deeds.

The dead Ameni needs to impress the living with his greatness in order to win from them the libations and the offerings of food upon which the dead depend—the "pathetic dependence of the dead upon the living" (Butterfield, 1981:48) that was at the heart of ancient Egyptian culture. Eagle-ribs, of course, hoped to win regard while he lived for many different purposes, on many different occasions. I have already mentioned that a warrior might recite his coups in order to win for himself a following of warriors. Eagle-ribs recalls that certain of his exploits won him the title of chief; he might have said that certain of his exploits *and* his constant recounting thereof won him this title. Warriors might also tell their coup tales in competitions between tribal societies, bouts in which warriors strove to outdo their rivals by telling coup tales and exercising generosity on a heroic scale (Llewellyn and Hoebel, 1967 [1941]:187).

Coup tales could even settle legal disputes, as once when a BIA official tried to settle a property dispute between two old Comanches, only to find the matter settled immediately when one of the Comanches told his coup tales and dared his rival claimant to match them (Hoebel, 1940). And the tales could be used to taunt the enemy. There are accounts, for example, of enemy war parties arrayed for battle, sending out individual warriors to parade in front of the enemy, telling their coup tales (Denig, 1928:550). And since the rankings of various military feats were recognized in some measure across tribal boundaries (M. W. Smith, 1951:349), a warrior's own coup tales could even function to determine the worth of his own defeat. That is, the honor to be won by killing, wounding, or humiliating a given warrior was in some measure proportional to the honors that warrior had listed in his coup tales.

This catalog of occasions could be greatly extended. Among the Cheyenne alone there were more than a hundred ritual situations that invited the ceremonial telling of coup tales (Hoebel, 1978 [1960]:75). But, finally, to see coup tales at work in a particular, richly depicted social context let us turn to DeMallie's edition of the complete Neihardt–Black Elk transcripts, the material Neihardt edited into *Black Elk Speaks*. When we understand the conventions and customs associated with the telling of the coup tales, for example, we see immediately why it was necessary for Black Elk to speak with Neihardt in the company of other Oglalas. Black Elk was making large claims about the greatness of the visions he had received and the deeds he had performed. In formal circumstances, a Plains Indian would seldom make such claims without proof. Standing Bear and Holy Black Tail Deer and the others, then, act as witnesses, to validate what Black Elk has to say. And their own right to participate in the important ceremony in which Neihardt was adopted as Black Elk's son is established by their telling their coup tales—just as Eagle-ribs's recitation of his coups established his right to his role in the Sun Dance. Here, for example, is one of Holy Black Tail Deer's coup tales:

> [I was] about twelve years old at that time, and there was a fight between the Crows and the Sioux, and they had quite a skirmish. The Sioux were camped, and the Crows were upon them before they knew it. I was out looking for horses. There was a blind man in camp, and I went and rescued him from among the bullets. The people said about this: "We knew you were going to do it." (In DeMallie, 1984:34–35)

Thus did Holy Black Tail Deer fix himself in the minds of his fellow Sioux. This is who he *is*.

INFORMAL AUTOBIOGRAPHICAL TALES

On other, less formal occasions, Holy Black Tail Deer, Eagle-ribs, and the rest felt free to be more expansive. At such times these same coup tales could be expanded to become entertainment and also to become a part of the detailed oral historical record. One sees immediately the difference between these informal tales and the coup tales. Here, for example, is the opening of Standing Bear's story of the rubbing out of Custer:

> That morning when we got up, most of the women went out to dig turnips and my uncles were out hunting. My grandmother who was very old and feeble, my uncle and I all stayed in the tipi. . . . My grandmother began frying some meat on the ashes of the fire. Then she fed us all. As we were eating, my uncle said: "After you are through eating you had better go and get the horses, because something might happen all at once, we never can tell" . . . Before I had finished eating there seemed to be quite a lot of excitement outside. Then I heard a crier announce that the chargers were coming and there were two men who went out to look for horses and one of them got killed. (184)

His own part in the battle is set against this same richly drawn backdrop throughout. He tells about the choking dust at the height of the battle, and about the spectacle at the end: "When we killed the last man, we could hear the women coming over and it was just a sight with men and horses mixed up together—horses on top of men and men on top of horses" (187). Virtually none of this detail would have appeared in Standing Bear's coup-tale version of the Custer fight.

Many of these autobiographical stories have been published. Indeed, one of the richest veins of oral Indian storytelling had to do with war and the hunt. And there are many warmly remembered accounts as well of the settings for such storytelling sessions. Alice Fletcher has written an account of an evening spent with her Omaha friends, where stories are traded back and forth. One young man's story about a frog reminds Wa-ja-pa of a time when he was hunting along the Loup River. He had killed several elk and was butchering them, when he saw a large gray wolf approaching the meat:

> "Taking my gun, I levelled it at him, and shot. He was a fine fellow, and, as he fell, I determined to have his skin at once. It was the work of a few moments to flay him. As I threw his skin to one side, the legs of the wolf began to twitch, and the blood to trickle. In a moment the wolf was on his feet, and walking off without his skin.
>
> "I have never believed in dreams, or the wonderful animals they tell about; but when I saw that wolf walking away, I felt uncomfortable, but I made up my mind to shoot again. I did so, and he fell, and walked no more." (In Clements, 1986:160)

When Wa-ja-pa finishes his story, his friend Badger corroborates it, and this reminds another man of a similar story he had heard, this time with a Buffalo playing Lazarus.

Grinnell has described a similar session among the Cheyenne:

> Some of the stories were short, others were long, sometimes told in great detail, and even in sections. A short story might be told, and when it was finished the narrator stopped, and, after a pause, said, "I will tie another one to it." Then there was a long pause; the pipe was perhaps lighted and smoked, and a little conversation had; then the story teller began again and told another section of the tale, ending as before. . . . At formal gatherings a man might tell a story and when it

was finished might say: "The story is ended. Can anyone tie another to it?" Another man might then relate one, ending with the same words, and so stories might be told all about the lodge. (Grinnell, 1962 [1926], xxiii–xxiv)

James Willard Schultz (see chapter 3), who remembers such evenings even more warmly than Grinnell, has published many Indian autobiographical tales. Such autobiographical stories are certainly the most accessible of the many kinds of early Indian literature that have come down to us in published form. Doubtless there are subtleties we miss as we make do with printed translations of what were oral performances;[12] doubtless nuances escape us because we are not intimately familiar with the assumptions of Crow horse raiders, Zuni deer hunters, and Cheyenne warriors. But what is at the heart of these stories crosses cultural boundaries with ease. It is not surprising that so many of these stories were first published for children. (There are other reasons for this, as well; see chapter 6.)

Certainly children were often in the audience when such stories were told in the old days. Indeed, we even have the remembrances of some scarred old warriors about their own responses to hearing such stories when they were children. Black-Wolf, a Gros Ventre, began his account of his war experiences in this way: "When I was a boy I heard about great deeds in war, and resolved to follow the tracks of such men" (197). And Two-Leggings:

> I was growing restless shooting rabbits and longed to join the war parties I watched going out. In the evenings I wandered through the village until I found a tipi where some old man was telling stories of famous raids. If I was not invited in I would sit outside, my ear pressed to the skin wall. Later that night, in my brother's tipi, I would imagine those same things happening to me. (11)

THE SELF-EXAMINATIONS

At one point in *Sun Chief* Don Talayesva recalls a salt journey. These journeys were important to the Hopi for more than salt; if all the rituals were properly performed, if all the taboos were properly observed, the rains would come and the harvest might be something more than a poor survival of the seed. Improper observance could bring on disaster. Upon Talayesva's return, he hears that his beloved nephew has died:

> I was very sad and went to my mother's place for food and a nap. I carefully reviewed my salt journey and found no fault with myself. I had no bad dreams, saw no evil spirits, and did not look back to see if Masau'u followed us. I did carve my initials on my Sun emblem, but certainly that would not have caused the death of the little boy. I returned to [my wife's] house for supper, and her father asked me to tell the complete story of the salt expedition. I began and talked until midnight, but I did not mention the fact that I had carved my initials on my Sun emblem. (246)

Talayesva is obviously a bit worried about having carved his initials, rather than his personal symbol, at the required place on the required rock—this was an innovation, something no preliterate Hopi *could* have done. And so the act worries Talayesva now. But on the whole he is able to excuse himself of responsibility for his nephew's death. And we may hope that his edited account of the journey satisfied his father-in-law as well. We see Talayesva engaged in this kind of self-examination at several points in *Sun Chief*. It is an activity that was common among the Indians, as indeed it was among preliterate and ancient peoples in general. Sometimes these self-examinations were so strikingly similar to what Christians recognize as confession that some early missionaries among the heathens decided that this could be nothing other than evidence of the missionary activity of the Apostle Thomas (G. Misch, 1951:29).

Sometimes confessions were a part of the preparation for some of the ceremonies. Brief confessions were, for example, required of certain participants in the Sun Dance in several Plains tribes.[13] Where failures are discovered in the course of such confessions, penances could be stipulated, as they were in the case of Sun Dance candidates among the Oglala, for example, who failed to observe all the taboos (Walker, 1917:71).[14] Such personal failures could even determine the fate of a whole tribe. This was the case for example in one famous instance among the Cheyenne, for example, when many of their late-nineteenth-century misfortunes were judged to have been brought about by Broken Dish and his wife, who had mistreated the sacred hat of which they were guardians.[15] But most commonly self-examination was a way of accounting for diseases, misfortunes, failures of ceremonies. The impetus is not difficult to understand. When the dance for rain, or for success in war, has been danced, if the rains do not fall, if the enemy is not defeated, an explanation must be found. The explanation that a dance can have no effect on clouds or enemies is culturally unacceptable. And so the fault must be found in the performers. In merely human communities one need not look far for *some* personal failure, and so explanations were usually readily at hand. (This is, of course, like the ways in which the failures of the Christian and the psychoanalytic faiths are often explained.) If three warriors died on a war party, if no horses were taken on a raid, the leader might examine his past—and lead his men in an examination of *their* past—to see what might have been omitted, what observance might have been slighted, what medicine might have been forgotten.

Early in *Black Elk Speaks,* for example, a shaman is brought in to minister to the boy Black Elk, who is sick nearly unto distraction. He would have asked Black Elk's parents to tell him what they might have done that would have brought on this illness. The parents evidently assured him that they had violated no taboos; finally the shaman decides, then, that the boy must have had some vision experience. The shaman urges Black Elk to tell it to him which the boy does. The same kind of questioning that Black Elk omits from his recollection of this confessional healing session we may find carefully recorded by Knud Rasmussen, who witnessed just such a session among the Iglulik Eskimo: "A woman . . . lay very ill, with pains all over her body," Rasmussen wrote. The shaman asks his helping spirit where the sickness comes from:

> "Is it due to something I have eaten in defiance of a taboo . . . ? Or is it brought about by the sick woman herself?"
> The patient answers: "The sickness is due to my own fault. I have not performed my duties well. My thoughts have been bad and my actions evil."

The shaman proceeds with more particular questions, and the woman confesses to have eaten caribou breast at a time when this was taboo for her, and she touched sealskin when this was taboo, combed her hair once when this was taboo, and other transgressions there were as well (Rasmussen, 1930:132–141).

Don Talayesva suffered a near-fatal illness while he was living far from the pueblo, in California, where he had been sent for his schooling. No shaman was by to aid him in his self-examination. But Talayesva was well educated in Hopi ways, and so he was himself able to examine his past minutely; he decides that he has fallen ill because he has left the Hopi gods behind. And *so* he decides he must leave the white world and return to the good, old Hopi ways.

Self-examination could even be life saving. The redoubtable Matilda Coxe Stevenson wrote an account of a witchcraft trial in turn-of-the-century Zuni pueblo (1904:400–406).[16] A group of warriors accuse a boy of making a girl ill by witchcraft. The boy saves himself from hanging not by proclaiming his innocence but rather by describing in ever greater detail his witching activities and powers:

> The longer the boy talked the more absorbed he became in his subject. He added many wonderful statements to those made during the day. At times his face became radiant with satisfaction at his power over his listeners. His final stroke made it evident that he intended to protect himself against all further persecution, for he closed with the remark: "I did possess all the power of my wizard forefathers. It came to me through many generations. I have been all powerful in witchcraft . . . [But now he feels that all his powers are gone], not only for a little while, but for all time. Alas! No more shall I be great among my people. . . . My power is gone . . . forever!" Hundreds cried out: "Good! Good! Thanks . . . Thanks!" (1904:406)

It is Stevenson's clear sense that the boy is making all this up (1904:406). But for our purposes it does not matter whether she is right or not. To whatever degree the boy's spellbinding narrative is a "fiction of the self," the incident demonstrates yet another way in which extended confessional autobiographical narratives could be made use of in preliterate times.

But the confessional tradition also serves, in some cases, as an organizational device, to tie together some of the best of the book-length as-told-to autobiographies. Black Elk, for example, was convinced that the unhappy condition of his people was his own fault:

> In my vision [the Grandfathers] had predicted that I was chosen to be intercessor for my people so it was up to me to do my utmost for

my people and everything that I did not do for my people, it would be my fault. If I were in poverty my people would also be in poverty, and if I were helpless or died, my people would die also. But it was up to me to scheme a certain way for myself to prosper for the people. (*Sixth Grandfather:* 294)

But as Black Elk looks back over his own life and over the history of his people during his lifetime, he sees that he has not yet accomplished what his great vision had predicted for him. "I have fallen away," Black Elk cries out to the Great Spirit from atop Mt. Harney, "thus causing the tree never to bloom again; but there may be a root that is still alive" (*Sixth Grandfather:* 295). So he collaborates with Neihardt; he reveals to Neihardt more of his visions and of his life than he had ever yet revealed. Neihardt, of course, had his own reasons for working with Black Elk, but Black Elk's motivations for undertaking what he knew would be an extended autobiographical project seem largely to result from what we may recognize as a tradition of self-examination.[17]

We know less about Two Leggings's motivations in collaborating with Wildschut in his autobiographical project. The transcripts of Wildschut's interviews of Two Leggings have not been preserved. And *Two Leggings* in its published form is even a revision of Wildschut's manuscript.[18] The book is, then, a thoroughly reworked version of a transcription of an interpreter's on-the-spot translation of a long series of oral narratives and questions and answers. But through all this may still be seen elements of this tradition of self-examination. After returning from a particularly unsuccessful raid, for example, Two Leggings examines his past in order to account for his failure:

> Young Mountain had died because I had not followed the medicine men's advice. It was hard to have to learn this way. In the past I had met with some good luck and had also experienced many close escapes, but now I had lost my best friend. I began to see how reckless and foolish I had been.

As he thinks back on another raid—this one wildly successful—he remembers his proud independence in the light of subsequent disappointments:

Crooked Arm still believed I should buy a medicine from some experienced medicine man and warned me not to let my luck make me forget the older people's valuable experience. But I felt my dreams were powerful and this last success made me very proud. The whole camp sang my praises and I was in no mood to listen to anyone. (100)

We should not make the mistake of assuming that Two Leggings's confessions have anything to do with piety. His concerns are, in fact, close to those of Homer's Ajax and Achilles. He went on his raids, like Ajax and Achilles, for booty and glory and revenge. When he prays to his gods he does so, again like Ajax and Achilles, in the hope of winning divine favor and not because of any belief that praying to the gods is a moral thing to do in any abstract sense. For Two Leggings, the gods and animals and even stones possess power, may confer luck, and luck and power are essential for the warrior.

But we find self-examination so frequently in the book, and it is so entirely in keeping with what we find elsewhere in the Indian autobiographies, that we can be fairly certain that this feature of the book did not result from Wildschut's questions and concerns. We can be fairly certain that this was one of the ways in which Two Leggings had thought about the course of his life before he ever met Wildschut. This is not to say that self-examination unifies the book. No, for Two Leggings these are ideas that have attached themselves to particular episodes of his life, to particular stories; he is also quite capable, as we have seen, of expressing a pride in the extravagance and daring of his youthful war deeds which is altogether unmitigated by regrets. Indeed, *Two Leggings* here comes closest, I think, to conveying a preliterate sense of "autobiography." He is telling not the story of his life, but rather the stories of his life. In general, the more tightly unified the published autobiography of a nonliterate Indian, the more likely we are to be seeing the sensibility of the Anglo editor at work. This is what strikes us most immediately as we compare Neihardt's *Black Elk Speaks* with Neihardt's interviews with Black Elk (De Mallie, 1984). The Indians themselves often seem, like Walt Whitman, to have been quite large enough to embrace contradictions.

THE SELF-VINDICATIONS

When a ceremony failed, when a war party met disaster, or when hunters came home with empty parfleches, Indians did not always search for explanations in self-examination. One could, of course, blame others. And this, in turn, often called forth an autobiographical self-vindication. *Sun Chief* provides several examples of just this kind of exchange. Because Talayesva's children died, one after the other, a fellow villager, Nathaniel, finally accused him of being a Two-Heart, a witch:

> I told him that he had no right to call me a Two-Heart, that I had never attended a secret meeting of the underworld people, that I had not caused the death of my children.

He goes on to accuse Nathaniel in his turn of being a Two-Heart, citing as evidence events of twenty years before, giving "all the details."

> He could not deny this and was speechless for a moment. Then I out-talked him, reviewing his complete record for the people, how crazy he had acted, how his wife and children had died one after the other, and how he even let the missionaries bury them without food and a grave ladder. My friends backed me and supported my statements with short sharp comments . . . and a few spat at Nathaniel. (308–309)

The scene Talayesva describes is complex, and played according to rules which all present seem to understand. When accused of being a Two-Heart, one may exculpate oneself by reviewing the relevant portions of one's life. One may also counter with accusations. In this case Nathaniel is unable to provide a satisfactory version of the events twenty years past (!) that Talayesva has recalled, and so Nathaniel is regarded as the Two-Heart.

This exchange—charge, self-vindication, countercharge—seems so immediately understandable, so universally human, that we should perhaps blush to clutter it with talk of "autobiographical traditions." But once we have a sense of how commonly such exchanges may be found in the literature, and how elaborate they sometimes are, it is easier to believe the affidavit at the beginning of *Black Hawk:*

> I [Antoine LeClair, Black Hawk's interpreter] do hereby certify
> that . . . Black Hawk . . . did call upon me, on his return to his
> people . . . and express a great desire to have a History of his Life
> written and published, in order, (as he said) "that the people of the
> United States . . . might know the *causes* that impelled him to act as he
> had done, and the *principles* by which he was governed." (36)

Of course, one might object, it is possible that this was simply
a notion that was urged upon Black Hawk by many of the sympathetic whites whom he had met in the course of his tour of the East.
And it is certainly the case that Black Hawk's—and Talayesva's—
narratives were heavily edited. Those who remain thus skeptical
should turn to chapter 2, to the discussion of Sarah Winnemucca's
Life among the Piutes: Their Wrongs and Claims. But I am convinced
that, in hoping to justify himself by producing an autobiographical
narrative, Black Hawk was acting in a perfectly traditional manner,
however innovative may have been the idea of having his self-vindication written down and published. And we may now see that
Yellow Wolf, Black Elk, Geronimo, and Chief Joseph were also
motivated by tribal custom to vindicate themselves and their tribes
by autobiography—however innovative, again, may have been
their idea of collaborating with white men in order to accomplish
their ends. In the case of Geronimo, we know that this motivation
was felt keenly, strongly enough to overcome real fears that all that
he was revealing was being taken down only to be used against
him and his fellow captive Apaches.[19]

EDUCATIONAL NARRATIVES

In some ways all the kinds of narratives here delineated were
educational. The coup tales and hunting stories, for example, prepared children for adult roles. Joseph Griffis tells us of how such
tales were retold by his Kiowa mother:

> Often my foster-mother led me into the Sleep-Land in the footsteps of
> some great hero of the past, the telling of whose wonderful deeds
> expressed the hopes of her mother-heart for me. (26)

And we remember the child Two Leggings, with his ear pressed
against the buffalo skin of the tipi, listening to the old men's stories

of war glory. And as late as 1980, Henry Beatus could remember that hunting stories had helped to prepare him for the hunt:

> The best story I like to hear when I was younger is the mens telling their hunting stories. There could be ladies in the houses, too, but seemed likely they just didn't bother listening when the mens is talking.
> Fellow named Johnny Oldman used to tell the good stories. He was a great hunter, too. That's the one I really enjoyed listening to. There were times later on when his stories help me out. Sometimes when I'm hunting, like tracking a moose with the wind, I think back at how the people used to do it. Think back to those stories and make that move. (42)

The self-vindications and the self-examinations would have been among the tribes' primary instruments of socialization. Any child who witnessed Talayesva's heated exchange with Nathaniel would have come away with a clearer sense of what kind of behavior might lead to charges of witchcraft. Such examinations as Rasmussen recorded must have been important to children faced with the considerable task of learning a tribe's taboos. But for some autobiographical narratives the primary purpose was educational. A wide range of Indian education could be provided in this way. Don Talayesva remembers that even sex education was managed autobiographically: "There are good and bad ways in love-making," Talayesva recalls. "My old uncle Kayayeptewa often told us about his own experiences" (282)—and so Talayesva goes on to summarize what he learned from Kayayeptewa's stories about women and lovemaking.[20]

And consider the Maxidiwiac narratives. In 1912 it occurred to Gilbert L. Wilson that it would be illuminating to get a single informant's account of Hidatsa agriculture, rather than a composite account from many informants. And so he spent a great deal of time with Maxidiwiac, hearing her tell mythic stories, moral fables, and many stories about her life in her fields.[21] She told him brief stories about working with her plants; she recalled sitting on platforms, as a child, guarding the corn from the crows; and she recalled for him the nurturing songs she and her companions sang as they watched the fields. The songs she sang for Wilson she had sung many times, and it is my sense that the stories she told him are also, for the most part, stories that Maxidiwiac had told before, stories that had been told to daughters and nieces, to the young women during the companionable hours spent in the menstrual lodges.

Some years later Wilson applied the same methods to his study of the Hidatsa horse-and-dog culture, and so we have more narratives from Maxidiwiac and from her brother Wolf-Chief. Again, it is my belief that Wilson took down stories that had been told before, stories that would have been typical of those which were routinely told to young people. In this way, at least, Maxidiwiac's narratives seem to be much like those we find—some forty years later—in *Sanapia, Comanche Medicine Woman;* indeed, Sanapia says that she collaborated with Jones on this book in order to assure that her healing lore would not be lost to future generations.

One of the most explicit statements of these assumptions—and a nice example of these assumptions at work—comes from the far North, from an Athabaskan, Joe Beetus.

> We were out hunting and it was noon, lunchtime. Cold, windy day. We were hunting moose or caribou or something. Old Ned said, " . . . I'll show you boys how to make a fire Old Ned style." He had moose skin mitts, sixty below mitts on his hands. "I'll show you how to do it so you boys can use it in your days," he tell us.
>
> We're all young guys, five or six of us. I watch him when he got some wood. He split it then make shaving with his ax! Most people make shaving with their hunting knife. They got to take their gloves off to build fire.
>
> It's cold weather day. We got no birch bark. Birch bark is no good anyway in cold weather to start fire. Got to split wood and make shaving. But when it's really cold weather your hands going to get cold if you take your sixty below mitts off. So Old Ned, he make shavings with an ax. Only time he take his mitts off is when he is ready to go for his matches in his pocket.
>
> That's handy thing. I use it a lot when I'm out trapping with dogs in cold days. Awfully important thing. *I tell my boys that story when we were out trapping last winter. I tell them stories every night because that's my own boys. They got to learn that way.* (15–16; emphasis added)

THE STORIES OF THE ACQUISITION OF POWERS

The most elaborate stories of the acquisition of power were told by the shamans.[22] Some of these are astonishing in their starkly mat-

ter-of-fact descriptions of dangers and deprivations courted and
withstood. During the early years of this century, for example,
Knud Rasmussen collected narratives from three Eskimo shamans,
Aua, Igjugarjuk, and Autaruta, stories of exposure to arctic cold,
encounters with polar bears and sharks, all in the quest for
shamanic powers. Many such autobiographical narratives have
been collected and published, a nice measure of how great has been
the interest in such matters among Anglo anthropologists and
amateurs. (See Appendix 1 for a good example of a preliterate
Shaman's Life.) Matters supernatural seem to excite the imagination of nonbelieving scientists and fellow-travelling mystics alike.
And when the stamp of the taboo is added, the attraction seems
well-nigh irresistible. Indeed, so many of these Shamans' Lives
have been published, and so nearly do they seem to cater to Anglo
interests, that one might with reason assume that this kind of
narrative was simply a response to persistent Anglo questioning.
But this is not the case.

The shamans had reason to tell about their lives long before they
began to attract Anglo audiences. I think that can best begin to
convey a sense of how these Shamans' Lives fit into a social matrix
by turning once again to Two Leggings, whom we find still driven
by yearnings for warrior glory. His self-examination has led him to
the conclusion that his own visions lack power sufficient to accomplish his ambitions. He decides, finally, to purchase medicine from
a shaman, Sees The Living Bull.

There is no reason here to rehearse all the rituals and negotiations which such a transaction entailed. But on the morning when
the medicine and its associated songs were finally to be transferred,
Sees The Living Bull first told the story of his vision quest and his
first raid, the story of the acquisition of the powers he is selling and
of their manifest effects in his first raid. This story is told before
witnesses. Two Leggings is able to recall this story in detail. It is
important to Two Leggings, for it is, as it were, the certificate of
authenticity for the medicine he is purchasing and its list of specifications. Should anyone later question whether Two Leggings has
power sufficient to lead a war party, Two Leggings will himself tell
the story. It has, in a real sense, become his own story, the authen-
tication of his purchased power.[23]

For shamans and warriors alike, then, these narratives of vision

quests were necessary as a means of setting before the tribe just
what was the extent of the powers claimed.[24] A warrior would be
much better able to win a following once it is known that his vision
and his medicine are powerful. And worried parents might well
hesitate to deliver their fevered child unto the ministrations of a
shaman who could lay claim to no more than a minor vision. This
could even provide a reason for telling the life from the beginning
so that the power of the man may be seen to have been evident
even in the special nature of the mother's pregnancy, or in the
remarkable circumstances of the great man's birth, or in a few
meaningful events of his childhood. Don Talayesva tells us that he
was twins in his mother's womb; Black Elk recalls that even as a
child he heard voices out upon the plains. Even childhood penury
could be pressed into service in this way. Two Leggings says that
once "an old man named Four Dance visited our tipi and told us
the story of his medicine dream. It made a great impression on
me" (58), so great an impression, in fact, that he is able to repeat
the whole narrative. The narrative, as Two Leggings recalls it, ends
with Four Dance saying, "My dream was powerful and though I
was a poor boy I grew to be a chief and a medicine man" (60).
The greatness of what was achieved is made to seem the greater,
then, by contrasting it with the humble beginnings. And we are in
little doubt about why this narrative made such an impression on
Two Leggings, for he has come to see himself in the same way,
emphasizing how great was the disadvantage to an aspiring warrior
to have been raised a poor orphan.

In these narratives detail is more important than it is in the war
and hunting tales. Often the details have to do with pains endured,
and such suffering seems to have been twice effective: once in the
winning of the powers themselves, and then again in moving the
audience to feelings of awe. And these narratives could be awesome
indeed. Igjugarjuk, one of Rasmussen's Eskimo shamans, tells
about being left to fast and suffer in the arctic cold, with only the
thinnest of clothing. But I know of no such tales so harrowing as
those of Crows Heart, a Mandan warrior. With Homeric detach-
ment, he tells about the wounds he inflicted upon himself in the
Sun Dance, and even these are as nothing in the telling compared
with those he suffers in the course of his eagle trapping. We cannot
doubt the courage of this man or his capacity to endure. And so

we find ourselves responding to the narrative with feelings that are akin to those which such narratives were designed to call forth in those societies where courage, endurance, and self-sacrifice were essential attributes in warriors and leaders.

There were other reasons for the wealth of detail which we find in so many of these power-quest narratives. The details of these experiences were carefully considered for several reasons. In the first place, the vision and the events of the quest had to be interpreted and graded.[25] The great Crow chief, Plenty-coups, gives us a good sense of this. After a four-day fast in the mountains, he is taken directly to the sweat lodge:

> While I was in the sweat-lodge my uncles rode through the village telling the Wise Ones that I had come, that I had dreamed and wished interpretation of my vision in council. I heard them calling this message to those who had distinguished themselves by feats of daring or acts of wisdom, and I wondered what my dream could mean, what the Wise Ones would say to me after I had told them all I had seen and heard on the peak in the Crazy Mountains. I respected them so highly that rather than have them speak lightly of my dream I would willingly have died. (70)

Later, he recalls,

> my uncle, White-horse, laid his hand on my shoulder. "Speak, Plenty-coups," he said. "Tell us your dream. Forget nothing that happened. You are too young to understand, but there are men here who can help you." (71–72)

Detail, they want detail. Plenty-coups is to leave out nothing, not even what may seem to him to be insignificant. When all has been told, Plenty-coups's fears prove groundless; the Wise Ones are impressed by his vision and find it full of meaning and prophecy. But warriors did not always receive high marks. Two Leggings, for example, who was a Crow contemporary of Plenty-coups, tells Sees The Living Bull all about his own vision: "When I had finished he said he believed me but that I had not seen anything great" (75). Three of the old ones then confer about the meaning of a particular element of Two Leggings's vision. The old men ask for more detail in order to help them decide the issue.

Such details were also important because they allowed the appropriate icons to be developed. Sometimes this was so simple a matter as deciding what device the warrior ought to wear about his neck as he rode into battle, or what helping spirit or animal ought to be painted on his shield. Before leading a raiding party, for example, Two Leggings made miniature sweat lodges after the unorthodox design of the four sweat lodges he had seen in his power vision (67). We find, as well, that the shaman may derive much of his curing paraphernalia and some aspects of his curing prayers and ritual from the details of his vision. *Black Elk Speaks* provides a marvelous example of this. He performed his first cure when he was nineteen, making use of just such a cup of water and such an herb as he had seen in his vision. He invokes almost every power that had been shown him in his great vision: "You see," he told Neihardt, "I had never done this before, and I know now that only one power would have been enough. But I was so eager to help the sick little boy that I called on every power there is" (202–203).

Visions could also be enacted. The people assumed that the vision had a store of power, and that this power could be shared by the people if the vision could be enacted. This performance could happen on a small scale: Two Leggings, for example, after building the miniature sweat lodges, sang for his raiding party the song he had heard in his vision (67). Visions could also be enacted on a much larger scale, as we find in *Black Elk Speaks*. When Black Elk was just seventeen, for example, the whole band was involved in performance of some episodes of his Great Vision.

CONCLUSION

Of all these traditional forms, the narratives of how-I-came-by-my-powers more nearly resemble modern autobiography than any of the other types of preliterate autobiography. They are often, as we have seen, richly detailed. They also comprehend more than a single episode in the life of the narrator. The Shamans' Lives, especially, often mention early childhood and even prenatal events. And because such narratives have so largely to do with prediction and with the provision of powers for subsequent shamanic or warrior feats, these narratives are also like modern autobiography in drawing connections between events.

But, still, even the longest of these narratives differ essentially from typically modern autobiographies. If two shamans from the same tribe tell each his story of the acquisition of power, the two will differ in the amount of power gained; they may differ about which animal, object, or spirit granted the power. But such narratives have as little to do with individualism as the ancient Philosopher's Life stories. The Philosopher's Life told the story of the wise man's pursuit of the logos. Insofar as the logos was assumed to be universal, the endpoint of the quest is not likely to differ from one Philosopher's Life to another (Misch, 1911:119). The shamans sought and exercised animistic power, just as the philosophers pursued the logos. These were not individualists.

Indeed, it is possible, I believe, to generalize about the way in which all the preliterate autobiographies, taken together, differ from typically modern autobiographies. What Karl Weintraub has said about autobiography among the Greeks and Romans could as well be said about the preliterate Indians:

> The ancients did not put a premium on the life devoted to settling the quandry: who am I? how did I come to be what I am? in what sense am I a distinctive personality? and what complex interplay of external forces and internal characteristics accounts for my specific configuration? There was no need to use autobiography as a basic quest for the self, or as a tool for self-clarification. (Weintraub, 1978:13)

Aua does not recall his arduous preparations and his visions and his spirit helpers as helping him to work out *just who he is;* they gave him power to do his work. And *telling* about his quest for powers is a culturally sanctioned means of setting forth his credentials. And so even the most elaborately detailed narratives of the acquisition of powers are really closer to the coup tales than they are to the autobiographies of Rousseau, Franklin, and Adams.

But the foregoing categorization should at least make it clear that when the anthropologists, poets, and amateur historians began collecting autobiographies from the Indians, they were not asking the Indians to participate in an endeavor that was entirely foreign to them. In fact, the Indians usually responded with autobiographical narratives designed according to their own autobiographical conventions. Often their editors overlooked these conventions as they reworked their material to suit their white readers' post-Rousseauian sense of what autobiography ought to be. But, as I hope I have demonstrated, if we look closely at even heavily edited as-told-to autobiographies, we can still make out the lineaments of ancient traditions. It is perhaps fitting that, even embedded as we see them in written words, in books, these oral traditions have still the power to struggle against the conventions of the dominant culture.

2

THE PRELITERATE TRADITIONS
AT WORK: WHITE BULL,
TWO LEGGINGS, AND
SARAH WINNEMUCCA

The first chapter described certain preliterate autobiographical traditions among the American Indians. I would like here to discuss in more detail how some of these traditions influenced three early autobiographies in particular. The first is that of White Bull, and it is very traditional indeed. The second is *Two Leggings,* the heavily edited autobiography of a nonliterate Crow warrior. The third is *Life among the Piutes,* the autobiography of Sarah Winnemucca,[1] a woman who learned English and writing with virtually no formal schooling. Taken together, these three autobiographies demonstrate neatly the ways in which preliterate autobiographical traditions may survive both editors and literacy.

THE PERSONAL NARRATIVE OF
CHIEF JOSEPH WHITE BULL[2]

White Bull (1849–1947) was a chief of the Miniconjou Sioux and a valiant warrior. He counted his first coup in 1865, at the age of sixteen. He went on to enjoy more than a decade of robust enmities, battles with Crows, Hidatsas, Shoshonis, Mixed-bloods, and whites. He surrendered in 1876, to live an eventful life on the reservation. In 1931 Usher Burdick of Fargo, North Dakota, persuaded White Bull to describe for him his remarkable life. White Bull responded with an autobiography that mixed traditional Sioux pictographs with an account written in Lakota, in the syllabary devised by the missionary Stephen R. Riggs. We owe the published version, which combines pictographs and Lakota text with an English translation, to the late James Howard.

The Personal Narrative is much closer to preliterate autobiographical traditions than are the as-told-to Indian autobiographies. Howard gives us *The Personal Narrative* in White Bull's own order, and nothing has been cut. Even the range of what is included was White Bull's own choice. The original bargain, evidently, had been for an account of White Bull's war deeds, but White Bull wrote to Burdick that he "would like to earn more" (2), and so he included other things. Since circumstances encouraged White Bull to be expansive, then, *The Personal Narrative* opens for us a window through which we may glimpse precontact conceptions of autobiography—perhaps even of the self.

But we might first consider what White Bull chose not to include. Most conspicuously, perhaps, there is nothing here about any of the events of childhood. Used as we are to autobiographies in the generic mold formed by Rousseau, Adams, and Franklin, it is difficult for us to imagine autobiography that does not take into account in *some* way what generations of psychologists have taught us to think of as The Formative Years. But the first episode of his life White Bull chose to tell about was a buffalo hunt. In so conceiving of the story of his life, White Bull is like other unacculturated Indians—and probably like preliterate people in general. The story of one's life is the story of one's deeds, one's adult deeds. Especially in the case of the warriors it may be said that, where one finds childhood episodes in as-told-to Indian autobiographies, either they will illustrate some very specific preparation for the adult deeds, or they will have resulted from the insistence of the editors that their informants tell *something* about their childhood.[3] Many editors must have had something like the experience Lucullus McWhorter had when he tried to question Yellow Wolf about his youth:

Hoping to incorporate something of Yellow Wolf's earlier life as a prelude to his war career, I broached the subject to him at our last interview. . . . The effort was futile. His native pride and modesty proved aversive to the measure. "I am now getting old," he protested. "I had seen twenty-one snows when the [Nez Perce War] was fought. It is not right for me to tell of my own growing-up life. That does not belong to history. Would not look well in this history we are writing. I do not want to hurt, to spoil what I did in the war. Only that should go in the story of the war. The other would not be well placed."
Insistence was not to be thought of. (24)

This passage provides the clearest example of this difference between the modern and the preliterate, tribal sense of autobiography. McWhorter agrees with Yellow Wolf that though this book is to be in one sense the story of Yellow Wolf's life, it is most importantly to be the *real* story of the Nez Perce War. It is a setting-straight of the record. Yellow Wolf feels that any account of childish deeds would diminish this record, which is his self-vindication, his tribe's vindication, and his own definitive coup count. Clearly, to preface his coups with his childhood deeds would be entirely out of keeping with his Nez Perce sense of autobiographical narrative. McWhorter, on the other hand, literate modern that he is, guided as he is by assumptions about autobiography that differ from Yellow Wolf's, McWhorter cannot bring himself to publish Yellow Wolf's story without that first chapter devoted to childhood:

> It was only by an assemblage of items gleaned from our previous interviews, covering more than a quarter of a century, that the meager glimpse of his early career as set forth in this chapter could be constructed. (24)

And so *Yellow Wolf: His Own Story* begins with a chapter entitled "The Youth of the Warrior." McWhorter knew the Nez Perce well. He was in deep sympathy with their cause and did all that he could to aid them in their struggles with land grabbers and corrupt Indian agents. But his sense of what it means to tell the story of a life is so fundamentally at odds with Yellow Wolf's that it seems not even to have occurred to him to publish the narrative as Yellow Wolf so manifestly wanted to have it published.

White Bull, then, includes no account of his childish deeds. Neither does he provide much at all that we would recognize as a connection—or even a transition—between episodes. There is no attempt to allow one episode to comment on another; no episode seems designed to explain how some later episode may have come about; no episode asks us to look back at a previous episode.

For the most part, in fact, *The Personal Narrative* is a recounting of White Bull's coups. Each coup is recounted doubly, once in a pictograph and once in a closely corresponding written account.[4] The page reproduced here as figure 1 is typical. Here is Norman's translation of the text at the upper left:

Figure 1. "This is White Bull running down an enemy." (From the White Bull Manuscript, Orin G. Libby Manuscript Collection, University of North Dakota, Grand Forks, North Dakota.)

Son of Makes-room
Nephew of Sitting Bull
They will verify this great deed

Then the principal text:

This is White Bull running down an enemy. This was at a battle with the Crows and both sides stormed each other's lines. I counted first coup in this great battle. One of the Crows was carrying a sacred bundle consisting of a white buffalo hide. He came out between the lines to encourage his men and everyone was afraid to go out and kill him. Finally I did it. I was twenty years old at the time and was riding an unusually fast horse. The Hunkpapas saw me do this. The battle took place at the mouth of Shell Creek. They praised my deed, friend. I was not wounded and came back safely to our own lines.

And the text at the horse's feet:

They took this white buffalo hide and spread it out and I saw it.

And the text beneath the horse:

It was a Crow Indian. (41)

Like Odysseus, White Bull is who he is according to the sum total of his deeds and his family, his clan, his people. Also like Odysseus, son of Laertes, even as he tells us of his deeds, White Bull tells us of his family: he is the "Son of Makes-room"; he is the "Nephew of Sitting Bull." It is in this spirit, too, that White Bull gives us an extended account of his family relations before he commences the recitation of his coups:

"I, Chief White Bull, say this . . . My father was Makes-room. . . . Good-feather-woman is my mother. One Bull is my younger brother. . . .

"Good-feather-woman was the younger sister of Sitting Bull." (5)

He expects us to believe him, in part, because of who he is in relation to his people. But coup tales are not to be believed simply because we know the family of the speaker. As we have seen in chapter 1, a Plains warrior could count as coups only such feats as his tribe recognized and graded as coups. And only such coups was he allowed to recount in public. On important occasions at least one witness would be present to corroborate what was being told. Finding himself in this new medium of writing, however, White Bull does what he can: he writes—again and again—that there are plenty of witnesses who would vouch for his right to recount these coups.

The narration of the coup itself is quite brief. White Bull provides virtually no details that do not serve to delineate the deed itself, or to describe the circumstances that made it special, or to distinguish for mnemonic purposes this battle from other essentially similar battles. And, in this instance, there is yet another assurance that White Bull is entitled to recount this coup: "The Hunkpapas saw me do this." The coup tales were traditionally brief, as we have seen, and so there is no reason to assume that White Bull was brief because of his unfamiliarity with this business of writing.

The Personal Narrative, then, is for the most part a traditional recitation of coups. But White Bull wanted to earn more money, and so he decided to add something to this recitation of his coups.

Figure 2. Smallpox, from three Dakota calendar histories. (By permission of the Smithsonian Institution Press, from *Calendar History of the Kiowa Indians* by James Mooney. © Smithsonian Institution, 1979.)

This is a great gift to anyone at all interested in the history of autobiography. Here we have a largely unacculturated Sioux Indian, a man whose habits of mind were largely formed before the move to the reservation. He recites for us his coups, which is to say that he tells us those autobiographical tales that describe him *essentially;* and then he provides for us some other material that, we may assume, is most nearly associated in his mind with the story of his life and his conception of himself.

What does White Bull add? He added, first of all, a calendar history of his people. Many of the Plains tribes kept such histories. In precontact times they were kept on hides; later they were sometimes kept on paper, in ledger books or notebooks. Typically, one image would be drawn to recall and to fix in time the events of a whole year.[5] White Bull purchased his calendar when he was twenty-nine. He was this calendar's third owner, and he soon called together a number of old oral historians to help him understand the course of events for which the pictographs were mnemonics (Vestal, 1984 [1934]:259). By this time, however, he had learned to write, and so he was able to transmit his calendar to Burdick in writing, without pictographs. This was an innovation, certainly, but his calendar is otherwise strictly traditional. Where a pictographic calendar would have included such an image as we find in other Dakota calendars for the winter 1781–1782 (fig. 2), White Bull writes, "There was smallpox" (9). He neither elaborates nor comments upon the images, except once to note the birth of his uncle, Sitting Bull, and once to note his own birth.

Many of the as-told-to Indian autobiographies include tribal history; indeed, that early Indians should tell about their own lives only after telling the history of their people has suggested to several scholars something essential about Indian habits of mind. It seems to confirm that these early Indians conceived of themselves as tribal beings, that it was unconventional for them to think about themselves apart from their people. This view has much to recommend it; the problem has been—and this has not been acknowledged—that the autobiographies that are adduced as evidence are as-told-to autobiographies. Carter Revard, for example, writes about how Geronimo opens "his autobiography" with a "Genesis-like history of the world" and of his people; and only then "does Geronimo speak of himself."[6]

But we know little, really, about the order in which Geronimo delivered himself of all the material that Barrett edited into *Geronimo*. And we do not know how much of the material in the book came as a result of Barrett's questions.[7] Certainly Barrett was himself interested in Apache history. It is, of course, possible that all the tribal history in the book arose from the editor's questions. And the same must be said about nearly every other autobiography by an unacculturated Indian. White Bull provides one of the very few exceptions. *The Personal Narrative* shows us that at least one largely unacculturated Indian *was* inclined without the interference or questions of an Anglo amanuensis to link the story of his own deeds with the history of his people. (It should be remembered, however, that White Bull was unusual in that he was himself the keeper of a calendar history.)

White Bull made other additions besides the calendar history. After writing and drawing his coup tales, he added an account of his later deeds:

> These are my deeds, recognized by the Dakota warriors: 1. I was made a chief. . . . 2. . . . I joined the Indian police. 3. Since then I have served as tribal judge. 4. In the Miniconjou district some time ago I was also a policeman. 5. There were twelve tribal policemen and I was one of them. 6. I was chairman of the tribal council. 7. Another office I held was sergeant-at-arms. . . . 9. I also served as leader of the young men's [church] group. . . .
>
> Another time some military men came to me and said, "Chief White Bull, come and bring one thousand men with you. We want you to

demonstrate how Custer and his command were killed." I did this and it was a beautiful reenactment. (76–77; the numbering of the deeds is White Bull's own.)

We see White Bull struggling toward another innovation here. Clearly, White Bull is listing these deeds for us because it seems to him that they add to his stature, to his fame. He is recounting these deeds *as though* they were coups. Yet there is a certain awkwardness, for these are not coups in the traditional sense, really. Although he assures us that these deeds are "recognized by the Dakota warriors," one guesses that no council of warriors met to decide whether White Bull's number 15 or his number 4 ought to be counted as a coup. And this is the only assertion of his veracity for the entire list of twenty reservation-period deeds. There is even less detail here than in his coup tales proper.

One might assume that White Bull told about the later deeds in this truncated form because they were less important to him than the warrior deeds. But this is not the case. The last deed he lists, for example, his command of the reenactment of the Custer battle (which was staged as the central attraction of the Semi-Centennial of the battle) was very important to him. White Bull later told Stanley Vestal that this was the happiest day of his life: "Thousands of people were there. . . . I was honored above all the Indians. I was a great man that day" (Vestal, 1984 [1934]:255).

There are no pictographs for any of these reservation-period deeds. His culture provided him with ways of representing the deeds of warfare, the hunt, and the raid. There was no tradition for the graphic representation of service as sergeant-at-arms—to say nothing of service as leader of a young men's church group. There was no tradition for the oral representation of such accomplishments either. And so White Bull innovates; he makes a numbered list.[8]

White Bull did not feel that his life ended when he moved to the reservation. Whatever pain he endured after his surrender, he continued to lead a life that made good use of his daring and his resourcefulness; he continued to perform deeds that seemed to him to be full of honor—but they could not be counted as coups. So the stories differ in their telling; the conventions are altered. One thinks of Charles Alexander Eastman, whose father sent him off to the white man's school with these words: "Remember, my boy, it is the same as if I sent you on your first warpath. I shall expect you to conquer" (*From the Deep Woods to Civilization:* 32).

TWO LEGGINGS

Two Leggings, a River Crow Indian, was born about 1847. He was a warrior, as tender of his reputation as Achilles, as eager as Ajax for honor and booty. Like White Bull, he delighted in war, the hunt, and the stealing of horses. In 1888, just two years before Wounded Knee, he led what was almost certainly the last Crow war party. He was a seeker after visions, and to this end he danced in the Sun Dance lodge, leaning back against the pull of the thongs slowly tearing through the flesh on his chest. To this end he fasted in prairie-dog villages and on mountain tops. And to this end he cut off the tip of a finger with a stone knife. And he cut into his arm the shapes of horses' hooves—the horses he hoped to steal from the Sioux and the Piegan. Not least remarkably, this man has left us an autobiography.

In 1918 William Wildschut, a Dutch-born businessman and amateur ethnologist, moved to Billings, Montana. Wildschut met Two Leggings in the summer of 1919, and soon they were embarked upon the autobiographical project that continued until Two Leggings's death in 1923 (Nabokov's introduction, xiii). Wildschut, then, was one of a number of Indian enthusiasts early in this century who collected memories in order to preserve something of "authentic" Indian life before it vanished utterly from the face of the West. The engine of nostalgia worked always in such books (see chapter 7). But in Wildschut these motivations were muted by the demands of science for objectivity, for Wildschut was a scientist, albeit an amateur. (His work was sufficiently careful that the Museum of the American Indian has seen fit to publish two collections of his notes, *Crow Indian Beadwork* [1959] and *Crow Indian Medicine Bundles* [1960].) And the scientists, too, were collecting autobiographical narratives. Franz Boas had taught a generation of anthropologists that collection was more important than theorizing, that the theorizing could wait until the data were in, and the data were fast vanishing along with the "authentic" Indians. He had taught them, too, as one of the corollaries of his cultural relativism, that it was important to discover the Indians' *own* sense of their culture. As Paul Radin wrote in his introduction to Sam Blow-snake's *Autobiography of a Winnebago Indian,* it was necessary to get "the facts in an emotional setting"; autobiography, Radin argued, allows this (2).

Autobiography, then, would not only allow us to recognize the Indians' own view, it would humanize the anthropological facts that were the Boasians' stock in trade.[9] It must have been balm to the soul of such an amateur as Wildschut to read Boas urging that collection of data was more important than the elaboration of theory. And as an amateur, he must have appreciated the concern which was then being expressed that the cold, hard ethnographic facts be humanized. So Wildschut was one of the earliest collectors of ethnographic autobiography. He was transcribing Two Leg-gings's remembrances before the appearance in 1919 of Goddard's and Wallis's accounts of the Plains Sun Dance, both of which made use of brief personal narratives for illustrative purposes. And Wildschut was well under way before Radin's publication in 1920 of Blowsnake's *Autobiography of a Winnebago Indian,* the book that is generally credited with having ignited the interest in autobiography for ethnographic purposes.

Wildschut edited all that he collected into 480 pages of florid prose. But, alas, he found no publisher. *Two Leggings* languished on the shelf for some forty years, until 1962, when Peter Nabokov engaged himself to reedit the manuscript. To read Nabokov's state-ment of his method and its rationale—and the before-and-after passages he provides to illustrate his method (213–217)—is to be convinced that he has worked a small miracle with his rewriting, making believable sentences out of Wildschut's fantasy of Indian drawing-room prose. But still, all of this places us at four removes from Two Leggings. Two Leggings spoke through an interpreter; the interpreter's words were transcribed; Wildschut reordered the transcription and embellished the prose; Nabokov rewrote Wild-schut. After all this tampering, we certainly cannot hope to identify any of the characteristic features of Crow narrative style. As Nabo-kov wrote, Wildschut "could not have been aware of the close attention Crows paid to antithesis, parallelism, repetition, hyper-bole, soliloquy, rhetorical queries, and symbolic expressions" (213), and so virtually all such sentence-level stylistic features are lost to us. But much as Two Leggings's words have been reworked, we may still recognize in the autobiography the lineaments of some preliterate autobiographical traditions.

Consider, for example, Two Leggings's motivation for collaborating with Wildschut. A hawk, it seems, appeared to Two Leggings in a vision. The hawk was The Bird Above All The Mountains, and it told Two Leggings that he would be known by "people all over the earth" (63). Two Leggings told Wildschut,

> I . . . think he was telling me that one day a white man would be sent to write my life in a book so that people all over the earth would read my story. You are the one to tell about my life and it will soon travel all over the earth. (205–206)

His motivations seem to have been exactly like White Bull's in writing his *Personal Narrative* and in his work with Vestal on his biography. "When our book is published," White Bull said to Vestal, "my name will be remembered and my story read so long as men can read it" (Vestal, 1984 [1934]:255–256). Two Leggings understood his own autobiographical labors in just this way. One of his visions had foretold that his glory would be known all over the world—and, lo, here was Wildschut to take it all down, to make a book of his deeds. Two Leggings must have imagined the book that was to be as the most wondrously extended set of coup tales the Crows had ever known.

Two Leggings, like White Bull, would tell his coup tales in order to establish and confirm who he is, his worth, and his rank in his tribe. Roy Pascal's dictum (1960:182–183) that the making of autobiography recreates the autobiographer achieves new meaning with the coup tales. The work with Wildschut, then, meant that he could recount his coups for all the world to read. We have seen how White Bull adapted the requirement for witnesses to the medium of writing. Two Leggings made sure that, when he talked with Wildschut, his old friend Bull Does Not Fall Down was usually in attendance, "verifying incidents" (xiii).

There are other ways as well in which *Two Leggings* is shaped by the Indian's sense of what it meant to tell autobiographical stories. In the first place, all of Two Leggings's desires were fixed in his heart as he listened to the old men telling their tales of warfare:

> As a boy I spent my evenings listening to the stories of our warriors and medicine men. I wanted to be just as brave and honored, and the following day would train myself that much harder, running and riding and playing war games with my friends. (6)

He is even able to recite the autobiographical tales of others. He recalls Sees The Living Bull's story of his vision quest, because he has purchased Sees The Living Bull's medicine, and so this story has become his own. And he recites the story of a poor orphan who became a great warrior. "I was excited by this story," he says, "and hoped to make a name for myself in the same way" (60). Although we know little about the kinds of questions that Wildschut urged upon Two Leggings, it does at least seem clear that Two Leggings himself was inclined to relate episodes of tribal history along with his own.

Two Leggings is also shaped by traditional autobiographical conventions in the Crow warrior's concern to tell us exclusively about his adult deeds. And since Two Leggings saw himself as a warrior, there was little question about which deeds he would recount. Despite all the questions Wildschut must have asked him about other aspects of his life, there is little in *Two Leggings* that does not have to do with raids, battles, hunting, and the preparations necessary for these pursuits. The little he has to say about his boyhood has all to do with his yearning to become an honored warrior (as we have seen). His wife is mentioned only in passing, his children not at all.

By the same token, Two Leggings refused to tell any stories about events after his last raid:

> Nothing happened after that. We just lived. There were no more war parties, no capturing of horses from the Piegans and the Sioux, no buffalo to hunt. There is nothing more to tell. (197)

Generally, this passage is understood as a poignant statement that "The Crow way of life . . . was over."[10] But if we recall how White Bull had to work his innovations upon the coup tale form before he could tell about his later achievements at all, we must realize that one of the reasons Two Leggings has "nothing more to tell" is that it has not occurred to him, as it had to White Bull, how he might change the familiar form in order to tell the story of his life in a new kind of way, to recount deeds which were not coups. Put baldly, without the form for telling about his postreservation accomplishments, he has difficulty seeing the content. There are no stories to tell about his life after warfare for the same reasons as there are no stories to tell about his life *before* warfare. His conception of his life is limited by the Crow warrior's conventions for telling about lives.

SARAH WINNEMUCCA

Sarah Winnemucca was born probably in 1844.[11] She was, then, just a few years older than Two Leggings and White Bull, but the circumstances of her life were very different. White Bull and Two Leggings grew up with little white interference; they were trained for the hunt; they were trained for war. The victories Two Leggings remembers with such relish were victories over the Crow's traditional enemies; the stories he tells about his exploits (discounting his editors' labors) could have been told nearly word for word by his grandfathers. White Bull's enemies were often dressed in cavalry blue, but his assumptions in fighting these men did not differ in any essential way from those of his grandfathers in their wars with the Crows. White Bull did work some innovations, as we have seen; but—orthography aside—White Bull recounted his deeds in ways that would not have seemed strange to his grandfathers.

The old ways began to crumble earlier among the Paiutes. The Crows and the Sioux had the vast fertility of the Plains and the Rocky Mountain woodlands at their disposal. If an enemy drove them from one valley, they knew of other valleys two hundred miles distant which promised buffalo and water, grass for their horses, and poles for their lodges. The Paiutes were wonderfully adept at winning their sustenance from dry expanses of the Great Basin. They hunted rabbits, dug for roots, gathered pine nuts and seeds, fished, and found insects to eat. Sometimes they hunted the antelope. But they were bound to the few lakes and thin rivers, as desert peoples must be. When the white man came among the Paiutes, he chose for his own use, of course, the banks of those same few rivers and lakes. And so, although her band of the Paiutes had no memory of any white contact before about 1848, white influence on the tribe was immediately and unremittingly disruptive of the old ways. Neither so numerous nor so warlike as the Sioux, the Paiutes, especially those who were led by Winnemucca's grandfather, Captain Truckee, tried to live among the whites by practicing cooperation and, where that failed, appeasement. They took up arms only rarely, and as a desperate last resort.

By the time she reached adulthood, then, Winnemucca had experienced a wide range of what late-nineteenth-century America had to offer. As a young child she had lived with a stone-age, hunter-gatherer people; by the time she was twenty she had made her stage debut, acting in Indian tableaux vivants and interpreting for her father in his attempts to explain the Paiutes to the good burghers of Virginia City. By twenty-four she was a figure of some influence in the Great Basin, serving as the Army's emissary to recalcitrant bands of Paiutes and Bannocks, to win them to the reservations. In 1870, when a letter she had written on the plight of the Paiutes was published by *Harper's Weekly,* she became one of the darlings of the eastern Indian enthusiasts. In 1881 she headed East on a speaking tour, spending most of her time in Boston, where she became the especial friend of Elizabeth Palmer Peabody (the woman who published the works of the Transcendentalists) and her sister, Mrs. Horace Mann. It was Mrs. Mann who edited Winnemucca's autobiography, and Elizabeth Peabody who published it. Winnemucca delivered lectures in the homes of Emerson and John Greenleaf Whittier (Fowler, 1978:38).

When her life is described in this way, we might expect that her autobiography would be like that of the educated Indian autobiographers. In a forthcoming article LaVonne Ruoff, for example, asks us to consider Winnemucca along with two other early, literate Indian autobiographers, William Apes and George Copway.[12] Copway, indeed, was very widely read. Ruoff argues that *Life among the Piutes* should be understood in the light of contemporary literary trends and types, such as the captivity narratives and the slave narratives. She points to a number of features which *Life among the Piutes* has in common with such narratives: some sexual violence, for example, and lots of daring adventures. But probably Ruoff is telling us more about Winnemucca's audience than about what might have influenced Winnemucca in writing her autobiography. I think it is unlikely that Winnemucca herself was familiar with

such literature; indeed, aside from the hymns she quotes occasionally, it is unlikely that Winnemucca was much aware of literary
influences at all.

In fact, it is not at all clear just how literate Winnemucca was.
She was certainly a fluent *speaker* of English, as numerous newspaper accounts of her lectures and interviews attest.[13] She was
employed as an interpreter on many occasions. And there is little
reason to doubt that she did, herself, write *Life among the Piutes.* But
her editor, Mrs. Horace Mann, had this to say in a letter to a friend
about Winnemucca's manuscript:

> I wish you could see her manuscript as a matter of curiosity. I don't
> think the English language ever got such treatment before. I have to
> recur to her sometimes to know what a word is, as spelling is an
> unknown quantity to her. . . . She often takes syllables off of words &
> adds them or rather prefixes them to other words, but the story is
> heart-breaking, and told with a simplicity & eloquence that cannot be
> described. (In Canfield, 1983:203)

The book allows us to see some of this for ourselves. As Catherine
Fowler has noticed, some of Winnemucca's "pronunciation spellings" slipped past Mann's editorial eye: "Acotrass" for "Alcatraz,"
"Carochel" for "Churchill," and even "shut off the postles" for
"shot off the pistols" (1978:40). Now, this is exactly what we would
expect of one who was a fluent speaker, but an infrequent reader—
as those of us who read undergraduate writing know to our cost.
Winnemucca herself candidly confirms this. She recalls reading a
four-line letter: "It took me some time to read it, as I was [at age
24] very poor, indeed, at reading writing; and I assure you, my
dear readers, I am not much better now" (82). And what little is
known of her education seems to indicate that she had virtually no
formal schooling (Canfield, 1983:30–31; Fowler, 1978:35). According to her own account in *Life among the Piutes,* she had just three
weeks at a convent school in San Jose before a group of anxious
parents convinced the pious sisters that it was unseemly that their
white and delightsome daughters be educated in the company of
an Indian (70).

One must be careful not to overstate this. Winnemucca could
read; and she carried on a remarkable correspondence, some of
which, in fact, was published, once in *Harper's,* as we have seen,

and more often in local newspapers. And, of course, Canfield and Fowler may just possibly be wrong in their estimation of Winnemucca's education.[14] But given what they tell us, given Mann's letter, and given what Winnemucca herself tells us in *Life among the Piutes*, it does seem that we should not simply *assume* the degree of literacy and the breadth of reading which Ruoff's argument would require of Winnemucca. *Life among the Piutes* probably was not influenced by written captivity or slave narratives.

Winnemucca's autobiography does, on the other hand, seem to owe a good deal to preliterate autobiographical traditions. Consider how different Winnemucca's autobiography is from other early autobiographies by literate Indians. William Apes (1829), George Copway (1847), Charles Alexander Eastman (1902, 1916), and Joseph Griffis (1915) all made the journey Winnemucca made, from the tribal world to the white world. The autobiographies of Apes and Copway have at their center their conversion to Christianity. Eastman and Griffis, as we shall see in chapter 7, saw themselves as embodiments of Social Darwinist ideas about the progression of the races. All four of these men wrote autobiography in such a way as to describe an individual self and to account for just how that self came to be. Their autobiographies describe certain clear turning points. Had Eastman not been taken away from the Santee Sioux by his father and sent to school, he would not have become the man he became. Had Apes not found Christianity, he would have remained in a state of sin. In this way, at least, all four are typical modern autobiographers in the Western tradition.

Winnemucca has virtually nothing to say in *Life among the Piutes* about turning points. Her biographer, Canfield, on the other hand, quite reasonably does include a chapter entitled "The Turning Point." The turning points are there for Western eyes to see; Winnemucca saw her life differently.

And she is again unlike modern, Western autobiographers in that she is unconcerned about self-definition. In 1870 a Sacramento reporter sought her out in a Paiute village:

She said: I am glad to see you, although I have not now a parlor to ask you into except the one made by nature for all. I like this Indian life tolerably well; however, my only object in staying with these people is that I may do them good. I would rather be with my people, but

not live as they live. I was not raised so; . . . my happiest life has been
spent in Santa Clara while at school and living among the whites. (In
Canfield, 1983:65)

The choices here seem to have little to do with the question of self-
definition. Winnemuuca enjoys living a comfortable life in the cities;
when she can live in a house, she gladly does so. When she must
live in a brush nobee, she is not unwilling to do so. She knows how
to live in the Paiute way. She stays with her people, however, not
because of a fervent love of their ways—she certainly does not stay
with them because of her love of the Nevada landscape,[15] say, or
roots, or rabbit's flesh. She stays, rather, out of a sense of obligation.
Winnemucca did remember some of the Paiute rituals fondly, and
she may be exaggerating her altruism a bit. But this passage does
seem to suggest that Winnemucca did not see the choice between
the Paiute and the white way as having to do with self-definition.
Eastman, Griffis, and Luther Standing Bear, on the other hand,
were concerned to work out an explicit sense of who they were in
relation to the two worlds they knew. Their autobiographies suggest
in many ways that, in moving from prereservation Indian life to
the white world, they were passing over a great divide. They speak
as from a great distance of the "superstitions" of their people.
Eastman and Standing Bear, especially, describe the prereservation
Sioux as being simple and "childlike."

Winnemucca does not seem to see any such fundamental difference between her Indian people and the whites. Certainly she is
aware of different customs; she is outraged at how dishonest the
whites are, and she contrasts this with the honesty of her own
people; she realizes that her people have to learn a great deal in
order to become self-supporting farmers, but she nowhere suggests
that there are *essential* differences. Indeed, the point of her chapter
on "Domestic and Social Moralities" would seem to be that the
Paiutes are *not* essentially different from whites: they are "taught
to love everybody"; their women are *not* allowed to marry "until
they have come to womanhood"; and, says Winnemucca, "We
have a republic as well as you. The council-tent is our Congress."
All of this is a part of the book's argument that the Paiutes ought
to be granted land in severalty and full rights of citizenship.

Quite aside from this line of argument, Winnemucca just does not seem to see differences beyond differences in customs. Indian agent Henry Douglas wrote of Winnemucca that "She conforms readily to civilized customs, and will as readily join in an Indian dance" (Canfield, 1983:62). He would probably not have been surprised to find that she has nothing to say in *Life among the Piutes* about her conversion to Christianity; nothing, either, about a moment when she decided that, really, she preferred the white to the Paiute way. She spent time among whites; she spent time among the Paiutes. In reading her book *we* may see implicit in some of her experiences features of a cultural identity crisis, but she seems herself not to have thought about her life in this way.

In many ways she is like White Bull and Two Leggings. Like those two warriors, she seems mainly concerned to set down her *deeds*. And I think she is like them, too, in conceiving of herself as something like the sum total of her deeds. Like White Bull and Two Leggings, she assumes that she may rise in the regard of her tribe by telling her deeds; and like Two Leggings she realizes that the written word may allow her to rise in the regard of a much larger tribe. At one point Winnemucca is explaining the position of women in the tribe:

> [The women] are always interested in what their husbands are doing and thinking about. And they take some part even in the wars. They are always near at hand when fighting is going on, ready to snatch their husbands up and carry them off if wounded or killed. One splendid woman . . . went out on the battle-field after her uncle was killed, and went into the front ranks and cheered the men on. Her uncle's horse was dressed in a splendid robe made of eagles' feathers and she snatched it off and swung it in the face of the enemy . . . ; and she staid and took her uncle's place, as brave as any of the men. (53)

Winnemucca wants to be remembered in this way, as a woman who was brave as any man, as a woman who did great things. She recalls leading a detail of soldiers to rescue her father and his band of Paiutes from the hostile Bannocks, for example. Her relish of this memory is nearly palpable: "we have come with you," she remembers the soldiers saying, "and [we] are at your command. Whatever you say we will follow you" (156). She talks about these soldiers as "my men," her "boys" (155). Later she says,

This was the hardest work I ever did for the government in all my life . . . having been in the saddle night and day; distance about two hundred and twenty-three miles. Yes, I went for the government when the officers could not get an Indian man or white man to go for love or money. I, only an Indian woman, went and saved my father and his people. (164)

Clearly, she is telling something like a coup tale. And she remembers her father's praise of her before the Paiutes:

Oh, yes! my child's name is so far beyond yours; none of you can ever come up to hers. Her name is everywhere and everyone praises her. Oh! how thankful I feel that it is my own child who has saved so many lives. . . . Now hereafter we will look on her as our chieftain, for none of us are worthy of being chief but her, and all I can say to you is to send her to the wars and you stay and do women's work, and talk as women do. (193)

Bataille and Sands claim that Winnemucca's autobiography is "heavily biased by her acculturated and Christianized point of view" (1984:21). A good Methodist—and Winnemucca was a Methodist—should recognize vanity in such passages, all vanity. White Bull, I think, would be puzzled by such a response. And Two Leggings? Every sinew of his being yearned to hear just such praise. He would—he did—quite literally kill to hear such words. Winnemucca is trying to establish her standing, trying to establish just how it is that she ought to be regarded, just as did Two Leggings and White Bull. In many ways, *Life among the Piutes* assumes an audience with Paiute habits of mind, not Christian. She is what she has accomplished; like White Bull and Two Leggings—and Achilles—she is the sum of her reputation. And so the maintenance of her reputation is of great importance to Winnemucca.

Like White Bull and Two Leggings, her first education was in a shame culture rather than a guilt culture. It should not surprise us, then, that she is concerned with self-vindication. As we have seen in chapter 1, when Nathaniel accused Don Talayesva of being a Two-Heart, his defense took the form of a detailed recounting of the events related to the charge and a detailed countercharge, urging that his accuser is himself a Two-Heart. Talayesva makes his case persuasive by bringing into his account details and events that it had never occurred to his accuser to mention. Much of *Life among the Piutes* works according to this pattern. Winnemucca remembers many such scenes in her book. At one point, for example, a Captain Jerome bade them come talk with him, since the Indian agent, Newgent, had accused the Paiutes of killing two white men:

> We went like the wind, never stopping until we got there. The officer met us. I told him everything from the first beginning of the trouble. I told him that the agent sold some powder to an Indian, and that his own men had killed the Indian. I told him how brother and I went to him and asked him and his men to go away, as we had heard that our people were going to kill him. I told him that he talked bad to brother and me, because we went to tell him of it. I told this to the officer right before the agent. The agent did not have anything to say, and then the officer asked my brother what he knew about it. (83)

This is typical of Paiute responses to accusations in the book. Does this seem merely "natural," universally human? I think not—at least not in Winnemucca's view. The whites in her book respond to accusations very differently. For example, the Paiutes had a great deal of trouble with another agent, Rinehart. Once they charged him and his cronies with stealing their government-issue clothing: "You are all wearing the clothes that we fools thought belonged to us." Rinehart's response?

> He turned round . . . and said, "If you don't like the way I do, you can all leave here. I am not going to be fooled with by you. I never allow a white man to talk to me like that. (126)

Nearly every Paiute answer to an accusation is "autobiographical" or "historical": "No, no—in fact, I (or we) did this, and then this happened, and then I (or we) did thus, whereupon you did such a thing."[16] The white people in the book, on the other hand, never respond to charges "autobiographically." They reply with dismissals, flat denials, and, especially, with assertions of authority. Another agent, Wilbur, simply refused, repeatedly, to speak with a Paiute delegation at all: "You are talking against me all the time, and if you don't look out I will have you put in irons and in prison" (239). Winnemucca's Paiutes even had an explanation for such behavior. After yet another promise had been broken, Winnemucca recalls,

My uncle, Captain John, rose and spoke, saying, "My dear people, I
have lived many years with white people . . . and I have known a great
many of them. I have never known one of them to do what they
promised. I think they mean it just at the time, but I tell you they are
very forgetful. It seems to me, sometimes, that their memory is not
good, and since I have understood them, if they say they will do so
and so for me, I would say to them, now or never. . . . They are a weak
people." (225)

The weakness has to do with memory. Small wonder, then, that
all of Winnemucca's Paiutes use autobiographical-historical self-
vindications, while the whites, in their weakness, must rely simply
upon authority. In this book it is the Indians who have the memory
that history requires. Indeed, Winnemucca's whole book may be
seen as an extended self-vindication, as an attempt to defend her
own reputation and that of her family and her tribe:

1. The Paiutes would have rescued the Donner party (the famous
party that tried to make it over the Donner Pass too late in the season;
they ended up eating one another) but they were *afraid* to approach
too closely, because the members of this same party had wantonly
burned the winter stores of the Paiutes on their way to the Donner
Pass. (13)

2. She includes a whole chapter on the moral education of the Paiutes,
which seems designed to demonstrate that they are not "savages,"
contrary to white assertions. (45–57)

3. The Paiutes are not "revengeful." (54)

4. "There is nothing cruel about [the Paiutes]. They never scalped a
human being." (54)

5. "The chiefs do not live in idleness." They are poor because they feel
it is their responsibility to give to the poor. (54)

6. She responds to a particular charge that "bloodthirsty savages"
killed "innocent" white men. (71)

Among many other examples that might be adduced are the letters
appended to the book, twenty-seven letters (!) bearing witness to
Winnemucca's good character and important work. (Witnesses, it

seems, are at least as important to Winnemucca as they are to White Bull and Two Leggings.) Just as part of Talayesva's response to Nathaniel was an attack upon his attacker, so Winnemucca sometimes attacks the whites (and other detractors):

1. The Paiutes were "less barbarous" before they fell under the influence of the whites. (10)

2. "There were very bad men there. Sometimes they would throw ropes over our women, and do fearful things to them." (228)

3. The "citizens" who follow the army are forever urging the extermination of the Paiutes, but when a battle is at hand, they fall to the rear, until the battle is over, whereupon they commence their looting. (177)

Examples could be multiplied; the broken promises alone would require a sizable list. But I would not wish to be misunderstood: I am not claiming that only a Paiute could have conceived of autobiography as a way to answer slander. My point is that we do not have to look to contemporary literary models to explain the form of *Life among the Piutes*. Indians of many tribes were answering their accusers with autobiographical narratives long before the Paiutes came into contact with the white man.

This does leave the question of the book's narrative polish. We may talk about ways in which the conception of self implicit in the book is closer to that which we find in White Bull's *Personal Narrative* than it is to the conception of self that is usual in the autobiographies of literate moderns, but these are differences we must teach ourselves to notice. If I am right about the book, Ruoff is wrong not at all because she is an insensitive reader, but rather because Winnemucca was so good at adapting Paiute oral conventions to the uses of the pen and to the entertainment and persuasion of white audiences. In this, of course, she had a good deal of practice before she ever sat down to write *Life among the Piutes*.

Winnemucca first appeared on stage in 1864, in Virginia City.[17] In that same year she appeared at the Metropolitan Theater in San Francisco. In these early performances she acted in tableaux vivants: "The Indian Camp," "The Camp Fire," "The Message of War," "The War Council," "The War Dance," "The Capture of a Bannock Spy," "Scalping the Prisoner," and others. She also interpreted her father's brief speeches on these occasions. Her father evidently undertook these exercises in Indian stereotyping in order to get money for his people (Canfield, 1983:41). But these experiences put Winnemucca before the public eye, and they must have given her an immediate sense of what she might accomplish with an audience. With her command of English, she soon became an important spokesperson for her people not only in their negotiations with agents and army, then, but also on the lecture platform.

She was evidently an effective lecturer. Even a reporter who doubted her personal morality could write that "she speaks with force and decision, and talks eloquently of her people" (Canfield, 1983:163). Another San Francisco reporter described one of her lectures:

> San Francisco was treated to the most novel entertainment it has ever known, last evening, in the shape of an address by Sarah, daughter of Chief Winnemucca. . . . The Princess wore a short buckskin dress, the skirt bordered with fringe and embroidery. . . . On her head she wore a proud head dress of eagle's feathers. . . . The lecture was unlike anything ever before heard in the civilized world—eloquent, pathetic, tragical at times; at others her quaint anecdotes, sarcasms and wonderful mimicry surprised the audience again and again into bursts of laughter and rounds of applause. *There was no set lecture from written manuscript, but a spontaneous flow of eloquence.* Nature's child spoke in natural, unconstrained language, accompanied by gestures that were scarcely ever surpassed by any actress on the stage. . . . [T]he Indian girl walked upon the stage in an easy, unembarrassed manner, and entered at once upon the story of her race. (In Canfield, 1983:163–164)

Perhaps Secretary of the Interior Carl Schurz bore the most convincing testimony as to her power to move an audience: he did everything he could to keep her from lecturing while she was seeking justice in Washington. He knew that her subjects would have been the evils of "the Indian Ring" and the wrongs of the Paiutes.

Much of *Life among the Piutes: Their Wrongs and Claims* must have had its original in one of her lectures. By the time she came to write it down, she would have delivered her tale, in parts, on many occasions, and she would have had a lively sense of how white audiences had responded to this version of a particular episode, and how they had responded to the other version of the same episode. Again, we need not assume that Winnemucca was at all aware of literary models.

Winnemucca's autobiography is far from White Bull's in some ways. She had learned a good deal about her white audience. She also works self-consciously with analogies in ways White Bull does not. For example, she tells a tale from the mythic history of her people. At one time the Paiutes' neighbors were cannibals. The Paiutes did everything they could to avoid war even with these "barbrians"; when finally they did rise up and smite these neighbors, they did so out of necessity. The tale serves, then, not only as a refutation of the charge that the Paiutes are "bloodthirsty savages"; it also suggests a neat historical analogue for one of the first groups of whites the Paiutes came to know—the Donner party. Winnemucca's work is "connected" in ways that White Bull's certainly is not. But Winnemucca's book is like White Bull's in that it is essentially an oral performance put down in writing.[18]

In her conception of her self, too, and in her conception of what it means to tell the story of one's life, she was not far from White Bull and Two Leggings. Eastman and Griffis felt a great gulf to open up between themselves and the Indians they had "left behind." They became full-time participants in the modern world, however much they may have yearned with a part of their being for the old life. Sarah Winnemucca, however much she may have preferred the comforts of a California house to the dirt and draft of a Paiute reed shelter, never seems to have felt such a distance between herself and her people. For all her acquaintance with the Transcendentalists, for all her Indian activism, Winnemucca retained an essentially tribal sense of self.

3

EDITORS, GHOSTS, AND AMANUENSES

The first two chapters have tried to look past the editors to the contribution of the Indian autobiographers. But any historical treatment of American Indian autobiography must consider the Anglo woof as well as the Indian warp. More than six hundred Indian autobiographical narratives have been published. Some forty-three percent of these were collected and edited by anthropologists and another forty percent edited by Anglos from many other walks of life. Very few of the narratives discussed in the previous chapters would have come down to us had it not been for these Indian enthusiasts. Some labored in the name of science, some for the greater glory of God and His Christian missions. Some invoked Clio. Others collected autobiography in the search for social justice.

The motives of the Indians in these autobiographical projects varied at least as widely. Some, like Don Talayesva, worked for prestige. Some worked, as we have seen, to set the record straight. Others worked to preserve their knowledge of the old ways for future generations. Some worked, quite simply, for the money. (None of the autobiographers were paid very much money; but, then, wages never have been real high out on the reservations.) Those of us whose motives are purer may blanch at this, but at least it was quite a traditional practice. Shamans in many tribes had to pay a master to learn their mystery. And the calendar histories—along with the course in oral history that alone endowed the pictographs with their wealth of associated meanings—usually changed hands only after some sort of payment. Two Leggings, as we have seen, was not embarrassed to buy another man's power vision. Visions, healing knowledge, and history were all thought to be worth paying for.

Some of these relationships, particularly those involving anthropologists, were quite impersonal. In some cases busy anthropologists delegated the work of eliciting and recording the narratives to Indian assistants. But in many cases the collaborators developed warm friendships. For an immediate sense of this, one has only to read through old issues of *The American Anthropologist,* where one occasionally finds obituaries of Indian informants written by the anthropologists. There is always real collegial feeling in these and often a personal sense of loss. And the preface to many an obscure monograph records the anthropologists' gratitude to his native teachers.

For their part, the Indian informants sometimes came to regard their anthropologists as something close to sons or daughters. Here were bright, attentive people, most of them young, who were keenly interested to learn what the old men and women could teach them. Indeed, here were bright, attentive young people who were willing to pay to learn curing rituals, food preparation, arrow making, planting, songs, dances—all the knowledge of the old ways, for which the Indians' own sons, daughters, and grandchildren seemed to have too little respect and less interest.[1] The first chapter of Frank Linderman's *Pretty-shield* provides an immediate sense of this. Linderman recalls that once he and Pretty-shield were talking about the difficulties of raising children in the present age:

> Just here a boy of about sixteen years entered the room with an air of assurance. Decked out in the latest style of the "movie" cowboy, ten-gallon hat, leather cuffs and all, he approached Pretty-shield [and asked her for money]. . . . The old woman dug down into a hidden pouch for a silver dollar, which she gave him without a word.
>
> "My grandson," said Pretty-shield, when the boy had gone. . . .
>
> "I wonder how my grandchildren will turn out," she said, half to herself, a dazed look coming into her eyes.

Then she turns to Linderman:

> "Young people know nothing about our old customs, and even if they wished to learn there is nobody now to teach them. I believe you know more about our old ways than any other man of your age, Crow or white man. This is the reason why I hide nothing from you. I have even spoken the names of the dead." (23–24)

Now, it is certainly true that Linderman includes this scene early in the book in order to vouch, as it were, for his own credibility. It is also true that some of the popularizing writers invented or exaggerated such scenes (Brumble, 1983). But what Pretty-shield feels here many Indians must have felt as they looked at the younger generation. I think that I shall never forget watching the anthropologist Omer Stewart, himself full of years, perform a long and complicated ritual song that he had learned years before out upon the reservation. He was justly proud of his performance, and he recalled the pleasure his informant had taken in teaching it to him—when none of the man's own people were at all interested to learn it.[2]

But whatever their motives may have been, Indians and editors collaborated on many, many autobiographies. Previous chapters have discussed some of the narrative assumptions that guided the Indian autobiographers. The assumptions and traditions that influenced their amanuenses are at least as various. A number of scholars have contributed to our understanding especially of the anthropological amanuenses. As early as 1935 John Dollard addressed his *Criteria for the Life History* to the social scientists, in an attempt to give the collection and use of life histories a sound methodological and theoretical base. Clyde Kluckhohn's *The Use of Personal Documents in Anthropological Science* (1945) took into account all the autobiographies, those edited by professionals and amateurs. It is still useful for its survey of the field and its critiques of particular autobiographies and methodologies. And Kluckhohn was so influential that the book can also serve as a guide to the editorial assumptions of a generation of Indian autobiographies (see chapter 4). In 1965 L. L. Langness set out to bring Kluckhohn up to date with his *The Life History in Anthropological Science*. In 1981 Langness returned to the study of the life histories. This second book, written with Gelya Frank, ranges much more widely, attempting to account for certain editorial/anthropological assumptions in historical terms. Vincent Crapanzano wrote a brief article in 1977 arguing that all the anthropologists' versions of the life history—the biography, the autobiography, and the case history—impose Western genre expectations upon the lives they seek to tell.[3]

Literary scholars have come to be interested in amanuensis-Indian relations more recently. Such attention was first focussed upon

Neihardt's role in the composition of *Black Elk Speaks,* in 1971.[4] This interest eventually led to the publication, in a fine scholarly edition by Raymond DeMallie (1984), of the Neihardt–Black Elk transcripts. And now, as the Indian autobiographies are attracting a wider audience, the contributions of other editors are also coming under the scrutiny of literary scholars, especially the work of Paul Radin, S. M. Barrett, and Ruth Underhill.[5] Chapter 4 will continue in this line of inquiry, in this case contrasting the editorial strategies of Leo Simmons in his work with Don Talayesva and the Leightons in their work with Gregorio, a Navajo hand-trembler. But it may be useful, first, to outline some broad categories into which the editors may be sorted, specifically according to their strategies for dealing with point of view.

At one end of the scale we find the Absent Editors, those who edit in such a way as to create the fiction that the narrative is all the Indian's own. This is both the most venerable and the most widespread editorial strategy. *Black Hawk,* for example, one of the earliest Indian autobiographies, was published in 1832. It begins in this way:

> I was born at the Sac Village, on Rock River, in the year 1767, and I am now in my 67th year. My great grandfather, . . . Thunder . . . was born in the vicinity of Montreal, where the Great Spirit first placed the Sac Nation. (41)

Fools Crow, one of the most recent Indian autobiographies, begins as follows:

> In July of 1974, I went to the Rosebud Sioux Reservation, located in southern South Dakota, and to the town of Rosebud to see a Sun Dance. While I was there . . . I was given an honor dance and the Sioux name *"Waokiye,"* which means "One Who Helps." (1)

One hundred and forty-seven years separate Thomas Mails, Fools Crow's editor, from Black Hawk's editor, John Patterson. But both labored to sustain the fiction of the Absent Editor. Neither narrative suggests in any way all of the questions the editors had to ask; neither suggests all the questions that must have been posed to the interpreter. Neither suggests where resistance to the editor's promptings was overcome, nor where the editor's promptings failed. Neither gives us any sense at all of the occasions for all the separate oral performances that went into the making of these books. I do not mean to suggest that there is anything dishonest in what Mails, Patterson, and many others have done. Often these editors provide introductions to the autobiographies which describe, sometimes in detail, just how they went to work. But once the autobiographies are underway, the fiction is that the Indians speak to us without mediation. As John Hollander has said of *The Divine Comedy*, the fiction is that there is no fiction.

Generally speaking, the Absent Editors are driven by the conventions of Western autobiography. Chronological order, for example, is usually strictly adhered to, even though the narrators themselves were often little concerned with chronology. Sometimes the editors feel the Chronological Imperative so keenly that they rearrange their material *despite an explicit awareness* that in doing so they are removing traces of their subjects' own habits of mind. See, for example, Charles Brant's introduction to his edition of the autobiography of Jim Whitewolf:

> Jim tended strongly to think and speak in terms of the qualities of actions and events much more than in temporal terms; this habit may well be due to the influence of his native language [Kiowa-Apache] which stresses aspects and qualities and does not pay the attention to time and chronology that English does.

But still Brant rearranged the material in order to "introduce some semblance of chronology into the life history" (viii). Brant intended his book for social scientists, not for the general public, but still he could not resist the Chronological Imperative so fundamental to the historical sense of his own culture. The central preoccupations of modern autobiography—the uniqueness of the self and how it came to be—are not at all characteristic concerns for preliterate Indians, nor for ancient or tribal peoples in general. But the Anglo amanuenses expected autobiography to speak to just such issues as these, and so they asked questions to elicit such information. Some asked their questions more insistently than others.

The Absent Editors also feel keenly a pre-Faulknerian sense of what we might call the Organic Imperative. Despite their awareness that the Indians told them the stories of their lives *as* stories, as separate stories, they feel compelled to turn all the stories into a continuous narrative with what Coleridge might perhaps recognize as organic unity. Leo Simmons turned some 9,000 pages of interview transcripts and Don Talayesva's handwritten manuscript into *Sun Chief*, an autobiography with a beginning, middle, and end. After many years of work with Maxidiwiac, his favorite informant, Gilbert Wilson sorted through all that he had taken down from her and made up *Wa-Hee-Nee: An Indian Girl's Story, Told by Herself*,[6] which is, again, a unified book, a book with a beginning, middle, and end.

In all of this the Absent Editors are responding to the promptings of their modern, Western sense of what belonged to autobiography. Some also felt that since this was, after all, *Indian* autobiography, the narratives ought to tell as much as possible about Hopi, Navajo, Papago, or Winnebago life. The professional anthropologists seem to have felt this most keenly. Underhill's work offers an extreme example.

In 1936 Underhill published *The Autobiography of a Papago Woman*, based upon material elicited from Maria Chona, an aged woman, who had cut something of a figure in the tribe in her day. At one point Chona tells about her father meeting an Apache in battle:

> They threw down their bows and arrows and started wrestling. My father was down. Far away, his brother saw that and came running. He clubbed the Apache from behind. My father got up and clubbed, too. So he was dead and my father and his brother were Enemy Slayers.
>
> They stopped fighting right away because an enemy's death lets power loose. You must take care of yourself until you have tamed that power or it will kill you. (42)

One senses that Underhill has interrupted Chona's story in order to explain just why they had to stop fighting right away. This is a common editorial strategy. For all their warm feelings for their Indian informants, many, if not most, of the editors were more interested in the culture than they were in the individual; and even interest in the individual was often interest in how a particular culture had come to shape this individual. Certainly Radin could not have assumed that his audience was panting to find out about how Sam Blowsnake had come to join the Peyote Cult. Radin assumed that his audience shared his own interest in cultures, and so, however fascinating Blowsnake may have been, however much Radin may have warmed to him personally, Radin published Blowsnake's autobiography because of what his narrative suggested about the Winnebago tribe in particular and premodern habits of mind in general. And so Radin was constantly tempted to interlard Blowsnake's lean narrative, a narrative that Blowsnake himself wrote in the Winnebago syllabary, with culture data.

At one point in his (translated) original, for example, Blowsnake tells about his initiation into the Medicine Dance: "they told me," he writes, "to keep everything secret, and that if I told anyone, I would surely die" (*Autobiography*, 20). Here Radin saw a golden opportunity to add some good culture data that he had earlier collected from Blowsnake. Radin wrote in a quick transition: "It was in the brush that the leader told me of the road that all medicine men travel." And then he gets to put in six pages of Winnebago Medicine Dance material. In this way *Crashing Thunder* came to be half again as long as Blowsnake's original, which Radin had already published with very little editing as *The Autobiography of a Winnebago Indian*. Radin was a man of some literary sensibility; he published Indian autobiographical material because he was interested in the Indian's own point of view, and yet, when he decided to publish Blowsnake's autobiography for a wide audience, he could not resist breaking up the flow of Blowsnake's autobiography with short and long hunks of topically related culture data.

One quickly develops an ear for this particular editorial frailty. Simmons's edition of Talayesva's autobiography begins, as we have seen, with the splendid story of Talayesva being twins in his mother's womb:

> When we were within our mother's womb, we happened to hurt her. She has told me how she went to a medicine man in her pain. He . . . told her that we were twins.

But Simmons just could not resist the opportunity to add some good, juicy culture data on Hopi natal customs, where, he felt, he could least obtrusively get it in. And so the story continues in fits and starts. The medicine man twists two threads together to make the babies one.

> It is a powerful way to unite babies. . . . My mother also helped to bring us together by her strong wish for only one baby.

My mother has described how carefully she carried me. She slept with my father right along, so that he could have intercourse with her and make me grow. It is like irrigating a crop.

Simmons works in some good data about what the father must do to assure a good baby, some data on birthing customs, then back to Talayesva's own nativity: "I was a big baby. I caused a lot of trouble and took a long time coming out" (25–27). Simmons tended to leave the seams showing. Others, like Underhill, worked much more diligently to sand it all smooth.

Underhill got most of the culture data she interpolated by halting Chona to ask questions. In the years before Dollard (1935) and Kluckhohn (1945) and others began to snap at their methodological heels, anthropologists tended not to worry much about the ways in which their questions might influence their informants. We get some sense of how insistent this kind of questioning could be from Ella Antone, who worked as Underhill's interpreter. She has recalled Underhill's interviews with Chona:

"She'd keep on until she really got what she's satisfied with," a word, information, or whatever she wanted to know. . . . Chona would "yell at Ruth sometimes when she'd keep asking a question over and over and Chona got aggravated." She would say, "You *mil-gahn* [American], you're so dumb, you don't know anything," and Ruth would laugh and be asking what Chona said, and when I told her, she would laugh more and say, "Well, I just didn't quite understand, but I've got it now." (In Bataille and Sands, 1984:56)

Underhill skillfully blended the responses to her questions with Chona's narratives. And so, since the transcripts of the interviews do not survive, it is impossible (as it is with *Sun Chief*) to be certain just where Underhill has plugged in this or that. Even the information about the power of a dead enemy *could* have spilled out of Chona spontaneously as she told the story. But it is quite certain that Underhill serves up culture data in this way throughout the book.

Underhill's editorial hand was heavy in other ways as well. As she explained in her introduction to the autobiography,

The writer felt most deeply the objections to distorting Chona's narrative. Yet if it had been written down exactly as she herself emitted it, there would have been immense emphasis on matters strange to her but commonplace to whites and complete omission of some of the most interesting phases in her development.

What seemed strange from Chona's point of view, Underhill often cut; what was commonplace from Chona's point of view—and so, hardly worth mentioning—Underhill consistently encouraged. According to Underhill, then, the book systematically embodies not Chona's but her own sense of what ought to be included in the story of Chona's life. And the arrangement of the book is entirely Underhill's as well. The autobiography is, in Underhill's own forthright words, "an Indian story told to satisfy whites rather than Indians." "Chona is ninety years old," wrote Underhill,

> and her memory works with the fitfulness of age, presenting incidents in repetitious confusion. The only possible system was to write each one down separately, add to it all the amendments which occurred to her during the years of our acquaintance, and then to question her patiently about the chronology.

"The only possible system," of course, means the only system which would produce a narrative in keeping with Western autobiographical conventions. And then certain concessions also had to be made as to "narrative style":

> Indian narrative style involves a repetition and a dwelling on unimportant details which confuse the white reader and make it hard for him to follow the story. Motives are never explained and the writer has found even Indians at a loss to interpret them in the older myths. Emotional states are summed up in such colorless phrases as "I liked it." . . . For one not immersed in the culture, the real significance escapes. (4)

And so "Chona was not allowed [!] to pass over the crises in her life with a mere word." Underhill was, on the other hand, very much concerned with the accuracy of the translation. There were difficulties here, since Underhill spoke only "a little Papago"; but the translation was "as accurate a translation as the writer, engaged in a study of Papago grammar, could work out" (4) with the aid of her fourteen-year-old interpreter.

Underhill seems, in fact, to have been concerned to preserve Chona's own point of view only at the level of the sentence.[7] Had Underhill been faithful to Chona's own habits of mind, sense of narrative, and point of view, the book would have had less to say about Chona's emotions; and more of Chona's "colorless phrases" would have survived. The individual narratives would have dwelt more upon "unimportant details," details, that is to say, which seemed unimportant from Underhill's point of view. The order of the autobiography, too, is all Underhill's; indeed, that there is order at all is Underhill's doing. What Underhill took down came from Chona as narratives, answers to questions, anecdotes, exasperated interjections, and conversation. Even the individual stories that Chona told about this episode of her life and that, even these stories, as Underhill edited them, are intruded upon by interpolations of culture data.

Underhill says that she did all this so that her white readers would not be "confused." Probably white readers would not, in fact, have been much "confused" had Underhill allowed Chona to dwell on "unimportant details" with her "colorless phrases." It is likely, on the other hand, that few whites *or* Indians would have *read* such a book in the 1930s. It would not have been the sort of thing that people were used to reading. It would not, in fact, have seemed at all like an autobiography. And so Underhill labored to win from Chona the kind of material that she could turn into something a literate audience *would* recognize and enjoy.

This is not to denigrate Underhill's work. Neither does all this amount to a lament that Underhill did not give us Maria Chona straight and unhomogenized. There is much to admire in *Papago Woman*. But it behooves us to remember just what we are admiring. Although virtually every (translated) word in the book may have come from Chona, *Papago Woman* embodies Chona's point of view hardly at all. We may learn much from the book about Papago ways and about Chona, but the point of view is not Chona's. At this end of the editorial scale,[8] the use of the first person is an editorial device and a pleasing fiction.

It is a measure of the success of the Absent Editors in general and of Underhill in particular that generations of readers have taken these books at face value, that they have believed the fiction that there is no fiction—as though the autobiography of Black

Hawk really *were* the autobiography of Black Hawk, as though
Barrett really did just sit down at Geronimo's feet and take dictation.[9] As late as 1984 Underhill's editorial craft so bedazzled two
scholars that they were moved to write several pages in praise of
Chona's "prose style," *Chona's* "lyric prose" (Bataille and Sands,
1984:54–59).

Many of the Absent Editors were more concerned than Underhill
to embody their Indians' point of view. And some of the Absent
Editors collaborated with Indians who had a sense of how this
business of telling a life story could be turned to their own uses.
One thinks here of Black Hawk, Two Leggings, and Geronimo, for
example. But there were also some editors who attempted in various
ways not only to preserve the point of view of their Indians, but
also to preserve as much as possible of the Indian's own mode of
telling, the Indian's own conception of what it might mean to tell
the story or the stories of a life.

Some of these are quite early. Lucullus McWhorter, for example,
began his work with Yellow Wolf in 1907. Their book was published
in 1940. Krupat has discussed at some length all that McWhorter
did to make clear where the line between himself and Yellow Wolf
could be drawn (1985:116–125). McWhorter begins each chapter,
for example, with a headnote describing the circumstances of the
telling of that chapter's stories; sometimes McWhorter interrupts
one of Yellow Wolf's narratives, as he does, for example, early in
chapter 5:

> Wanting to obtain the Nez Perce version of the status of Chief Looking
> Glass at the outbreak of the hostilities, I interposed, "General Howard
> states that some of Looking Glass's band had joined Chief Joseph's
> band before this time . . . " To this came the quick response. (78)

McWhorter also explains that Yellow Wolf spoke with him in
the presence of witnesses, in keeping with the traditions for the
telling of coup tales (34). He does a good deal, then, to give us a
sense of the circumstances under which the narratives were delivered, even a sense of where some of the oral originals began and
ended. McWhorter, however, was not the first to work in this way.
Linderman had published Plenty-coups's autobiography in 1930
and Pretty-shield's in 1932. And virtually all the devices we find

in McWhorter we find in Linderman. But the first Self-Conscious Editor of Indian autobiography was probably James Willard Schultz.

Schultz was born in Boonville, New York, in 1859. But, as he wrote in his autobiography, he "hated the conventions of society." "The love of the wild life and adventure" (1907:11) was born in him. And when he was just seventeen his parents succumbed to his pleas that he might flee the East and live out his dreams among the Indians. He spent the next six years trading and living with the Blackfeet. He lived *as* a Blackfeet. He learned to speak their language with fair, if not native, fluency; he hunted with them, made friends among them—even went on raids with them. He married Natahki, a Piegan (the Piegans are a subdivision of the Blackfeet). He also heard many, many stories; and he came to be a storyteller the Blackfeet themselves could appreciate. He began writing these tales down for publication before the turn of the century. And so we have autobiographical narratives by Hollow Horn, Three Suns, Big Brave, Bear Head, Heavy Eyes, and many others.

For the most part Schultz's work appeared in popular journals, but he did careful work, careful enough to win him the respect of George Bird Grinnell, who published many of his stories. Keith Seele has argued persuasively that, in general, we may take as genuine the autobiographical tales that Schultz edited.[10] And even so careful an anthropologist as David Aberle (interview, 1985) is willing to vouch for the general authenticity of Schultz's work. This is not to say that Schultz's stories are meticulous translations of their originals, nor even that he took down all these stories verbatim. Usually Schultz worked from notes, fairly extensive notes taken down the same evening he heard the story. We should probably regard Schultz's editions, then, as careful redactions by a man who lived on intimate terms with the people whose stories he is retelling, a man who knew the language and the patterns of Blackfeet stories from the inside.

We would not expect Schultz's versions to correspond, phrase for phrase, with those in the original. But his work does convey, much better than Underhill's, a sense of autobiographical narratives as they might have been told by individual Indians. Schultz tried to preserve the Indian's own point of view. Consider, for

example, the following lead-in to one of Red Eagle's tales. The tale
itself happens not to be autobiographical, but it is typical of the
way Schultz presents his material:

> Of all the noted story tellers in the Blackfeet camp, away in the
> buffalo days, I loved best to listen to old Red Eagle. That he was my
> wife's uncle, and therefore very friendly to me, perhaps had some
> influence in my preference. But, anyhow, he was a born story teller;
> he got in all the little details that enhance the value of a tale, and he
> always told one that was worthwhile.
>
> It was on a winter evening when the Blackfeet camp was trailing
> the buffalo around in the Bear Paw country . . . in the winter of 1877–
> 78 . . . that he told me the story of . . . The Loud Mouthed
> Gun. . . . That I have the story right is certain, for here before me on
> four leaves of my old notebook is the memorandum I jotted down about
> it at the time. . . .
>
> There were only four of us in the lodge. Old Red Eagle and his wife
> on their buffalo robe couch at the back of the lodge, and Natahki and
> I on the soft robe guest seat to their right. . . .
>
> Said the old man as he knocked the ashes from his black stone pipe
> and laid it away: "Apikuni, my son, did you ever hear of the loud
> mouthed gun?" (Schultz, 1974:65–66)

And so, Red Eagle begins his tale. Ten pages later he finishes:

> "Kyi, my son, I have finished. It is time for sleep."
> And so saying, old Red Eagle smilingly waved us the good night
> sign and we went out into the night and home. (Schultz, 1974:75)

Here we can see Schultz employing many of the devices that
McWhorter and Linderman were later to take up. Like Schultz,
McWhorter and Linderman explain the circumstances under which
they recorded the stories of the lives of Yellow Wolf, Pretty-shield,
and Plenty-coups. Linderman provides a fuller sense than
McWhorter of the social situations, of the personal interactions,
which gave rise to this story and that. But like Schultz, both
Linderman and McWhorter encourage us to experience these
stories in something like the way they were told, *as* individual
stories, rather than as seamless, Western autobiographies.

But both Linderman and McWhorter were engaged in enter-
prises that were foreign to their Indian collaborators. Neither was

anything like so insistent in their questioning, so determined in their aims as were Underhill and some other Absent Editors. But both did pursue the *whole* life; both were insistent in finding *meaning* in the whole life, even though, as we have seen, their Indian collaborators would not on their own have thought about their lives, nor told about their lives, with such goals in mind. It may well be the case that Yellow Wolf, Plenty-coups, and Pretty-shield responded to these questions with tales that, for the most part, work within the conventions of preliterate autobiography; indeed, I am convinced that this is the case. Still, we can hardly doubt that McWhorter and Linderman led their Indian autobiographers to think about their experiences in new ways.

Schultz, on the other hand, did little to influence the way the tales were told in the first place. He was a participant in the Blackfeet oral culture. He appeared there at the campfire with neither notebook nor scientific agenda. When we hear Blackfeet telling about their lives through Schultz, we are experiencing preliterate autobiography fairly directly. We have seen in chapter 1 that preliterate autobiographical tales were likely to be discreet stories of episodes in a life, rather than the story of a life. This is quite apparent in Schultz. There are very few connections between narratives, but where we do find them they are of a particular kind. Red Eagle, for example, tells a story about his experiences with a tame wolf named Laugher. At the end of this tale we read:

> "And what became of the wolf," I asked.
> "Ha! That is another story," the old man answered. "But not to-night. Go. Go home all of you. It is time to sleep." (190)

Schultz begins another story in this way:

> Apsi and Jackson had not been present the evening Old Red Eagle related the story of Laugher. . . . But while we were skinning some wolves at one of our baits down on Cow Creek I retold the story and they were as anxious as I was to hear more. . . . To that end Apsi told his mother one evening to prepare a little feast for us, and himself invited Red Eagle to come over and eat and smoke.
> "Ha! That is why you invited me here; you want to hear more about the wolf!" the old man exlaimed, after the feast was over and Apsi had lit a pipe for him.
> "Well, you shall hear." (191)

This is typical of the few connections between autobiographical stories we find in Schultz. They have nothing to do with stages of personal development, nothing to do with "turning points"; these tales do not build toward a personal crisis. These are stories, individual stories. In ways that Momaday has taught us to appreciate (see chapter 8), the connections are left to the audience.

Perhaps this helps to explain why Schultz wrote so many stories and so few books. (Most of the books that later appeared under Schultz's name were collections of his stories; even his own autobiography is really a collection of stories about his life among the Blackfeet that had first been published in Grinnell's *Forest and Stream.*) We should certainly not assume that Schultz edited the autobiographical material into short narrative units because of his own conception of what the story of a life ought to be. In 1916 Schultz did put together one Absent Editor autobiography, *Apauk, Caller of Buffalo,* from material he had collected from one old Piegan warrior from 1879 to 1880. But even here we see Schultz working with a clearly defined sense of the differences between Blackfeet and Anglo autobiographical conventions. As he wrote in his introduction:

> I did not, of course, get Apauk's story of his life in the sequence in which it is here laid down. On consecutive evenings he would relate incidents far apart in time, and only by later questioning would I be able to fill in the gaps. (4)

But because of his reverence, I think, for the oral originals, Schultz did little to fill in the cracks between stories, and so *Apauk* is episodic, far from a seamless narrative. But this experiment with book-length Indian autobiography Schultz did not repeat. We may be grateful that in most of his work, Schultz was content to let the stories breathe with the gaps intact. He was content to tell the stories with something very like the motives of the original tellers. We cannot get from Schultz a sense of the whole range of preliterate autobiographical tales, but we probably cannot do much better than Schultz if we want to experience something like the excitement preliterate people felt listening to hunting stories and war stories, stories of raids and remarkable encounters told informally, for uplifting entertainment.

Krupat argues convincingly that McWhorter's self-conscious editorial style was a marriage of two distinct lines of influence. First, McWhorter was influenced by contemporary intellectual currents: for example, his "technique constitutes what the Russian Formalists, his contemporaries, referred to as a 'baring of the device,' a refusal to naturalize what is, after all, art(ful)" (1985:119). Second, Krupat argues, McWhorter was influenced by the Nez Perce custom of telling coup tales in the presence of witnesses who were free to comment and correct. McWhorter's willingness to present more than one point of view, then, was "an adaptation" of an Indian practice (1985:121). We should probably remember as well that William Faulkner's *The Sound and the Fury* (1929) and *As I Lay Dying* (1930) appeared early enough to influence McWhorter, and perhaps even Linderman, quite directly. Faulkner's experiments with point of view are more radical than what we find in Linderman or McWhorter; but these men were no less concerned than Faulkner to work out ways in which a single book could embody—indeed, insist upon the differences among—multiple points of view, multiple voices.

But Schultz, I think, must also have influenced both McWhorter and Linderman. Widely as they had read in matters Indian, they could hardly have been unaware of Schultz's work. What Linderman did, and what McWhorter did after him, was to work out at book length Schultz's framing devices for Indian narratives, Schultz's specification of the roles of editor and narrator, and Schultz's concern for the integrity of individual stories.[11]

Sometimes the anthropologists accomplished something close to the same effects inadvertently. The anthropologists made extensive use of first-person narratives for illustrative purposes. Grenville Goodwin, for example, wrote a massive account of *The Social Organization of the Western Apache* (1969 [1942]). His method was to intersperse his own description and analysis with long quotations from his informants. And so, scattered about in this book we find thirteen pages of autobiographical stories by Neil Buck, thirty pages by Anna Price, and thirteen pages by John Rope. All three of these Apaches were born before 1865. Goodwin does not, of course, provide lead-ins to these narratives, as do Schultz, Linderman, and McWhorter; and many of these narratives would have come as responses to Goodwin's questions, but Goodwin presents the narratives themselves with little editorial interference. Leslie Spier enlivens the pages of his *Havasupai Ethnography* (1928) with autobiographical narratives by his principal Havasupai informant, Sinyella—tales of Sinyella's relations with shamans, his hunting, and other experiences. All of these tales, taken together, are quite enough to give us a sense of this man, even though we read the tales separately with no kind of fabricated narrative connections. But David Mandelbaum has perhaps given us the best of these inadvertent autobiographies in *The Plains Cree* (1934). His principal informant for this book was Fine Day, a man who was, according to Mandelbaum, the most renowned Cree warrior still alive in 1934. Fine Day was, for example, the leader of the Plains Cree in their rebellion against the Canadian government forces in 1885. He also enjoyed a considerable reputation as a shaman. Mandelbaum's book includes many long quotations from Fine Day. This is finely detailed autobiographical material, especially where Fine Day is telling about his visions and his war deeds.[12]

This method of culture description, the interspersing of the ethnologist's theories and descriptions with long passages quoted from native informants for illustration and evidence, was quite conventional when Mandelbaum wrote *The Plains Cree*. But the vogue for this method of presentation passed as social scientists, after about 1950, became increasingly skeptical about the value and authenticity of extended autobiographical studies. Anthropologists, it was urged, needed to become more self-conscious about the ways in which their own attitudes might affect their collection of data.[13] Chapter 4 will discuss the work of Simmons and Alexander and Dorothea Leighton in particular in relation to these issues. For the moment, let us turn to that end of the scale where the anthropologists have become very self-conscious indeed.

In 1969 Vincent Crapanzano published *The Fifth World of Enoch Maloney: A Portrait of a Navaho.* Had Enoch Maloney found his Boswell in the 1930s or 1940s, he might have become an autobiographer. But Crapanzano's book did not turn out to be an autobiography, not even according to my own elastic sense of the term. This *Portrait of a Navaho* is, rather,

> a personal account of the reactions—sometimes naive, often arrogant—of an "Anglo," an East-Coaster who had been oriented more toward Europe than toward his own country, during one short summer on the Navaho reservation.[14]

Crapanzano's prose does not flow with milk and honey, but it does seem clear that he worries about the cultural imprint that anthropologists inevitably leave upon the data they collect. For this reason Crapanzano feels compelled to stress that his "portrait" is a "personal account"—a personal account not just by an Anglo, but a particular sort of Anglo. Crapanzano must specify that he is an "East-Coaster . . . oriented . . . toward Europe." It is not enough for Crapanzano to provide this foreword wherein he describes himself in order to alert us to his prejudices and his limitations. No, "the 'I' of the book" is not to be Maloney, but, rather, "a graduate student in the social sciences." In this book Crapanzano will speak to us directly, not Maloney. To present his material in the form of an autobiography by Maloney would be to pretend that the material was unmediated, and so Crapanzano opted for late 1960s full disclosure.[15] He decided to give us a "portrait" of Maloney by publishing his field notes, a journal, then, of his experiences with Maloney, there in "the Arroyo." Of course Crapanzano tidied up his notes a good deal before sending them off to Random House; still, this is "baring the device" with a vengeance![16]

Crapanzano's article on "The Life History in Anthropological Fieldwork" (1977) provides a rationale for his editorial method:

> Like the autobiography and the biography, the case history and the life history are distinctly Western genres . . . And, as such, they shape a particular, pre-selected range of data into a meaningful totality. They reflect not only the more superficial concerns of a particular historical epoch or a particular cultural tradition but also the more fundamental attitudes toward and evaluations of the person, of time, nature, the supernatural, and inter-personal relations. (1977:4)

He goes on to assert that "Generic differences are more than formal differences," that they are "cultural constructs" that reflect the "most fundamental assumptions about the nature of reality" (1977:5). Any attempt, then, to prepare a life history, autobiography, case study, or biography that fails to include the "I" of the recorder/observer must fail:

> The ethnographic encounter is lost in timeless description; the anguished search for comprehension in theoretical explanation; the particular in the general; the character in the stereotype. (1977:5)

In this article Crapanzano is referring in particular to his method in another of his "portraits," this one of a nonliterate Moroccan tilemaker named Tuhami (1980). But it is clear that Tuhami and Maloney were painted with the same brush. He explains that he includes not only his subject's words, but also his own "questions, explications, musings, and theoretical confabulations" in order to "avoid the presuppositions of the case history of [sic] the life history" (1977:6). And so we never see Maloney or his neighbors without Crapanzano's flag-waving mediation. Early in the book, for example, Crapanzano meets an old medicine man, who refuses to tell him anything about his sings:

> I was overwhelmed. I hadn't said anything about learning a sing. I was just interested in talking to him. I decided to change the subject and ask about his family.
>
> "My parents are dead," he said, "so you can't know them. I was just like a lizard. I left home when I was three and didn't know my parents." And then, "A lot of anthropologists, they come here and they say they want to be my friend, and then they go away and put down what I say in books and make a lot of money."
>
> "I don't know about the other anthropologists," I told him. "When I tell someone that I want to be friends, I mean it. I don't sell out my friends."
>
> "What are you going to do with what I tell you?" he asked. And before I could answer he said, "Anthropologists, they make a lot of money on what I say. When they publish those books they should give me half."
>
> "If I published anything you told me, I would give you half. That would only be right among friends."
>
> "I don't want to be paid," he announced proudly. He was arguing for argument's sake, and there was a twinkle in his eye. (1969:32)

It is impossible to tell just how Crapanzano expects us to understand this exchange. Is he looking back upon himself here as the fresh-faced fieldworker, full of good intentions and youthful naivete? Or was he still proud of this ringing statement of his principles as he prepared his field notes for publication? The answer is not important; the point is that these are the kinds of questions we ask ourselves as we read through this *Portrait of a Navaho;* we ask questions about Crapanzano. In fact, the book reads remarkably like chapters out of *Crapanzano's* autobiography. Another example:

Thursday, July 21

> "Today we go to Grand Canyon, see Rita," [Enoch] said at breakfast. He had mentioned a trip to the canyon several times before and had invited me to come as soon as he learned I had never seen it. No date had been set for the trip.
>
> I asked Enoch what time he planned to leave.
>
> "Ten o'clock. Rita does not get out of work until three. We bring her back then. You have plenty of time to see canyon."
>
> I returned to my hogan to type notes, and at nine I looked out the door to see if anything was going on. Enoch and the two girls, Dorothy and Ella, were waiting patiently for me.
>
> "I'm ready whenever you are," Enoch called.
>
> We loaded a gallon jug of water in the car and piled in. The girls were quiet throughout the trip. I tried making conversation but as usual failed. (1969:149)

Crapanzano places himself in the foreground. He keeps Enoch and the girls waiting. He seems to be confessing his insensitivity in this. And he fails to make conversation. Crapanzano delights in confessions and frank admissions. (He seems to share with Rousseau a sense that one may rise in the esteem of one's readers by confessing to venial sins as though they were deadly.) In his article on "The Life History" (1977), for example, he confesses that late in his relationship with Tuham, the Moroccan "yielded" to him: "He came to speak my language," Crapanzano writes, "the language of the real rather than the imaginary. . . . The colonial relationship was restored" (1977:6). But again, we find ourselves trying to account for Crapanzano. He is at the center of this book that is supposed to be about Maloney and the Navajos. Later, still on the way to the Canyon, Crapanzano tries "to stimulate conversation," but Maloney "showed no interest."

> I had no choice but to lose myself in the scenery, which was spectacular. The mountains and the pine forests stood in marvelous contrast to the dried Arroyo and the desiccated corn stalks. (1969:150)

Crapanzano tells us about his own clichéd sense of the landscape. Whether Crapanzano's sense of the landscape differs from Maloney's we do not know. Here, as so often in this book, Crapanzano has trouble communicating with Maloney, just as he failed "as usual" to strike up a conversation with the girls. Indeed, this is one of the themes of the book. Thus the last paragraph describes yet another failure to communicate:

> Enoch came in to tell me he was going to town for a few minutes but would be back in time to say good-bye. He never returned. Later in the day, from Gene's car, I saw Enoch enter a supermarket in Flagstaff with Dorothy and Ella. The light turned green before I had a chance to call to him. (1969:234)

And this is a theme of Crapanzano's work in general. He wrote, for example, as follows about his "portrait" of Tuhami:

> It resembles less the case history or the life history than the modern novel of the alienated individual who cannot communicate. Both Tuhami and I emerge as alienated antiheroes. One genre has replaced another. We are, I suppose, destined by the idiom into which we have been caste [sic]. (1977:7)

Crapanzano considers it "an irony" that, finally, despite his awareness, he himself has resorted to a Western genre. But perhaps there is less irony here than obtuseness. Given his awareness that editing his material into a Novel/Field Notes/Confession has not saved him from the toils of Western genres, why ever should he persist with a genre so far removed from both Enoch Maloney and Tuhami as "the modern novel of the alienated individual." And perhaps his persistent failure to communicate has less to do with essential cultural differences than it has to do with not knowing the Navajo's language and with the brevity of his sojourn among them. This explanation would at least seem to be in accord with his informants' sense of the matter:

> "There are too many white men coming around here lately," [Bill] said suddenly. "They come here for a week or so and then go back East and write their PHs [sic] and think they know everything." Bill was referring to me. He knew that I was planning to stay two months. "Sometimes they stay two months and then go back," he added, making himself clear. (1969:28)

Bill overestimated at that: Crapanzano stayed just forty-seven days. A "portrait" of a Navajo after just forty-seven days' experience of the Navajo. But Crapanzano himself is convinced that the problem has to do with the breadth of the chasm separating the two cultures.

Crapanzano, the Hero Anthropologist: he has discovered that absolute objectivity is impossible; he has discovered that it is impossible to escape completely the perceptual nets cultures weave. And so he eschews as-told-to autobiography. He puts in its place his own autobiography, one which "resembles . . . the modern novel of the alienated individual who cannot communicate." If complete objectivity is impossible, he will forthrightly trumpet his subjectivity from the rooftops: he will confess his biases, describe his doubts and anguish, and his guilty triumphs as though objectivity does not admit of degree. Crapanzano tells us that every act of mediation is distortion: to assume the possibility of objective knowledge of another culture is an act of "antrhopological [sic] presumption, the anthropologists' *hubris*" (1977:3).

One is reminded of the deconstructionist literary critics who argue, as does J. Hillis Miller, that undecidability "is always thematized in the text itself in the form of metalinguistic statements" (1975:30–31)—and so the Hero Critics call our attention not to the text but to their own forthrightly subjective play with the text.[17] Underhill's Papago autobiography is closer to Anglo autobiographical narrative than it is to Papago autobiographical narrative. Schultz was a romantic, as was Linderman, to a lesser degree. McWhorter included material in *Yellow Wolf* that Yellow Wolf specifically urged should not be included. But these editors at least went to work with a clear sense that their readers were likely to be—and *ought* to be—more interested in Indian autobiographers than in editors.

Some recent work demonstrates that it is possible to be aware of the problems of genre interference that so troubled Crapanzano, while avoiding Crapanzano's heroic extremes of subjectivity. A loose confederation of Alaskan teachers, scholars, and native Alaskan citizens has produced a number of Athabaskan and Eskimo autobiographies. Eliza Jones published *The Stories Chief Henry Told* in 1979. Yvonne Yarber and Kurt Madison published no fewer than nine autobiographies from 1980 to 1981.[18] Bill Pfisterer, Alice Moses, Jane McGary, and Catherine Peter worked together to produce a volume of autobiographical narratives by an aged Athabaskan woman, Belle Herbert. These editors, transcribers, amanuenses, and translators are motivated largely by their desire to provide materials for Alaska's bilingual-education programs. (Some of their publications, then, include native-language texts on facing pages with English translations.)

These people have worked closely with linguists and anthropologists, who have encouraged them to collect stories rather than to ask questions designed to elicit all the information necessary to tell the story of the whole life. The linguists Ronald and Suzanne Scollon and the anthropologist Ray Barnhardt have been particularly important influences on this work.[19] In general, the aim has been to find forms that best translate oral performance. This effort has profited from recent studies of oral storytelling and the problems of presenting oral narrative—the kind of work for which Dennis Tedlock (e.g., 1972, 1977, 1983) and Dell Hymes (e.g., 1977, 1981) are well known.

Herbert's *Shandaa: In My Lifetime* (1981), I think, is the best these Alaskan scholars have produced thus far. In the first place, Herbert's storytelling took place in circumstances as natural as the humming of a tape recorder could allow. When Pfisterer and Moses asked Herbert if she would tell her stories to them, she said that she would and that she had been expecting them to come to her. Further, Moses, who served as Pfisterer's interpreter, knew Herbert well; indeed, Herbert addresses her stories to Moses, and frequently calls her "my grandchild" in the course of her storytelling.[20] Herbert was allowed—indeed, encouraged—to tell stories of her own choosing. And the published version preserves the order in which Herbert told her stories—on Ronald Scollon's advice that such oral storytellers as Herbert may well be working in accord with formal principles that are not apparent to literate moderns. Pfisterer has told me that he did occasionally get a session moving by asking a question, but Herbert almost invariably ignored the question and simply got on with a story of her own choosing. But of most interest is the form of the published narrative. I quote from Pfisterer's introduction:

> The accounts appear here with a minimum of editing, in the order Belle told them. The text is set up with the idea that there is more to telling a story than just the words and sentences. For instance, the places where a storyteller pauses while speaking are important in adding meaning and feeling. They set the pace of the story. The stories,

in either language [Athabaskan and English appear on facing pages], should be read aloud. The reader should pause at the end of each line briefly, as if for breath; where there is a wider break between the lines, the pause should be longer. . . . When one reads the text in this manner, one should be able to give an impression of a storyteller rather than a writer. (5)

Simple as it seems as advice to readers, in practice the decisions about where lines ought to be broken did not come easily. It was Ronald Scollon who taught Pfisterer, Moses, and Peter (the transcriber) how to recognize several levels of "markers" in Herbert's Athabaskan-language narratives. These markers are linguistic features, some of which, for example, might be roughly translated as "then," or "and then." But for Pfisterer and his colleagues, these markers served to indicate line breaks and paragraph breaks.[21] At any rate, their method gives us such passages as the following:

> When I was going to get married,
> I was still very young;
> my mother got a man for me even before I had my first period.
>
> Ah!
> your grandfather was up river, you see.
> I had only seen him once
> and after that my mother got him.
>
> When
> that was happening,
> I hadn't even had my first period yet.
>
> So he went back upriver with his older brother and stayed there
> until I became a woman, and after that
> he came and lived here. . . .
>
> Finally
> one time he came in and asked me.
> "They say I'm going to get married to you; when do you think we'll do it?" he said to me.
>
> Grandchild, really
> I didn't like it, but they kept asking me, so finally I did it.

I was so innocent, I guess, that what they said was like
nothing to me.

So
then
it turned out he was going to take good care of me;
my poor mother
put me there.
I was an orphan, so my mother didn't make a potlatch for me.

                              (115–123)

Matters of form aside, one of the most striking things about this
passage is that so much is left unsaid—particularly in the last seven
lines. This is quite unlike what previous editors would have produced. Were Underhill at work here, for example, she would "not
allow" Herbert to remain silent. What, precisely, was "nothing" to
you? When did you realize that he "was going to take good care"
of you? Why should your mother not "make potlatch" for you? Why
shouldn't orphans have potlatches? too expensive, or what?
McWhorter and Linderman, too, would have been puzzled, although they would probably have been less insistent in their questioning. They would, probably, have waited until an opportune
moment might allow them to ask a question to elicit another narrative that might make some of this clear. And they might give us a
sense of the scene in which they asked their question. Like Nick
Bottom, the weaver, Crapanzano would have written himself into
the scene with as large a part as possible—writing down all the
difficulties he had in getting Herbert to say even this much, telling
us how anguished he was to realize that he had his ham sandwich
for lunch while Herbert had only jerky, telling us how pained he
was when she declined to tell him any more about the potlatch,
and how little he understood it all, after all—how difficult it is to
carry on conversations across culture lines!

Pfisterer and his colleagues, on the other hand, keep themselves
tactfully in the background. They provide very brief introductions
to Herbert's narratives, locating some of the places she mentions,
providing this bit of historical and that bit of ethnographic background. But they eschew interpretation. And they respect Herbert's
silences as well as her words: they allow the differences and the

difficulties to speak for themselves. We end up with less Athabaskan culture data than we would have gotten had Underhill worked with Herbert. We know a good deal less about the editors' sensibilities than Crapanzano would have provided us with. But we are closer here to oral Athabaskan storytelling—and much closer to one aged Athabaskan woman's own point of view.

4

DON TALAYESVA AND GREGORIO: TWO INDIAN AUTOBIOGRAPHERS AND THEIR SOCIAL SCIENTISTS

Many of the Indian autobiographies, as we have seen, were collected by social scientists. During the 1930s, 1940s, and 1950s they published narratives collected from Apaches, Navajos, Sioux, Kwakiutls, Hopis, Papagos, and Kiowas among others. And the published autobiographies are but a fraction of those now moldering in the dark reaches of forgotten file cabinets.[1] Most social scientists, however, lost interest in such narratives after the mid-1950s. It was easier to collect the narratives, it seems—and *much* easier to be fascinated by them—than it was to figure out just what to do with them.[2] Still, the social scientists did publish a remarkable number of these narratives. We owe both the social scientists and their Indian narrators a debt: these narratives are to us a legacy, affording us some sense of what it means to see the world and the self according to traditional tribal—perhaps even ancient—habits of mind.

But a puzzling legacy they are. In the first place, the bicultural character of Indian autobiography is perhaps nowhere more striking than in the narratives collected for scientific purposes. Take, for example, the Belle Herbert narratives. Pfisterer and his colleagues worked very hard to retain as many features as possible of Herbert's oral originals. But considerable learning was necessary to achieve such ends. And in order to understand *Shandaa: In My Lifetime* thoroughly we need to understand Pfisterer's assumptions as well as Herbert's. To understand the as-told-to Indian autobiographies, we need to work toward an understanding of both the teller and the amanuensis. I think that a discussion of *Sun Chief* and "The Life Story" of Gregorio, the Hand-trembler, will help to make this general point. These two narratives may also help us to see more clearly the differences between ancient and modern conceptions of the self and of what it means to tell the story of one's life.

Sun Chief is the autobiography of Don Talayesva, a Hopi Indian born in the pueblo of Old Oraibi in 1890. The book was widely praised when it was first published in 1942. *The Saturday Review* (1942) called it "absorbing reading," a book that "answers about all the questions one might have about Hopi life and behavior." And the eminent Harvard anthropologist Clyde Kluckhohn declared that it was "the most satisfactory presentation of a personal document from a nonliterate society yet to appear" (1943). There is some irony here, however. Talayesva's society may have been nonliterate, but Talayesva himself was not. This book that tells us so much about the premodern Hopi is, in fact, the autobiography of a man like the heroes of many novels about Indians. He was a man caught between cultures, unable to reconcile the white way and the Hopi, fully at home in neither, keenly and sometimes painfully aware of what the choices allowed and denied. He was brought up in the traditional ways until the age of ten, at which time he was whisked away to boarding school to learn the white man's way. Then, like Martiniano in Frank Waters's *The Man Who Killed the Deer* (1970 [1942]) and like Abel in Momaday's *House Made of Dawn* (1966), Talayesva had a revelatory brush with death:

> My death experience had taught me that I had a Hopi Spirit Guide whom I must follow if I wished to live. I wanted to become a real Hopi again, to sing the old Katchina songs, and to feel free to make love without fear of sin or a rawhide. (134)

And so, like Martiniano and Abel, he returned to his people. At the age of twenty he returned to the pueblo, renounced his Christianity, joined the Hopi secret societies, worshipped the Hopi gods, and danced as a katchina in the plaza:

> I had learned a great lesson and . . . I could see that the old people were right when they insisted that Jesus Christ might do for modern whites in a good climate, but that the Hopi gods had brought success to us in the desert ever since the world began. (178)

But these thoughts, of course, did not suffice to turn him into such a Hopi as his grandfathers had been. This is immediately apparent when we juxtapose the first lines of Talayesva's autobiography with those of Gregorio's. Let us turn yet again to the opening of *Sun Chief:*

> When we were within our mother's womb, we happened to hurt her. She has told me how she went to a medicine man in her pain. He worked on her, felt her breasts and belly, and told her that we were twins. She was surprised and afraid. She said, "but I only want one baby." "Then I will put them together," replied the doctor. He took some corn meal outside the door and sprinkled it to the sun. Then he spun some black and white threads into a string, and tied it around my mother's left wrist. It is a powerful way to unite babies. We twins began, likewise, to twist ourselves into one child. My mother also helped to bring us together by her strong wish for only one baby.
>
> My mother has described how carefully she carried me. She slept with my father right along, so that he could have intercourse with her and make me grow. It is like irrigating a crop. . . . She had intercourse only with my father so that I could have an easy birth and resemble him.
>
> My father took care to injure no animal and thus damage my body. (25)

And here is Gregorio, a nonliterate Navajo shepherd and Hand-trembling diviner:

> I am about thirty-five years old. Juanito is the man that knows my age. Twenty years ago we moved down about 2 miles east over there. The place called Big Fields, that where we lived before. They tell me I was born there. When we moved down, I remember it very good. It was just about this time when Juanito has his sheep lambing. He has about one thousand head of sheep. He don't do anything besides, only herding this man. Stayed all summer, do nothing else, only herding. In the fall, me and Juanito went down to Aspera. There is a man used to have a lot of sheep there, his name, Tervie. He says he need two men, wanted to hire us, take his lambs over to South Mountain to . . . that store, big store at Smiths. (45)

Like many other unacculturated, nonliterate Indians, and like the ancient Egyptians, Greeks, and Romans,[3] Gregorio conceives of his life story as a history of deeds done, of adult deeds done. And it is already clear that Gregorio will have little to say about the connections between the deeds or about the implications of one deed or another on the later course of his life. In this, he is again like the ancients and like other nonliterate, unacculturated Indians. Red Crow's "Life History," for example, is really little more than an editor's knitting together of Red Crow's stories of his war deeds. The history of his life is a stringing together of the episodes of his deeds. There is little here of what Karl Weintraub has called "the inwardness of true autobiography" (1978:1). Red Crow's sense of himself, like Gregorio's, was essentially tribal. He was a Blood Indian and a warrior. He may feel superior to other Blood warriors, and certainly he feels that Bloods are a different order of being from the Crees. But we search in vain for any examination of his self, any self-definition, any sense that he might have been other than he was. Many of the early, as-told-to Indian autobiographical narratives have similar qualities: White Bull and Two Leggings, as we have seen, and Crows Heart's harrowing accounts of his eagle trapping and the Sun Dance, *Yellow Wolf: His Own Story*, Sinyella's autobiographical narratives, the Maxidiwiac narratives, and many others.[4]

Sun Chief is different from these. Talayesva articulates a clear sense of how what happened to him as a child helped to make him the man he is. He was twins in his mother's womb. His father was careful to avoid actions that would mar him in the womb. Already it is clear that Talayesva regards himself as a remarkable man: he wants to account for how he came to be the man he is, to understand the connections between events. Had he gone no further than recounting the wonders attendant upon his birth, this would not be unusual. Many premodern life stories describe such wonders as a way of showing how inevitable it was that the life to come should be remarkable. One may recall the story of the Virgin Birth of Jesus, the dipping of Achilles in the river Styx, the dedication of Samuel in the temple. But for Talayesva there is meaning implicit in a wide range of the episodes of his childhood. Some ninety pages of *Sun Chief* are devoted to the events of his life before he returns to the pueblo. This period of growing up, which we and Talayesva regard as obviously formative, Gregorio does not even mention.

Talayesva is, then, much closer than Gregorio to the thoroughly literate Indian autobiographers. For these writers self-definition is

inextricably related to the development of the self, and for them
the definition and development of the self are at the heart of the
autobiographical project, as it is for other writers in the mainstream
of the autobiographical tradition after Rousseau. Momaday's *The
Way to Rainy Mountain* tells us how he discovered himself as he
discovered his past. *The Names* treats only Momaday's first fifteen
years, the years that formed him. Alexander Eastman wrote an
autobiography to describe his journey "from the deep woods to
civilization," all the way from the prereservation forests of the
Santee Sioux to Boston Medical School. The Winnebago Albert
Hensley produced two brief autobiographies, the first explaining
how peyote made him the man he is, the second giving the credit
to the Carlisle Indian School (see chapter 6). Leslie Silko, in *Storyteller*, tries to place herself as one who is neither "pure" Indian nor
"pure" white, tries to work out what it means to be Indian at all
at a time when Indians are not as they once were.

But in order to understand clearly the differences between Gregorio's and Talayesva's autobiographies, we must also consider
some of the ways in which the Navajos and the Hopis differed. And
we must understand, too, how the methods and assumptions of
their white collaborators differ. Let us begin with the cultural
differences.

Gregorio and many other Navajos in these years led remarkably
isolated lives—much more isolated than their Hopi neighbors.
Talayesva's Oraibi is the oldest continuously inhabited town in
North America. Gregorio was a shepherd who spent more time
following his sheep than he did in the society of other Navajos. And
we may not even assume that he spent the evenings swapping
stories about the campfire with a fellow shepherd. After they had
taken down Gregorio's autobiography, Alexander and Dorothea
Leighton asked him some questions:

> *What did you and Juanito talk about out there herding alone?* I was taking
> care of the camp, Juanito is herding all the time, every day. Juanito
> used to tell me that I must . . . have some water ahead all the time . . .
> cook some food . . . and have it ready for him at noon time, and when
> he comes at supper time. He told me not to burn bread, make my camp
> nice [and perform other chores]. That is all he tell me.
>
> *Ever tell you any stories?* Never did tell any stories. Once in great while
> he say something about his own home over here, talk very little about
> that, not very much. . . .

> *What did you do for fun?* We never had any fun.
>
> *No dogs to play with or goats to rope?* Juanito was the only one used to play with dog at that time. . . . He used to rope that dog, tie him down, and have all kinds of fun with him . . . used to put a rope on the two hind legs and put the rope over a branch of a tree and hang him, hang him up. . . . [Juanito] Used to play with the dog that way. . . .
>
> *How often did you come home?* Sometimes once in two months, sometimes three months. (78–79)

I do not mean to suggest that all Navajos were like Gregorio. But to read *Gregorio* and such autobiographical narratives as are collected in Broderick Johnson's *Stories of Traditional Navajo Life and Culture* (1977) is to realize that many Navajos in these years led lives that were solitary to a degree that is almost unimaginable to the rest of us. Some of these men and women recall being sent out onto the arid, windy plateaus at the age of five or seven to watch the flock, with only a dog for company and protection. Life was much more tightly knit in Oraibi, and storytelling a much more important part of life, and there was storytelling of a kind to aid a future autobiographer. At one point, for example, Talayesva recalls camping on the way back from a salt expedition:

> We . . . ate supper, smoked, and rolled ourselves in our blankets. While we lay under the stars, we reviewed our experiences on the journey, and my father repeated the old story of how the War Twins established the salt expeditions long ago. (245)

On their return their relatives made for them a feast, and Talayesva's father told the story of their journey "with all its details" (246). These details are important, for such expeditions are undertaken not only for the salt. If all has been done with proper regard for the katchinas and the rituals, the rains will come. There were traditions of first-person storytelling among the Hopis, then, as there were among other preliterate peoples. This kind of storytelling, as we have seen in chapter 1, could even be introspective: "Was there anything we did on our salt expedition which might have angered the katchinas?" "Have we done all that we might do to assure that rain will fall?" And we see, too, that for the Hopis the history of their own doings may be explicitly related to the history of their people. Talayesva's father tells the story of the origin of the salt expeditions as they are recalling their own salt expedition. These same kinds of personal stories are told after another salt expedition (255). On another occasion Talayesva thinks back over the events of his life to see if he might, by some bad action, have been responsible for the death of his child (262). And later we read that Talayesva's old uncle Kayayeptewa would tell stories about his sexual escapades in order to instruct the young men in matters of love (282).

Such Hopi traditions must account for much that we admire in *Sun Chief*. Before he began his work on *Sun Chief*, Talayesva was practiced in most of the traditions of oral autobiographical story-telling described in chapter 1. Gregorio seems largely to have been isolated from such traditions. But such individual and cultural considerations are not sufficient to explain all the ways in which Talayesva's and Gregorio's narratives differ. For the rest we will have to consider not only the assumptions of the Hopis or the Navajos, but also those of the social scientists who served as their amanuenses.

In what was probably his last paper, the father of modern anthropology, Franz Boas, took to task the anthropologists, many of them his own students, who were collecting autobiographies from native informants (1943). These narratives, argued Boas, were of little worth, valuable only to those interested in the ways memory may pervert truth. Boas's response to these autobiographies is not surprising. Boas was after culture data, and there are less clumsy ways of collecting culture data. The offending anthropologists, however, were drawn by the siren song of psychology to consider the effects of culture upon personality. And so they collected autobiographies. As early as 1920 Paul Radin wrote in the introduction to his edition of Sam Blowsnake's *Autobiography of a Winnebago Indian* that it was necessary to get "the facts in an emotional setting"; autobiography, Radin argued, allows this:

> Such personal reminiscences and impressions, inadequate as they are, are likely to throw more light on the workings of the mind and emotions of primitive man than any amount of speculation from a sophisticated anthropologist. (2)

We may notice this same confident and hopeful spirit in much of the anthropology of the 1930s, 1940s, and early 1950s. There were real expectations that the social sciences were going to effect important changes for the good. Great things were going to be accomplished. Boasian particularism was on the run. Large projects were afoot, and the walls around the disciplines were crumbling. Alexander Leighton knew personally many of the social scientists at work in these years. In a 1985 interview, he recalled these heady times:

> Many people thought . . . we were in for a new period of cooperative relationships in problem solving. It was the spirit of the operational approach and interdisciplinary approach. We felt that we could tackle some of the major problems of Western civilization with some chance of being able to do something . . . particularly the problems relating to rapid social change and acculturation. . . . Through the mid-fifties, there was a lot of activity in this regard in the Ramah Project. Cornell developed a Center for Applied Anthropology, which involved departments of sociology and anthropology and social psychology. . . . Psychiatrists came [there] for training.

And Harvard built William James Hall, which was to house the new, interdisciplinary Department of Social Relations.[5] And Kluckhohn organized two projects, the Values Study Project and the Ramah Navajo Project, which brought anthropologists, psychiatrists, sociologists, historians, psychologists, a physiologist, an immunologist, a specialist in education, botanists, and a physician together to work among the culturally diverse peoples of the Four Corners area in the American Southwest.

One of these young hopefuls entered into the life of Don Talayesva. In 1938, some eighteen years after he had chosen the Hopi way, Talayesva was employed as an informant by Leo Simmons, a Yale sociologist. Soon they were engaged in the writing of autobiography. Simmons conducted many hours of interviews with his Hopi informant, and paid him as well to keep a minutely detailed diary. There was also a considerable correspondence. All of this was in English, in which Talayesva was, according to Simmons, "exceptionally fluent for a Hopi of his age" (5). By the time, then, that Simmons sat down to turn all of this into a single narrative, he was facing a huge trove of material, transcripts of some 350 hours of interviews and over *8,000 pages* of diary. *Sun Chief,* at 460 pages, includes only about a fifth of this material.[6] Simmons describes the result:

The account is . . . a highly condensed record in the first person, and almost always in Don's own words or in words which he readily recognized in checking the manuscript. [It] is . . . selected and condensed narration, interwoven with additional information obtained by repeated interviewing. (7)

Simmons's editorial hand was heavy, then. He was also insistent with Talayesva about what kinds of material he did and did not want. A time came, for example, when Simmons told Talayesva that he had quite enough about matters of daily routine (5). He wanted more that was personal. Like so many of his fellows in the social sciences, then, Simmons was interested in the psychology of the individual.

He was also directly influenced by Kluckhohn. And when Kluckhohn wrote up his 1945 survey of the life history in anthropology, perhaps his most important criterion in judging the usefulness of life histories was the degree to which they were personal, the degree to which they revealed an individual personality. And so it was that Kluckhohn criticized Clellan Ford's *Smoke from their Fires*, the autobiography of a Kwakiutl chief, Charles Nowell, because it seemed too objective, too little personal. Kluckhohn quoted approvingly from Barnett's review of the book, that in Nowell's autobiography "it is difficult to catch a mood, an attachment, a strong conviction—in fact any persistent personality trait threading through the collection of incidents which represent his life." The Kwakiutl autobiographer seems to be "an amateur ethnologist himself," and so "his story lacks the warmth, the humanness, and the vitalizing quality" (Kluckhohn, 1945:93–94) which Barnett and Kluckhohn and Simmons want to find in autobiography. For the collection of data about the *culture* the anthropologist turns to other methods as being more reliable. Autobiography, on the other hand, was to provide evidence that was subjective, evidence that would demonstrate the effects of culture on the individual.

At work in the minds of Kluckhohn, Barnett, and Simmons is an assumption about the nature of autobiography. They assumed, I think, that autobiography has no historical or cultural dimension, that autobiography as a genre is ever and always essentially the same. They assumed that, while people in a given culture may for one reason or another feel disinclined to tell their life stories to an anthropologist, while they may feel inhibited, say, or reticent, there is nothing in the making of autobiography itself which is beyond them. Where the anthropologist fails to elicit a subjective autobiography from an informant, the problem may be that the anthropologist simply did not ask the right questions, or was too aggressive in his questioning (Kluckhohn, 1945:93–94). Some informants, Kluckhohn recognizes, are more apt to cooperate than others; indeed, Indians of some tribes would be less likely to cooperate than Indians of other tribes. To make this point Kluckhohn quotes from the introduction to Leslie White's "Autobiography of an Acoma Indian":

> It is especially difficult to secure them [autobiographies] from Pueblo Indians of the Southwest. . . . They are not individualists; they are not given to reflective introspection and analysis. They do not conceive of human experience as something dependent upon an intimate and personal encounter and compact with a supernatural being, a guardian spirit (as do the Plains Indians, or the Winnebago). (White, 1943:326–327)

Kluckhohn recognized, then, "that there must be a cultural dimension to this problem" (1945:119), that pueblo Indians (like Talayesva) would be particularly disinclined to do autobiography. Kluckhohn even wonders if perhaps "most American Indians who give autobiographies [will] be those who are actually badly adjusted in their own culture?" (1945:96). But all of this, Kluckhohn assumed, raised no more than problems of fieldwork methodology. The problem, as he saw it, was reticence, reticence in this case to speak with a white anthropologist or to transgress tribal taboos with regard to sacred matters. (Both Talayesva and Gregorio, for example, struggled with such taboos.)

It is not surprising that Kluckhohn and Simmons should assume that people of all cultures are capable of defining themselves in autobiography. In this they were in agreement with Georg Misch, who was the foremost theoretician on matters autobiographical during these years. For Misch, as the facts of a life are recalled,

> there will spontaneously awake in the mind of the autobiographer the emotional feelings that were produced by their occurrence. . . . Finally, the man who sets out to write the story of his own life has it in view

as a whole, with unity and direction and significance of its own. In this single whole the facts and feelings, actions and reactions . . . all have their definite place, thanks to their significance in relation to the whole. This knowledge, which enables the writer to conceive his life as a single whole, has grown in the course of his life out of his actual experience. (Misch, 1951:7)

The dearth of autobiographical writing in classical Greece, Misch argued, is "quite an isolated phenomenon—one which needs explanation" (1951:17). Small wonder, then, that for Kluckhohn and Simmons the problem was overcoming the subject's feelings of reticence. If the fieldworker can once get beyond this, feelings and events will naturally associate themselves as the autobiography is elicited. For Misch, as for Kluckhohn and Simmons, autobiography *is* precisely a way of defining the self, and if people can deliver first-person narratives at all (as of course they can), then they are capable of delivering themselves of narratives that *are* personal, subjective, that offer psychological insights, narratives that are like the autobiographies in the Western tradition. If only the anthropologist can break through their reserve, if only the field methods are right.

Although Kluckhohn had a keen sense of the problems of editorial interference in such a book as *Sun Chief* (Kluckhohn, 1945), he did not realize that even the anthropologist's assumptions about the nature of the autobiographical enterprise could influence the Indian's narrative. This is not surprising, since nothing had been written about autobiography which could have led Kluckhohn or Simmons to think of autobiography differently. It did not occur to Kluckhohn or Simmons, then, that the degree to which the Indian's autobiography is as they would like it to be is a fairly precise measure of how deeply the Indian has drunk at the well of Euro-American culture. The social scientists' very questions could be powerful instruments of acculturation, Kluckhohn's brief discussion of Crow Wing's *Pueblo Indian Journal 1920–1921,* elicited and edited by Parsons, is another case in point.

As an account of the sequence of events in a Southwestern Pueblo it has distinct value for the ethnologist. But as a record of the reaction of a personality to these happenings the journal has slight significance. (1945:104)

But if Crow Wing has little to say in his journal that is individual, then his reticence is perfectly in keeping with all that we know about the Pueblo Indians' intensely tribal, nonindividualistic habits of mind. His journal, then, even in its silences, is telling us something significant, something essential about Crow Wing's personality. As late as 1971 the autobiography of Albert Yava, a Tewa-Hopi, reveals the same sort of inclination to talk about the people rather than the self.

It is ironic, then, that the harder Simmons worked to win from Talayesva material that was personal, material that would show how this individual Hopi *really* felt, the farther he moved his subject from being a typical Hopi. In his efforts to get information about the secret ceremonies, for example, we may see how hard Simmons was willing to push.

Soon after they began their work together, Talayesva stated that he could not tell Simmons anything about the secret ceremonies; "for he would get into trouble with other Hopi and with his gods if he told these things." It occurred to Simmons to suggest that Talayesva would not be required to talk about any aspect of the ceremonies "that was not already published." Later, however, Talayesva was shocked to find just how much had been revealed in a 1901 book by George Dorsey and H. R. Voth. "One evening," recalls Simmons,

> we began with Dorsey and Voth's account. Don [Talayesva] examined the pictures and drawings of the altars and seemed distressed, making such remarks as, "This is awful. It makes me unhappy. That man Voth was a thief. The secrets are all exposed" . . . [Later that evening] an important officer in the Soyal ceremony came into the house and the interview was abruptly ended. (6–7)

Still, Simmons insisted on their bargain, assuring Talayesva that he would pack up and leave the pueblo immediately unless Talayesva told all. Simmons, then, was willing to press hard to break through his informant's reserve. He also pressed Talayesva to think about and respond to questions that it would never have occurred to a nonliterate Hopi to ask of himself. Simmons introduced Talayesva to characteristically modern questions and concerns. Such questions—indeed, even the very idea that such a man as Simmons was eager to devote effort and money to the taking down of the details of his life—had a profound effect on such a status-conscious Hopi man such as Talayesva. This important white man was interested in *him,* in Don Talayesva, and not the other inhabitants of the pueblo. When his feelings were being minutely questioned, could he avoid coming to think of himself as a man of feeling? Simmons's questions and his interest furthered the transformation that had begun for Talayesva in the white man's schools. Simmons helped Talayesva to discover or to create a self whose limits were not set by the tribe.

Questions designed, for example, to elicit information about what Kluckhohn calls "the critical events of childhood" (1945:93) are essential to autobiography as Kluckhohn and Simmons understand it. Again, Simmons and Kluckhohn were heavily influenced by their reading in psychology. But one need not have read Freud to feel that the childhood years are essential in autobiography. We cannot imagine Rousseau's *Confessions* or any of the great Western autobiographies without the childhood years. One of the reasons Talayesva has so much to say about his childhood, then, is precisely that Simmons so insistently asked him about his childhood, so insistently asked him how this event in his adult life might have been connected to that event in his childhood.

Gregorio, on the other hand, clearly does not consider his childhood years to have been "critical." He does not even mention his childhood years. This silence is certainly not a result of the Leightons' lack of interest in the development of the personality. They shared many of Simmons's interests; indeed, the Leightons were important influences on Kluckhohn in this thinking about the whole scope and purpose of the Values Study Project that brought Simmons—and the Leightons themselves—to the Southwest.[7] They shared interests with Simmons, but they differed considerably in some of their assumptions and in their field methods. Important as they regarded anthropology to be, the Leightons were themselves doctors and psychiatrists; and trained as they were at Johns Hopkins under Adolf Meyer, the Leightons considered the taking of life stories to be an important part of diagnosis and therapy. Consequently they tried to elicit and record life stories with as little distortion and interference as possible. Sometimes they would "trade" stories with their informants, to make the storytelling mutual and thus more nearly natural.[8] And so the Leightons published Gregorio's life story as it came to them from the interpreter, with *very* few changes.[9]

And this is significant, for unlike Talayesva and virtually every other Indian whose autobiography comes to us via an Anglo amanuensis, Gregorio himself chose to tell an autobiography, and he composed his own autobiography. Gregorio, it seems, dropped by on several occasions to listen while the Leightons interviewed other Navajos in his neighborhood. He heard them eliciting life stories from some of their informants. He then volunteered his own. He told his 15,000-word life story in five sessions over a period of five days in the spring of 1940. Gregorio, who knew no English, spoke through an interpreter (a Navajo friend who knew Gregorio well); but he was interrupted by few questions (all included in the text). On other occasions—*after* he had told his autobiography—the Leightons asked him many questions.[10] But the life story they wanted to be his own, with as little interference and suggestion as possible.

Gregorio's autobiography, then, is a window back through time. Gregorio was twelve years Talayesva's junior, but he represents his life in an ancient way. This is a man with his Navajo religion and his tribal sense of identity intact. This is a man, as we have seen, who has had little contact with white culture. Gregorio has been given the idea that it is possible to tell his life whole; he has heard his neighbors questioned as to the details of their lives. But otherwise the story is his own, as he chose to tell it, with virtually no direction. And the Leightons did no reordering, no cutting, no inserting of details gleaned at other times. Of all of the published (and a number of unpublished) autobiographical narratives by American Indians I have read, I know of no other like Gregorio's. There are other long autobiographical narratives by unacculturated, nonliterate, non-English-speaking Indians but none that is so little influenced by the white collaborator-editor. There are other narratives that are published just as they came from the interpreter, but these tend to be either very brief autobiographies or narratives of single episodes in the life of the narrator.[11] Because the Leightons chose to work with Gregorio and his narrative as they did, we are allowed to see clearly here just how a preliterate, unacculturated, tribal man conceives of his life and of what it means to tell the story of a life.

We have already seen that Gregorio and Talayesva have different ideas about their childhood. A second striking difference is in the degree to which their narratives are integrated, connected. This, for example, is all that Gregorio has to say in his autobiography about his mother: "My mother died when I was a little feller, so I don't get to know my mother" (47). The Leightons later asked Gregorio about his upbringing: it seems that after his mother's death he was raised by his mother's sister and her husband, Jaunito (62). But it did not occur to Gregorio to mention this in the course of his autobiography. There is no suggestion in the autobiography that his early separation from his parents has any bearing on the later course of his life, no suggestion that he might have been a different man had his parents raised him rather than Jaunito. This is not to say that Gregorio was unaware that he was at a disadvantage because he was an orphan. But as Gregorio imagines how his life's story ought to be told, this has no place. The story of the life is the story of his deeds.

For another example, consider Gregorio's accounts of his two wives. Gregorio tells us in some detail about the arrangements that led to his first marriage, tells us who did the negotiating, what the bride price was. He tells us what kinds of foods were served to the marriage guests; he recalls the admonitions which were issued to his bride and to himself by his father-in-law at the time of the wedding:

> Told the girl that she's got the home of herself now. What she have to do is take care of her home. . . . Told her she have to wash the dishes, take care of the fire, sweep the floor. She have to mind [Gregorio]. . . . Told me . . . that me and the girl, we got our own home and (should) tried best to make a good living between the two. Told me to do the farming, make good house, good hogan, do the outside work. (50)

And then he is alone with his wife, a woman he had never seen before the day of their marriage. Soon the difficulties begin. His wife does not "mind" him. She cannot cook. She does not like to stay in the hogan all day. She is "bad" and "mean." Finally, they separate. But Gregorio does not relate in any way the difficulties he has with his wife to his sense of himself. He makes no connections between his first marriage and his later life. He provides no explanations of her behavior, no suggestion that she behaved as she did because of this or that event in her past, because of this or that bad influence. He provides us with no explanation of his own inability to keep his wife; no episode in his life as he tells it prepares us to understand his marital woes. Later he marries Nazba, a good wife. But he draws no comparisons between Nazba and the first wife. His experiences with Nazba are stories in their own right, quite separate from his stories about his first wife. No connections are made.

Talayesva's autobiography, on the other hand, is full of connections. There are many women in Talayesva's life, for example, and he is always ready to compare the one with the other, ready to show how the one prepared him to appreciate, or to recognize the deficiencies of, another. As he is preparing to marry Irene, for example, he receives a passionate letter from a former love, Mettie. "I think that I would have been more excited over my wedding," says Talayesva, "if she had been the bride" (220).

There are, to be sure, some fascinating discontinuities in *Sun Chief*, particularly in Talayesva's ambivalence toward the white world. And it must also be said that we may be missing connections in Gregorio's "Life Story" that we would recognize if we knew more about Gregorio and about his culture. And certainly we are missing all of the nonverbal cues that are inevitably a part of such a sustained oral performance as was Gregorio's telling of his life story. But even if we take all this into account, the differences between *Sun Chief* and "The Life Story" are striking.

Consider the ways in which the two narratives are ordered. Gregorio's "Life Story" is in chronological order. This happened, and then this happened, and then this. But had Gregorio not so ordered them, we would find little in the episodes themselves that would allow us confidently to place one before another. We are told about the onset of his Hand-trembling powers, and he tells how he learned to cook; these, then, must precede any of the episodes that have him cooking or doing his Hand-trembling; his marital difficulties must follow his marriage, but there is virtually nothing else which we would be able to place before or after anything else in the narrative. He herds sheep here, he herds sheep there; he does his Hand-trembling here, he does his Hand-trembling there; he works sheep, he works horses. Had they been deviously inclined, the Leightons could even have reversed the order of Gregorio's two wives, and we could not have sensed that anything was amiss.

Simmons, on the other hand, had to pay strict attention to the implications of the stories Talayesva told him. The depth of feeling that Talayesva expresses for his adopted son Norman must follow his accounts of the deaths of his natural children—and of his eventual impotence. Talayesva talks about taking care in his katchina performance not to go too far in frightening the children of the pueblo. He also tells of having himself been severely frightened by the katchinas when he was a child. The one is a consequence of the other. His conversion to the Hopi way must follow his experiences in the white man's schools. Even if we were reading the unedited material in the order in which it came to Simmons, we would still be able to work out much of the order for ourselves, because of the sense of consequences, connections, causes, results, effects upon himself, which permeate Talayesva's material.

For another, closely related, example, Talayesva clearly conceives of his life in stages: his thoroughly Hopi childhood, his schooling and immersion in the white world, and his return to the pueblo. Simmons's editorial hand has certainly made these stages clearer for us. He has, for example, divided Talayesva's material into chapters, and he has arranged the material into chronological order. Doubtless, too, the stages are clearer for all the cutting that Simmons did. But the stages are not Simmons's invention, however active he may have been in encouraging Talayesva to think in terms of connections, comparisons, causes, and results. Talayesva's remarks about his illness, for example, make this quite clear: "my death experience had taught me that I had a Hopi Spirit Guide whom I must follow if I wished to live. I wanted to become a real Hopi again" (134). And after his initiation into the Katchina society, Talayesva says:

> I thought of the flogging and the initiation as an important turning point in my life, and I felt ready at last to listen to my elders and to live right. (87)

Gregorio, on the other hand, says nothing, implies nothing, about stages or turning points. His autobiography begins with his shepherding, but Gregorio does not say "And so I reached that age at which I could begin upon the work of a man." As we have seen, he seems to begin where he does because of his sense of what it means to tell the story of a life. His marriage to his first wife seems to mark no epoch either. Immediately after his account of his wedding ceremony, he says, "Next day I start to haul wood there to the place" (50). And so we are back to his work, the herding, the lambing. He conveys no sense that he is himself a different man either for his marriage or his marital trials.

Gregorio does not even tell about the advent of his Hand-trembling powers in such a way as to suggest that this is a new stage in his life. He tells how the Hand-trembling began once while he was quite ill; he tells several stories about how he made use of his Hand-trembling to diagnose ills, to suggest which healing ceremonies would be appropriate, which singer would be the best. But although this is important work—and even dangerous work, since a Hand-trembler may himself become sick if he does not use his gift in moderation and exercise other precautions—Gregorio never says anything to indicate just how important he regards this work of Hand-trembling to be. Is this his life's work? Is this more important than his skills in lambing? He does not say. And there is nothing in the narrative that would allow us to infer an answer. There are no earlier episodes that foreshadow what his life's work is to be.

Gregorio is as he is because he is a Navajo man. He is certainly aware that, had things worked out differently, he might have had more sheep, more horses—or fewer. But there is no sense in his autobiography that he could have been a different kind of person entirely. Gregorio's autobiography does not, finally, articulate a sense of the self. Alexander Leighton (interview, 1985) has confirmed this sense of Gregorio's autobiography. Indeed, having collected numerous nondirected life stories over the years from people in many different cultures—Navajo, Eskimo, Japanese, French Canadian, American, Yoruban—he was able to add that he could remember no nonliterate participant in a preliterate culture who produced a life story that seemed designed to articulate a sense of how the self came to be. On the other hand, he said, his literate subjects seldom failed to tell about their lives in such a way as to suggest how they came to be as they are.[12]

In this way Gregorio and the other nonliterates from whom Leighton collected life histories are precisely like the ancient Greeks, as Weintraub has described them:

Individuals were embedded in the social mass of given blood relations. In fundamental ways, often so hard for us who live in a highly differentiated society of individualists . . . to understand, these earlier lives are enmeshed in and derive their meaning from basic social and kinship relations. (1978:2)

And so it did not occur to Gregorio to question how he came to be as he was. Talayesva's sense of himself as "special," on the other hand, is put into service to explain much of his life, to aid him to understand his life whole, to allow him to reconcile his life's contradictions.[13] He talks with Simmons, as we have seen, about many of the secret matters of the Hopi ceremonies. But Talayesva is a special person, and so he may rise above the taboos. Indeed, Talayesva came to see his work with Simmons and other academics as part of the fulfillment of his early promise. His work on the story of his life, then, came to be an important part of his life. It fed his Hopi sense of status, and it enlarged his sense of himself:

> One day a white woman came to our house and said she was from Ann Arbor, Michigan. I said, "Perhaps you know my friends there, Professors Mischa Titiev and Volney Jones?" . . . and I explained that I had helped Volney get his degree in botany and Mischa his in anthropology. . . .
> When the new postmaster handed out five letters to me at one time, he said in surprise, "You must have many white friends all over the United States." "Yes," I answered, "I have lots of friends from the different universities and I am proud of them." He stood staring at me for a while, thinking, perhaps, that I was a big man. (374)

So important did this association with the academics become to him, that it shaped his sense of what his life would be: "When I am too old and feeble to follow my sheep or cultivate my corn," says Talayesva late in *Sun Chief,* "I plan to sit in my house, carve katchina dolls, and tell my nephews and nieces the story of my life" (381). One thinks, again, of Roy Pascal's dictum that the making of autobiography recreates the autobiographer (1960:182–183).

Talayesva is, then, a man who has moved—and was moved— much closer to the modern world than was Gregorio. I think that this accounts, in large measure, for the impact and the ready acceptance of the book. Robert Hine wrote in his foreword to the 1963 edition that "The remarkable thing about *Sun Chief* is that the cultural outsider is swept along into acceptance." This could certainly not be said of Gregorio's "Life Story." We struggle against the strangeness of Gregorio's narrative, wondering at the silences, wondering always if what is left unsaid is left unthought. Some, I know, wonder if Gregorio might simply have been a stupid man. Hine says that we respond as we do to *Sun Chief* because the book "is a warm, universally human account." Again, this could hardly be said of Gregorio's "Life Story." Hine continues:

> Within [*Sun Chief's*] literary framework, we are convinced, removed from our pretensions, momentarily certain that the Spider Woman and the Two-Heart exist. What happens to the reader in Rousseau's *Confessions* . . . also moves him here: *Sun Chief* communicates a compelling human experience. (vii)

Just so. It is in large part the literary framework, which Simmons supplies, which makes Talayesva seem to us so much more "warmly human" than Gregorio. Talayesva's autobiography *is* like Rousseau's *Confessions*—because Rousseau and other modern autobiographers so completely shaped Simmons's sense of what it means to do autobiography that he worked with Talayesva tirelessly until he won from him the kinds of details, the accounts of failings, foibles, hopes, connections, feelings, and turning points, which would allow him to put together a narrative that moderns *would* recognize as being like Rousseau's, as being "warmly human." One suspects that this means, really, "surprisingly like ourselves." The Leightons, on the other hand, worked diligently to influence Gregorio as little as possible. And so his "Life Story" may give us a glimpse of a more ancient humanity.

5

SAM BLOWSNAKE:
ADAPTING ORAL FORMS TO
WRITTEN AUTOBIOGRAPHY

I have elsewhere suggested that the history of American Indian autobiography recapitulates the history of Western autobiography (1981:1–5). The earliest autobiographical writings in the Western tradition, for example, are what have been called the *res gestae*, the stories the Greeks and Romans wrote about their great deeds;[1] this kind of writing corresponds very closely to the coup tales and hunting tales that were discussed in chapter 1. Later, some of the ancients began to write memoirs, narratives about great events they had witnessed; we find that the Indians came to produce this sort of narrative as well. Sometimes the Indians themselves wrote memoirs; more often their memoirs were taken down by historians and anthropologists. (A remarkable number of Indian memoirs having to do with the Custer battle alone have been published.)[2] Then, with Augustine's *Confessions,* we find a very different kind of autobiographical writing, something much closer to what has been called "true" autobiography—autobiography that articulates an individual sense of the self. I would like to argue that there is here as well a parallel in the history of American Indian autobiography. A Winnebago Indian, Sam Blowsnake, alias Crashing Thunder, "reinvented" the autobiography.[3]

Since Blowsnake's autobiography, like so many Indian autobiographies, comes to us via an intermediary, in this case the anthropologist Paul Radin, it is important first to consider just how much of this book is Blowsnake's and how much of it is Radin's. We must remember, too, that Radin issued Blowsnake's autobiography in more than one form. *Crashing Thunder* (1926)[4] was based upon an earlier book, *The Autobiography of a Winnebago Indian* (1920). Radin wrote in his introduction to this 1920 version that it was simply a translation with very little editing of a text written in Winnebago by Blowsnake himself. Radin stated as well that "No attempt of any kind was made to influence [Blowsnake] in the selection of the particular facts of his life which he chose to present."

Crashing Thunder is a reworking of this *Autobiography*. Radin fit in excerpts from material that he had collected from Blowsnake over the years. Where Blowsnake mentioned in the *Autobiography*, for example, that he had prayed at a certain time to the spirits, Radin here interpolated an appropriate prayer, which he had at some time taken down from Blowsnake's dictation. As Arnold Krupat (1983) has demonstrated, Radin was not above changing the wording and the style in places, but the pattern of the two versions is the same. Radin did no reordering of the narrative sequence.

Given all this, Ruth Underhill's comment on *Crashing Thunder* is of considerable interest:

> *Crashing Thunder* is not strictly an autobiography, although every word of it came from the Indian's mouth. Rather it is a drama, centering around a religious experience. From the jumble of reminiscences which anyone pours out when talking about himself, one feels that the ethnologist has selected first, those bearing on religious education and myths, then the fall to drunkenness and murder, and finally, the salvation through peyote. . . . His vision achieved, Crashing Thunder's drama closes. . . . Here Radin was artist rather than ethnologist. (1971:ix)

Paradoxically, Underhill makes her mistake because she knows a great deal about American Indians and their autobiographies. Underhill is simply assuming that *Crashing Thunder* was the result of the method she herself had employed to produce her own *Autobiography of a Papago Woman*, the same method, that is, that has produced so many of the Indian autobiographies: ethnologist encourages informant to relate life history, asking questions along the way to guide informant and to ensure adequate detail; ethnologist then edits this great bundle of material (now usually in translation) into something like chronological order, cutting repetitions and making the other changes necessary to transform a collection of transcripts of individual oral performances into a single, more or less continuous narrative. But the ethnologist does not add to the words of the Indian. And the ethnologist does not impose a pattern, other than the chronological, upon the material.[5] According to Underhill, Radin did impose a dramatic pattern upon Blowsnake's material, which is to say that Underhill mistook Blowsnake's own structure for Radin's.

What was it about Blowsnake's narrative that fooled Underhill? She herself says that the narrative's dramatic pattern led her to her conclusion. But by this she could not have meant that no Indian could produce either a dramatic narrative or a patterned narrative. Certainly many of the episodes that Underhill elicited from Maria Chona and then edited into *Papago Woman* were dramatic in the everyday sense Underhill seems to intend. And Underhill must certainly have recognized patterns in many of the stories Chona told her. No, what she saw in *Crashing Thunder* was that the episodes were tied together to form a larger pattern; she saw that the episodes worked together to explain just how it was that Blowsnake had come to be the person he was. This was not at all the sort of thing Underhill would have expected in an Indian autobiography elicited by an anthropologist. Blowsnake had written an *autobiography*. He wrote a narrative that was so like the autobiographies of our own tradition that even so keen a student of the American Indian as Ruth Underhill could mistake the form for Radin's rather than Blowsnake's.

Indians who had been educated by whites had written integrated life histories, certainly. Charles Alexander Eastman wrote the first of his autobiographical books in 1902 and a second in 1916. Born a Santee Sioux, trained for hunting and war until he was taken away to school at the age of fifteen, Eastman certainly had a sense of how the peculiar circumstances of his life had made him the person he was: he saw himself as an embodiment of Social Darwinist ideas (see chapter 7). But by the time he began writing autobiography, Eastman had graduated from Boston Medical School. Later in his life, Eastman did question the value of "civilization," but he was thoroughly acculturated, however ill at ease he may have been, and widely read. En-me-gah-bowh was educated by missionaries and had for years served as their interpreter before he wrote *En-me-gah-bowh's Story* (1904). The remarkable George Cop-way had only twenty months of formal schooling, but he was thoroughly Christianized and sufficiently familiar with Anglo-American literature to be able to preface his 1860 autobiography by lamenting that he could "not wield the pen of a Macaulay or the graceful wand of an Irving."[6]

Blowsnake, on the other hand, had virtually no white education;[7] indeed, Radin introduced him to the world as a "representative middle-aged [Winnebago] of moderate ability" (*Autobiography*, 2), and as a man who could give us an "inside view" of what a "real Indian" is, "how he thinks, feels, reacts, adapts himself to the varying conditions of life" (*Crashing Thunder*, 8). This is a bit disingenuous. Blowsnake was a convert to the Peyote Cult; he had been a participant in more than one Wild West show; and he could write, albeit in a syllabary adapted for the writing of Winnebago (he was not at all fluent in English). And he was a man, as we shall see, of more than "moderate" ability. A "real Indian" he doubtless was, but he was a different kind of Indian than his grandfather had been. And yet as we read Blowsnake's autobiography, we find ourselves in the presence of a man who is very far from being acculturated in the way that Eastman, En-me-gah-bowh, and the rest were. Amazed as we may be by the lives these men lived, and moved as we may be by their accounts of their immense journeys, that they should be able to write autobiography should not surprise us. Autobiography was simply one part of the culture that they had assimilated. But Blowsnake had read no autobiographies. And he was not eager to undertake the work that Radin had assigned him. It was only when he found himself badly in need of money that he accepted the work, for which Radin had promised to pay him.

When he did set to work, he managed, like Augustine before him, to adapt the confessional forms to the demands of autobiography, but in a very real sense—and again he is like Augustine in this—his work was without precedent in his own experience: Blowsnake stands in relation to the history of American Indian autobiography as Augustine stands in relation to the history of Western autobiography. In whatever sense it may be said that Augustine was an innovator in writing his *Confessions*, the same may be said for Blowsnake.

I do not mean to suggest that Blowsnake was the first Indian to write a confessional autobiography. Samson Occom wrote such a narrative in 1762; William Apes wrote his *Son of the Forest* in 1829; Peter Jones wrote the story of his sins, conversion, and Christian mission in 1860.[8] But, again, these men were literate in English, and they had read just such narratives as they themselves wrote. Apes even edited an anthology of Indian conversion and confession stories in 1833. Blowsnake, like Augustine, had never read such a narrative as he came to write.

There are, I think, five important reasons for Blowsnake's accomplishment. The first reason was that Radin *asked* him to do a life history. Obviously, Blowsnake would never have written an autobiography had Radin not nagged him and paid him to do so. But we must also remember that the very suggestion that one could write the story of one's life *whole* could allow an unacculturated Indian to look at himself in a new way. Indians had long told stories about their personal experiences: one thinks, again, of the coup tales and the hunting tales; but they did not tell their lives whole. The historian Karl Weintraub discusses the same phenomenon among the early Greeks and Romans. He suggests that they did not write whole autobiography largely because of the importance to them of kinship ties:

> Ask a Homeric hero who he is, and most likely he will answer: I am Telemachus, the son of Odysseus, the son of Laertes. . . . Individuals were imbedded in the social mass of given blood relations. In fundamental ways, often so hard for us who live in a highly differentiated society of individualists and individualities to understand, these earlier lives are enmeshed in and derive their meaning from basic social and kinship relations. (1978:2)

This is very much like what we read about the prereservation Indians. There is very little sense that individuals can be thought of—except pejoratively—apart from the group. Heroes there may be, but they stand out as ideal expressions of their society's values (Weintraub, 1978:4), and so there is no reason even for a hero to try to account for how the peculiarities of his life made him the hero he is. Long hair, abstention from strong drink, and the favor of the Lord are enough to explain even the prowess of a Samson.

Imagine, then, what might have been the effect upon one of the brighter Homeric heroes of an ethnologist's insistent questioning. Well, yes, I understand that you slew your wife's suitors, but how did you *feel* about that? You are a sometimes devious man. What was it, do you think, about your childhood that made you cunning? Yes, I know that you resisted Circe's advances, but why was that? Why were you able to do so when none of your men did? Yes, doubtless you were a better man, but why? Yes, I know your family. I have already done the kinship study. But now I want to know what it was about your family, really, that makes you act the way you do. How were you raised? Was your father much away from home?

Before he wrote his autobiography, Blowsnake had spent a good deal of time with Radin working as an informant, answering Radin's questions about this ceremony and that, about this family and that clan. By the time he finally set to work on his autobiography, he had a good sense of what Radin wanted: he wanted to know *why* and he wanted to know in detail. And so Blowsnake wrote not only that he had led a life of sin and that he then joined the Peyote Cult, but also what it was about himself and his life in particular that led him to join the Peyote Cult. He describes himself as one who has been searching throughout his life for something "holy." He tries the Winnebago fasting and vision quests; he finds nothing holy. He tries the Medicine Dance; he finds no power there, nothing holy. He tries alcohol. He even takes his father's advice and goes out upon the warpath; he kills a Potawatomi blacksmith, but he finds that he has won no power from the act. In peyote his life's quest is finally satisfied: he has his vision; he experiences the holy; he gains sacred power. All this he tells about in detail.[9]

Ironically, then, the work with an anthropologist, the work of dredging up answers to questions about the shape of the old ways, the old life, provided Blowsnake—like Don Talayesva—with training in modern, Euro-American modes of thought. Like Talayesva, Blowsnake was encouraged by his anthropologist to ask *why?* of his life as a whole. But however much Talayesva came to be interested in such questions, the form of *Sun Chief* is the work of Simmons. The form of Blowsnake's autobiography is all his own. I know of no other life history by an Indian so little acculturated that has this form, that so consistently and so self-consciously relates the details of a life to a unified conception of the self.[10] (It is important, by the way, to mention that this claim is made only with reference to published life histories. There is an immense amount of material in anthropologists' field notes which has never been published.)

The second reason Blowsnake was able to write as he did was that, like Augustine, Blowsnake had available to him the form of the confession. Both men were able to adapt this form to autobiography. Public confession was a part of Christian ritual in the time of Augustine; and confessions were well known to Blowsnake because of his participation in the Peyote Cult. The Peyote Cult, as it was spread among the Winnebago by John Rave and Albert Hensley, was heavily influenced by Christianity,[11] and public confession was very much a part of the ritual.[12] Oliver Lamere, Radin's Winnebago interpreter and himself a participant in the Winnebago Peyote Cult, has described the Winnebago ritual as it was in Blowsnake's time. He mentions the public bearing of testimony as a regular part of the ritual. And usually this bearing of testimony would include public confession, because, as Lamere put it, "If a person eats peyote and does not repent openly, he has a guilty conscience, which leaves him as soon as the public repentance has been made" (Radin, 1970 [1923]:347). Lamere also mentions that those who try to eat the peyote without first repenting are likely to "suffer a good deal" from the effects of the peyote. Radin summarized the Winnebago Peyote meetings as follows:

> During the early hours of the evening, before the peyote has begun to have any appreciable effect . . . [there are] speeches by people in the audience and the reading and explanation of parts of the Bible. After the peyote has begun to have an appreciable effect, however, the ceremony consists exclusively of a repetition of the ritualistic unit and confessions. (1970 [1923]:341)

When Radin asked him to write down the story of his life, then, Blowsnake wrote in the confessional mode. He and many other devout Winnebago Peyotists had talked about their lives in just this same way on many occasions at the Peyote meetings. Indeed, John Rave, whom Blowsnake would have heard speaking at many Peyote meetings, remembered his own life in much the same way as did Blowsnake:

> Throughout all the years that I had lived on earth, I now realized that I had never known anything holy. Now, for the first time, I knew it. Would that some of the Winnebagoes might also know it! (In Radin, 1970 [1923]:343).

And when Radin asked Oliver Lamere to tell him about the history of the Winnebago Peyote Cult, Lamere included, as a matter of course, an account of the wicked lives that Hensley and Rave had led before their conversion:

> The Bible was introduced [into the Winnebago peyote ritual] by a young man named Albert Hensley. He, too, had been a bad person, although he had been educated at Carlisle. Like Rave, he was a heavy drinker and fond of wandering. (Radin, 1970 [1923]:346)

He was able to say this, of course, because he had heard Rave's and Hensley's stories often in the course of the Peyote meetings.[13] Blowsnake heard them too. And so, toward the end of his autobiography, his Confessions, Blowsnake, too, can say, "Before (my conversion) I went about in a pitiable condition, but now I am living happily, and my wife has a fine baby" (*Autobiography*, 67). On another occasion Blowsnake expressed this more fully, and Radin included this in *Crashing Thunder*, the expanded version of the *Autobiography*:

> Before I thought that I knew something but really I knew nothing. It is only now that I have real knowledge. In my former life I was like one deaf and blind. My heart ached when I thought of what I had done. Never again will I do it. This medicine alone is holy, has made me good and rid me of evil. (184)

The peculiarities of the peyote ritual among the Winnebago, then, provided Blowsnake with the confessional form for his autobiography, but these same peculiarities also largely determined which of his remembrances Blowsnake was to include in his autobiography. The Peyotists were very much opposed to drunkenness, and so Blowsnake tells us about his drinking. The Peyotists urged marital monogamy, and so Blowsnake tells us about his insatiable womanizing. The Peyotists opposed fighting and killing, and so Blowsnake writes about his fighting and his murder of the Potawatomi. The Peyotists opposed the use of (Indian) medicines and amulets, and so Blowsnake writes about his love potions and his pretended powers. And there was bitter conflict between traditional and Peyotist Winnebagos in the first decade of this century, and so Blowsnake tells us a good deal about the old ways. All he writes about the old ways, then, he writes in order to describe a moral wasteland. His vision quests were fruitless. The old ways were never able to fulfill his better longings.

He describes the Medicine Dance, for example. Since the secrets of the Dance were closely guarded, the very detail with which he describes it must be seen as a deliberate act of defiance and iconoclasm. He is careful to explain not only that the central drama of the Medicine Dance—the shooting and the coming again to life— was a clever fraud; and he must also confess that he was himself a willing participant in the fraud:

> They showed me how to fall down and lie quivering (on the ground) and how to appear dead. I was very much disappointed for I had had a far more exalted idea of it (the shooting). "Why, it amounts to nothing," I thought. "I have been deceived," I thought. "They only do this to make money," I thought. . . . However, I kept on and did as I was told to do. (*Autobiography*, 20: *Crashing Thunder*, 110–111)

Small wonder that it occurred to Radin, resourceful as he was and knowing the Peyotists as he did, to convince Blowsnake to write his life history by urging that he do so, in order "that those who came after [him], would not be deceived" (*Autobiography*, 67; *Crashing Thunder*, 203).

A third reason for Blowsnake's accomplishment was his literacy. He wrote in a syllabary then commonly in use among the Winnebago, a syllabary that they had adpated from one in use among the Sauk and the Fox Indians. His literacy, then, came to him from the Indians, and not from the schoolroom. But still, one is likelier to question one's past when one sees it written upon a page, where ideas and sequences remain fixed. Ideas in the mind are slippery, plastic things indeed. Jack Goody and Ian Watt (1963), in their work on "The Consequences of Literacy," provide fascinating examples of the ways in which oral histories have changed to accommodate changing social realities.[14] Certainly Radin, who knew Blowsnake and the Winnebagos very well indeed, believed that Blowsnake was able to accomplish things in writing that he could not have done orally:

There is one aspect of the use of the syllabary that deserves special consideration because of its possible bearing on the general subject of the influence of the adoption of writing on oral literature. Not a few syllabary texts were obtained that contain personal reflections of [Blowsnake] and a few contained highly unorthodox composition. One exceedingly long text [by Blowsnake] is quite manifestly composite in origin. There is little question, in my mind, that both are specifically connected with the new opportunities for self-expression and literary individuality which writing introduced.

Radin goes on to talk about some of the ways in which Blowsnake's written versions of myths and other narratives differ from what Radin would have gotten had Blowsnake been dictating the material to him. He concludes:

What we have here, therefore, is something quite new, something intimately connected with the new medium, more particularly with one feature of it, its elimination of an immediate, visible, and controlling audience and the leisure provided for reflection, selection, and correction.

Radin is certainly not saying that there are *necessary* consequences of literacy. None of the other Winnebagos who could write in the syllabary had written anything like Blowsnake's texts:

Only to a literary artist of Sam Blowsnake's skill, of course, would this mean anything. For the average man [writing] meant only another method for the perpetuation of the accustomed narratives in the accustomed manner. (Radin, 1949:4–5)

And this is the fourth reason. Blowsnake was, as Radin described him, a "literary artist of unusual gifts and possessed of a style of his own" (1949:5). He had a real sense of what the written word would allow. Certainly Radin gave him the opportunity to practice and develop his talent: Blowsnake wrote ninety percent of the texts Radin collected which were written in the syllabary (1949:4).

The fifth reason for Blowsnake's autobiography, I think, was that he lived in a time of spiritual and cultural turmoil. This was also, of course, the case with Augustine. Augustine's *Confessions* may not be as relentlessly individual as Rousseau's, but there is in Augustine's *Confessions* an inwardness and a sense of the writer as an individual which is without earlier precedent. Weintraub begins his discussion of this phenomenon as follows:

The historian of autobiography often finds a rich harvest in the great periods of crisis when the lives of Western men take decisive turns. In the "classical" ages, possessing the more coherently elaborated cultural configurations . . . , individuals less urgently face the need to account for the meaning of their existence. The ages of crisis, in which the firm assumptions about man and his world are being called into question, force upon the individual the task of doubting and reinvestigating the very foundations on which his self-conception traditionally rested. (1978:18)

The parallel with Blowsnake's condition is striking. I hardly need to rehearse the cultural dislocations attendant upon Indian-white contact in general. Blowsnake's autobiography itself provides a vivid sense of the consequences among the Winnebago. His father urges him to go on the warpath; it is a "good" thing to do, but all it amounts to is the pathetic murder of the Potawatomi and legal entanglements. Blowsnake cannot even tell of his "war" experiences around the campfire—cannot tell his coup tale—for fear that he will be found out by the police. He tells about "chasing the payments," courting women who have just collected their government payment. He assures us that the old ways are without power; the old ways offer no visions. And yet, clear as it seems to Blowsnake that he has cut himself off from his past utterly, we see clearly that he is formed by his past, that his desires have their roots deep in his Winnebago upbringing. Even the visions that peyote granted him, the visions that convinced Blowsnake that *here* at last was something holy, even these visions would not have had so profound an effect upon him had he not been reared with the traditional Winnebago belief in the importance of visions, had he not as a boy been taught to seek visions.

One might here expect a conclusion that would speak of Blowsnake as being like the heroes of so many novels by and about American Indians, a man caught between two cultures. But Blowsnake did not think of himself in this way. Augustine's idea of himself—like his *Confessions*—was a work of synthesis, the synthesis of Neo-Platonism and Christianity. Blowsnake's autobiography, his Confessions, is also a work of synthesis. Blowsnake's traditional Winnebago yearnings for prestige and transcendental experiences are finally satisfied in the Peyote Cult, in something like the way

Augustine's Neo-Platonic yearning for transcendence is finally satisfied by his Christianity. Augustine, however, was quite self-conscious about his work of synthesis. He wrote several times that the wisdom to be gotten from the pagans was like the Egyptian gold that the Hebrews, with God's blessing, took with them out of the land of bondage.[15]

Blowsnake, on the other hand, seems entirely unaware that he is straddling cultures. Like other Winnebago Peyotists early in this century, he sees himself as entirely apart from the misguided ways of the traditional Winnebagos. His whole autobiography is constructed to condemn his evil past. That we can recognize his intention in the book, and yet see so clearly that the book reveals Blowsnake to be his *whole* history's continuing creation, this is the fascination of Sam Blowsnake's own invention, the autobiography.

6

ALBERT HENSLEY: ALTERNATE VERSIONS OF THE SELF

Blowsnake's peyote, the divine cactus, the vision sender, came to the Wisconsin Winnebago in the last decade of the nineteenth century. These were difficult years for the Winnebago. Most Americans were still convinced that America was the great melting pot, and so it was the manifest duty of Indians to melt as soon as possible. The official expression of this sentiment was the Dawes Act of 1887, which aimed to break up the tribes and tribal feelings by breaking up the reservations into individual allotments for individual Indians. Like the Indians of many tribes, the Winnebagos were divided in their response to these pressures to abandon the old ways, to melt—to become "civilized."

Some, like Blowsnake's father, were adamant that their Winnebago traditions ought to be maintained, that their children ought still to be initiated into the old ceremonies, that they ought still to fast for visions. Blowsnake's father even urged his son to go on the warpath. And so Blowsnake helped to kill the unfortunate Potawatomi blacksmith. But times had changed. They could tell no coup tales, for fear of the police.

Other Winnebagos, like Oliver Lamere and Blowsnake's sister, Mountain Wolf Woman,[1] were convinced that it was not only expedient but right to melt into the larger American society. Still others managed to live in both worlds, to respect the old ways and to farm their land, as the BIA encouraged them to do, as a first step on the road to civilization. And an alarming number of Winnebagos were choosing alcohol.

Then came peyote. Ancient of use in Mexico, but new to the

northern plains and woodlands, peyote, with its elaborate attendant ritual, made sharper the divisions, made more bitter the conflicts, among the Winnebago. The traditionalists were appalled by this new religion with its antitribal, Pan-Indian tendencies, with its scorn for the old ways, with its elaborate Indian-Christian rituals. But for the converts these were exciting times. They were seeing dream eagles larger and more colorful than any Winnebago had ever been able to call forth by mere fasting; the promise of their religion, their church, was as yet undiminished; and probably not least there was the antipathy of the traditional Winnebago to unify the Peyotists and to make clear their difference.

One of the most important figures among the Winnebago Peyotists during these years was Albert Hensley. He is best known for having introduced the Bible and other Christian elements into the Winnebago peyote ritual.[2] This man left not one but two autobiographies. Both narratives are interesting for what they tell us about Winnebago history and Peyote Cult history; both are also interesting to set beside the remarkable number of autobiographical narratives by other Winnebago Peyotists.[3] But Hensley's two narratives are even more important as moments in the history of American Indian autobiography.

Nearly everyone who writes about American Indian autobiography mentions at some point that autobiography was not a genre indigenous to Indian cultures.[4] Hensley's two autobiographies, however, like Blowsnake's *Autobiography of a Winnebago Indian,* show us how deeply and how early—in terms of the Indians' adoption of Anglo ways—Western autobiographical forms could enter into Indian cultures. Not only could Hensley make use of autobiography for his own rhetorical and hortatory purposes, as we shall see; he could compose autobiography according to the conventions of two quite separate autobiographical traditions. And both of these forms were available to him and to other Winnebago Indians as a part of their oral culture! Taken together, these two narratives must complicate our sense of Hensley and of the history of American Indian autobiography as well.

The first narrative was elicited by Paul Radin in 1908. Radin published it in his chapter on the Peyote Cult in *The Winnebago Tribe* (1970 [1923:349–350).[5] The second was written by Hensley himself in 1916, in a letter to Millie V. Gaither, the superintendent of his daughter's boarding school.[6] One of Gaither's letters explains something of the circumstances:

> Last September Albert Hensley and Levi StCyr of Thurston, Nebraska, both former students of Carlisle, placed their little girls in this school. They took the children home for the holidays and brought them back after Christmas. Mr. Hensley brought his sister's two little girls with his children[7] on their return, and while in Sioux City had all their photographs taken with himself.
>
> He is such a splendid man. I wrote asking him if I might send the photograph to the "Arrow." In his reply, he wrote a history of his life. I enclose it thinking you might get extracts from it for the "Arrow." Am sorry not to have a picture of Mr. StCyr and his children also.
>
> Yours very truly,
Millie V. Gaither

Both narratives are printed below. Except for some regularization of Hensley's punctuation in the 1916 narrative. I have altered nothing. His handwriting is quite clear, even in xerographic reproduction.

—1908—

I am 37 years old. It was 37 years ago that my mother gave birth to me in an old-fashioned reed lodge. When I was a year old she died and my grandmother took care of me. I had come into the world a healthy child, but bad luck was apparently to pursue me, for when I was 7 years old my grandmother died. Then my father took care of me. At that time he began to be a bad man; he was a drunkard and a horse thief. He would frequently get into trouble and run away, always taking me along with him, however. On one occasion we fled to Wisconsin, and there we stayed two years. We got along pretty well, and there my father married again. By his second wife he had three children.

After a while he got into trouble again, and misfortune followed misfortune. People were killing each other, and I was left alone. If at any time of my life I was in trouble it was then. I was never happy. Once I did not have anything to eat for four days. We had fled to the wilderness, and it was raining continually. The country was flooded with high water, and we sat on top of a tree. It was impossible to sleep, for if we went to sleep we would fall off into the water, which was very deep. The shore was quite far away. As we were prominent people, we soon heard that my father had been freed. We were very happy, and went back to our people.

At that time a young man named Young-Bear was starting for Nebraska, and he said that he would take me along. I was very happy. So in that manner I was brought into this country. Here I have had only happy days. When my father got married everyone disliked me. When I worked I was working for my father, and all the money I earned I had to give to him.

After a while I went to school, and although I liked it I ran away and then went to school at Carlisle. I wanted to lead a good life. At school I knew that they would take care of me and love me. I was very shy and lacked a strong character at that time. If a person told me to do anything I would always obey immediately. Everybody loved me. I stayed there six months. I was also taught Christianity there. When I came back to my country the Episcopalian people told me that they wanted me to be diligent in religious matters and never to forsake the religion of the Son of God. I also desired to do that. I entered the church that we had in our country and I stayed with them six years.

At that time the Winnebago with whom I associated were heavy drinkers, and after a while they induced me to drink also. I became as wicked as they. I learned how to gamble and I worked for the devil all the time. I even taught the Winnebago how to be bad.

After a while they began eating peyote, and as I was in the habit of doing everything I saw, I thought I would do it, too. I asked them whether I could join, and they permitted me. At that time I had a position at the county commissioner's office. I ate the peyote and liked it very much. Then the authorities tried to stop the Indians from eating peyote, and I was supposed to see that the law was enforced. I continued eating peyote and enjoying it. All the evil that was in me I forgot. From that time to the present my actions have been quite different from what they used to be. I am only working for what is good; not that I mean to say that I am good.

After that I married and now I have three children, and it would not have been right for me to continue in my wickedness. I resolved that thereafter I would behave as a grown-up man ought to behave. I resolved never to be idle again and to work so that I could supply my wife and children with food and necessities, that I would be ready to help them whenever they were in need. Here in my own country would I remain till I died. This (peyote) religion was good. All the evil is gone and hereafter I will chose my path carefully.

—1916—

Thurston, Nebr.
Febr. 22nd, 1916

Miss M.V. Gaither
Springfield, S.D.

Dear Miss Gaither:

I received your letter and I was very glad to hear from you and the girls. We are all well here at home.

I have no objection if you wanted to put our picture in the "Arrow," and I will give you the brief history of my miserable life.

My mother died while I was yet a baby, so my grandmother (my father's mother) raise me on gravy, and she also died when I was five years old. Then I was kicked here and there in different families, and when I was seven years old my father took me and made me work for him, what little I could do, till I was Sixteen. The Allotting Agent, Miss Alice Fletcher[8] came, year 1887, and she saw me twice, and both time she said to me, I ought to be in school. We talked through an interpreter, and I told her, I have tried to go to school. Even at Agency School, my father would not let me, and I told her, if she can obtain permission from my father, I would go any where to school, but she fail, and I supposed she was very sorry for me, and next time I saw her, she asked me if I was still in notion to go to school, and I told her I was, and [she] asked me if I would run away from my father, if she get me the ticket to Carlisle, Pa.? And I told her I would, so she arrange certain night and certain place to meet, so we carried out, and I was taken to Bancroft, Nebr., Thirty-two miles from the Winnebago Ag'cy.

I started to ran away from father, Dec. 18th, 1888, and I got to Carlisle Dec. 22nd, 1888, and in April 24th, 1889, I went out in the country,[9] Rushville, Bucks Co., Pa., and I happened to struck a very mean man to work for, but I stayed there for two seasons getting only ten dollars a month, but I worked just as hard as though I was getting $40.00 a month.[10]

And went back to Carlisle Sept. 12th, 1890. And I was out again April 14th, 1892, at Bryn Mawr, Montgomery Co., Pa. At last I worked for very kind man, and he gave me $35.00 a month,[11] and I only worked there for five month and went back to Carlisle, Sept. 12th, 1892, and I stayed til I was send back to Nebraska to die. They thought I was consumped. I left Carlisle, June 15th, 1895. I never graduate, although I was in the senior class for three month. And I learn to be steam-plumber, including carpentering and blacksmithing. When I came back to Winnebago Agency, I was well in side of two month, and I was offered the position of chief of police, and beside I was promise a better place later on and gladly accepted it. And about two months late[r] I was promoted to be the Agency blacksmith, and three years late[r] I was promoted again as an Agency interpreter, and again eighteen months later I was given a better place. I worked with John K. Rankin, an Allotting Agent.

I worked with him three years, and then I was elected as a county commissioner in our county (Thurston Co., Nebr.), and I serve one term and refuse the Second Term, and in mean time I got married to Martha Henry. She never have any schooling, because her parents were oppose of schooling. There were five girls and two boys that they never went to a day to school, but she was a good worker.

And then we move on farm of one hundred and Sixty acres, near Thurston, Nebr.

We now got five healthy children and we are always happy and made good living on farm and independent.

I will now conclude with best wishes to your future welfare.

> I am your friend,
> Albert Hensley

The first thing to notice about these narratives is that they do not simply string together episodes; each is *connected,* unified by a single idea of the self. This sharply distinguishes Hensley's little autobiographies from many other early Indian autobiographical narratives. Nonliterate Indians were quite capable of telling stories about their deeds without learning anything about "autobiography" from Anglos, as we have seen in chapter 1. Fine Day, for example, tells about his battles and his curings. Gregorio tells about his work as a Hand-trembler, about his marriage, about his shepherding. Wolf Chief tells about his battles with the Crows, about his Sun Dances, and his eagle trapping. Maxidiwiac speaks movingly of her work as a farmer, of her relation to the earth and her plants. But we do not find such Indians telling stories in such a way as to suggest just how it was that they came to be just the men or women they were. These Indians tell of deeds done, of hardships endured, of marvels witnessed, of crops harvested, of buffalos killed, of ceremonies accomplished. They do not relate their tales each to each; their tales are not designed to work together to convey a unified idea of the narrator as an *individual* and how he came to be the person he is and how he differs from what he might have been.

Where the Indian's sense of identity is still largely tribal, there is no autobiography such as Rousseau, Henry Adams, and many other modern autobiographers have led us to expect. Rousseau, for example, tells us early in the *Confessions* that he was born in weakly condition, and that his mother died delivering him. And so we are to see that suffering was his lot from the beginning. Patterns emerge; the form takes shape. Adams became the man he was, he tells us, because in him the eighteenth century and the machine age found their intersection:

> He and his eighteenth-century, troglodytic Boston were suddenly cut apart—separated forever—in act if not in sentiment, by the opening of the Boston and Albany Railroad; the appearance of the first Cunard steamers in the bay; and the telegraphic messages which carried from Baltimore to Washington the news that Henry Clay and James K. Polk were nominated for the Presidency. This was May, 1844; he was six years old; his new world was ready for use, and only fragments of the old met his eyes.
>
> (*The Education of Henry Adams*, 1961 [1918]:3)

Rousseau is confident that his life might have been otherwise had his mother lived; confident that with different beginnings, different turnings along the way, he might have been a different man. Adams is keenly aware that he would have been a very different man had he been born fifty years earlier. He is the man his education has made him. Adams and Rousseau are typical of modern autobiographers, then, in that they are aware of themselves as individuals, and in their complex awareness that they might have been otherwise. On the other hand, an Indian living in the old way had little sense of an individual self apart from the tribe or clan, little sense that he might have been a different self had he been born in a different lodge, or had he, say, spent more time learning about plants and less time hunting. Once again, it is worth recalling Weintraub's attempt to account for the same habit of mind among the ancients: "In fundamental ways . . . these early lives are enmeshed in and derive their meaning from basic social and kinship relations." The hero may stand out, "but only as the representative of his society's values."[12] No other definition of the self is a possibility to be considered. Homer's heroes, for example, may sometimes wonder if the rewards of the soldier's life are worth the expense of fear and blood; they may wonder if they ought to leave the war to return home to hearths and wives, but it would no more occur to them to do what Adams does, to describe how they came by their particular constellation of values and desires, than it would occur to them to wonder just how it was that their horses were horses and not sheep.

Carter Revard (1980) makes just this point in the course of a comparison of *Geronimo* and another Apache autobiography by the Carlisle-educated Jason Betzinez. We can account for the shaping of Betzinez's self, Revard suggests, "by the harassment, imprisonment, and education at Carlisle. . . . How do we account for the sense of identity in Geronimo's book? Here there is no clear description by Geronimo: he gives us the self, but he does not show us how it was shaped" (89).[13] And so we find among the traditional Indians—as we do among the ancient Greeks and Romans—the accounts of deeds done, the episodes of autobiography. Where no other way of life is imagined as a possibility, it makes no sense to discuss how one's experiences have led exactly to *this* life, *this* self, and no other. (Where there seem to be exceptions among the Indians, one should beware the hand of the white editor.)

Hensley, with his (incomplete) Carlisle education, was much more nearly "civilized" than was Fine Day or Wolf Chief or Black Elk. On the other hand, Hensley is a good deal less well educated, and a good deal farther from "civilization" than were the other Indians who wrote their own autobiographies at about this same time. Although Hensley was twenty-one when he left Carlisle, the school provided what was essentially a grammar-school education, along with some training for the trades. Considering the short distance he has travelled along the narrow road between the two cultures, Hensley is able to tell his life story in a remarkably consistent way—indeed, in *two* remarkably consistent ways. The conception of self differs in the two narratives, but each narrative is unified by a consistent conception of the self.

In the 1916 narrative, Hensley is inviting Gaither to understand his life in much the same way Charles Alexander Eastman asks his readers to understand *his* life in *From the Deep Woods to Civilization*, which was published in the same year, 1916. Both Eastman and Hensley see themselves as having progressed, as having climbed the ladder of civilization. Eastman, who climbed several rungs higher than Hensley, realized that, in going from the "Deep Woods" of the Santee Sioux to graduation from the Boston University Medical School, he was a living embodiment of Social Darwinist theories of racial-cultural progression. (Chapter 7 will make this argument in more detail.) Hensley would not have read Darwin or Spencer, but he had drunk deep of the closely related assumptions that guided Carlisle.

Captain Richard Pratt, "the Father of Indian Education," founded Carlisle in 1879. The school was to be the working out of his faith that Indians were equal in potential to whites, but that this potential could be realized only if the Indian purged himself of all within him that was tribal, if he evolved, then, from a lower level of human development to a higher. "Kill the Indian, save the man" was Pratt's motto. And if a man were to be saved, he had to be educated to work in the American way. The Indian must be made ready to progress, to "melt"—the metaphor was current— into American society. Self-help was what was needed; self-help, education, and hard work could turn Indians into Americans.[14]

And so we see in the 1916 narrative that Hensley, by dint of hard work and education, has left behind the squalor of his Indian childhood. His own children are not being raised "on gravy." He has even managed to achieve what the BIA hoped its Indians would accomplish as their first step in their progress, their evolution, toward civilization; he has become a successful farmer. This idea of steady progress through self-help and education unifies the 1916 narrative; this idea gives unity to Hensley's conception of himself.

There are other Indian autobiographies from about this time that share these assumptions, others that are unified by this same conception of individual and racial progress. We see this in the subtitle, for example, of Joseph Griffis's 1915 autobiography, *Tahan: Out of Savagery, into Civilization.* In the introduction to the book, Griffis is spoken of as having progressed from being a leader of savages to being "the friend of the scientist and the literary critic" (8). And Thomas Wildcat Alford, although he yearns in his autobiography, *Civilization* (1936), for primitive innocence, never really

doubts that he was driven by an "inner voice" to seek in modern
America a "better way of living than [his] people knew" (77).
Hensley, in his 1916 narrative, like these Indians, is asking us to
see him as an individual example of racial progress.

Let us now turn to Hensley's earlier autobiography. Radin
worked intensively among the Winnebago in the years 1908–1913,
in the period, then, during which the Winnebagos were split down
the middle in their attitudes toward the old ways. For the Peyotists
the old ways were the ways of darkness; peyote was the light. With
the Christianizing of the Peyote Cult, which Hensley was largely
responsible for accomplishing among the Winnebago, the old ways
were made to seem even worse. With their Bible and their belief
in Christ, the newly baptized Peyotists could not regard the traditionalists as pagans, could regard their long-haired brothers as the
Israelites regarded the Philistines. The Medicine Dance was an
abomination and the medicine bundles were pagan fetishes with
power only to mislead. It is not surprising, then, that Radin found
his most willing informants among the Peyotists. Having grown up
in the old ways, they could tell Radin what he wanted to know
about the old ways; being converts to the Peyote Cult, and therefore
convinced of the evil of the old ways, they were not at all hesitant
to speak to Radin concerning matters that traditional Winnebagos
still regarded as taboo. Hensley was one of the first Winnebagos to
serve Radin as an informant; Radin asked him for the story of his
life in the first year of his sojourn among the Winnebagos.

The first questions raised by the 1908 narrative must have to do
with the language, which differs markedly in sentence structure
and "correctness" from that of the 1916 narrative. It is possible
that Radin collected the narrative in English—Hensley did serve
for a time as Agency interpreter—and edited toward standard
English. It is much more likely, however, that the narrative is a
translation of Hensley's Winnebago. In his preface to *The Winnebago
Tribe* Radin wrote that he tried "whenever it was possible . . . to
obtain information in Winnebago." In general it was Radin's practice to take down narratives from his Winnebago informants in
phonetic script.[15] Then Radin's Winnebago assistant, Oliver Lamere, provided translations. Radin, finally, checked Lamere's
translations (Radin's Winnebago was, evidently, quite respectable)
and polished the English. We know enough about Radin's work as

an editor of such texts (Krupat, 1983) to know that he was quite
capable of working some changes upon the material he edited, but
that these changes would be little likely to affect the shape or intent
of such a narrative as Hensley's.

The way in which this autobiography is unified, then, is almost
certainly Hensley's own device. Here too Hensley conveys a unified
conception of himself. Now, however, the unifying principle is not
the school and self-help, but rather peyote, peyote and the religion
of Christian renewal. In fact, the narrative is structured like Sam
Blowsnake's autobiography and like so many other Christian conversion stories. Hensley early in his life was under the influence of
wicked people: his father was "a drunkard and a horse thief." And
so Hensley himself was weak and inclined to sin: "Although I liked
it," he says of his first school, "I ran away." He was "shy and
lacked strong character." But even weak as he was, he "wanted to
lead a good life." He was taught Christianity at Carlisle, but weak-
ling that he was, *Winnebago* that he was, sinner that he was, he sank
deeper and deeper until he "even taught the Winnebago how to be
bad." Then the peyote eaters entered into his life, and so he is able
to say, in the present tense now, "I am only working for what is
good"; although with Christian-Peyote humility he is quick to add,
"not that I mean to say that I am good."

In the 1908 narrative, then, it is not Carlisle that made Hensley
the man he is; indeed, according to this conversion narrative, it
was while he was at Carlisle that he was weak and easily led. In
the 1916 narrative, however, we saw that it was during the time at
Carlisle that he was willing to work hard, even though he was not
well paid. According to the later narrative, Carlisle fitted him to
make his way in the modern world, and so after Carlisle his life
was a steady progress from reservation, to Carlisle, to chief of
police, to Agency blacksmith, to Agency interpreter, to assistant to
the allotting agent, to county commissioner.

Although Hensley was still an active Peyotist in 1916, there is
no mention of sinful ways nor even of peyote in the 1916 narrative.
In the 1908 narrative, on the other hand, Hensley is intending to
demonstrate the efficacy of the Christian-Peyote way, and so peyote
must be seen to work a transformation, a reformation. And so
Hensley tells of his sins. And if his sins are to be emphasized, so
must his schooling be minimized. In the 1908 narrative he gives

himself just six months at Carlisle! Clearly, Hensley must regard *both* peyote and Carlisle as transformative—and so in each narrative the one must be minimized in order to allow the other full credit for making him over.

How can we account for the differences? In the first place, Hensley certainly had a sense of two quite different audiences. He wrote his 1916 autobiography for a school superintendent—his daughters' school superintendent, a person not likely to approve of peyote. In 1908, on the other hand, he was speaking with Radin, who was asking him questions not about Carlisle, but about Winnebago ways and about the Peyote Cult. And Radin, as a part of his field methodology, was asking questions in such a way as to make his Peyotist informants feel *religiously obligated* to respond. For example, Jasper Blowsnake, Sam's brother and another important figure in the Winnebago Peyote Cult, wove Radin into "the whole fabric of his life," making of Radin "the pre-ordained one who had sensed what was the proper time to come among the Winnebago" (Radin, 1983 [1927]:x). And as we have seen in chapter 5, Radin was even able to elicit information from Sam Blowsnake that it was taboo for traditional Winnebagos to reveal, by urging him to tell about the old ways so that future generations would not be misled.[16]

But it is not enough, I think, to point to two different audiences, because the differences in the two narratives have to do with more than merely selecting incidents that would please a certain audience. Hensley was actually working self-consciously in two distinct autobiographical traditions: the Peyote Conversion Narrative and the Carlisle Success Story.

As chapter 5 seeks to demonstrate, Sam Blowsnake's autobiography is an excellent example of the Peyote Conversion Narrative. Hensley, of course, would not have read Blowsnake's autobiography, but *with* Blowsnake he would have heard many, many Peyote Conversion/Confession Narratives during the peyote meetings. The confessional autobiography that Hensley narrated for Radin must, then, be like similar narratives that he had delivered during peyote meetings, and like the many other confessional narratives he heard at peyote meetings.

Hensley would not have heard quite so many Carlisle Success Stories, but he must have heard some of these, since they were an important a part of the recruiting effort of Carlisle and the other boarding schools—or "away schools," as some Indians poignantly called them. It is easy to imagine the sorts of stories that would be necessary to persuade anxious parents to send their children to such a faraway place. Luther Standing Bear's autobiography, *My People the Sioux*, has a chapter devoted to "Recruiting for Carlisle":

> About this time [1882] Captain Pratt thought that it would be a good idea to send some of the more advanced Indian boys back to the reservation, in order to show the Indians there that they were really learning the white man's ways. By doing this, he hoped to induce more of the Indian children to come to the school.

Back on the reservation, young Standing Bear was soon allowed to "work in the blacksmith shop, making stovepipes and elbows, as a demonstration of [his] education acquired in the school." He continues:

> We were all very sincere in our desire to show what we had learned, in order to interest more of the children to go back to Carlisle School.

But so many of the Rosebud's children had died at schools far from home, and the people of the Rosebud had experienced so little that would incline them to trust white people and their institutions, that parents were fearful of sending their children away.

> To settle the matter it was decided to hold a big council. I was designated to speak. I felt very important, as many of the leading chiefs were to be present. . . . I told them all about the training we received in the East . . . And after I had finished talking, my father rose and told of his visit to Carlisle . . . and what an improvement the children had shown in learning and acquiring the ways of the white people. . . . He then said: " . . . I know this learning of the white man's way is good for my children." (161–163)

Standing Bear and the other children from Carlisle stopped at other reservations as well. They returned to Carlisle with fifty-two new children for the school. Hensley, who began at Carlisle in 1888, can hardly have missed hearing such speeches. He may even have read some. During Hensley's sojourn at Carlisle, the school published a weekly newsletter, *The Indian Helper*. As one might expect, *The Indian Helper* specialized in inspirational material that conveyed the school's particular philosophy of Indian education. One model student, a Tsimshian Indian named Edward Marsden, wrote a Carlisle Success Story in an 1892 issue of *The Indian Helper*. His fatherless family was so poor that he began to work as a boy:

> One of our streets was then in course of construction, and my work was to smoothe the earth and sand which were thrown into it.
>
> I did not have any spade so I was obliged to use both of my hands and bare feet.
>
> My whole summer's work brought me three round dollars, one pair of school pants and a sack of Irish potatoes.

One recalls Hensley being raised "on gravy." But Marsden soon began to learn the kinds of skills that Carlisle recommended to its students. He learned brick-laying, house-painting, gardening—eight different trades in all, *before* coming to Carlisle, where he learned printing.

> My first wages was three dollars and a few potatoes for the summer's work in 1880; but since that time, in 1890, I received three dollars a day.
>
> These are a few of the many facts that will help us to understand that, to reach the top of the hill, we must begin at the foot, and with patience and courage, struggle onward and upward, till the summit of the hill is reached.
>
> Be a *Man-Of-The-Best-Specimen!* (1, 4)

But even if we grant that such influences were at work upon Hensley, still a good deal is left to discuss. The suggestion that Hensley composed his two autobiographies according to two different autobiographical traditions does nothing to explain, for example, why the 1916 narrative is so much more tightly unified than the earlier one. It is difficult to find a single detail in the letter to Gaither that does not work to convey Hensley's conception of himself as a Carlisle success story. Even the propriety of the heading and the salutation, and the conventionality of the closing suggest Hensley's mastery of the norms that Pratt sought to impart to his charges at Carlisle.

In the 1908 narrative, on the other hand, while we recognize the unifying idea, we see as well a number of details that do not seem to fit. In the fourth sentence Hensley says "bad luck was apparently to pursue me." We are prepared, then, for a story about a figure beset by "misfortune after misfortune," but the story turns out to be about sin and redemption and reformation. Hensley tells us that his father was "a bad man . . . a drunkard and a horse thief," and then suddenly he says, "we were prominent people." The whole episode of the flood is strange, disoriented. We understand Hensley to mean himself and his father when he says, "we sat on top of a tree," but then *they* heard that his father was *freed*. Then Young Bear takes Hensley to Nebraska, where he had "only happy days," and there he became "wicked." He was a peyote eater, and he was responsible for rooting out the wicked peyotists.

These discontinuities are probably partly a result of the circumstances of the narration. This autobiography was probably delivered orally, as we have seen. In talking with one another we typically leave unspoken much that would have to be made explicit were we to tell our story in writing. And since Hensley's narrative was almost certainly not taken down in shorthand, it could not have been delivered continuously. There would have been pauses, questions, backtracking, starting again. It would have been difficult even for Anthony Trollope to maintain a narrative thread under such conditions.

Still, it is tempting to see a disjointed life in this disjointed telling of a life. Where Hensley tried to force the odds and ends of his life into the unifying mold of the Peyote Conversion Story, it is tempting to see a consciousness struggling to conform itself to a new ideal. Hensley was a dirt-poor Winnebago for a time, then a Carlisle school boy, then an Episcopalian, then a Peyotist. He was also (although he does not mention this in either autobiography) for a time a member of the Society of American Indians, an important, early Pan-Indian movement. He attended the first conference of the Society in 1911 and several other conferences as well. This means that Hensley was during the same years a Peyotist and a member of an organization whose members were divided in their attitudes toward peyote, but who finally voted, in 1916, to support the Gandy Bill to outlaw peyote (Hertzberg, 1981 [1971]:83, 124–125, 247–248).

Hensley remembers his father as "prominent" and as "bad." At one moment he seems to be speaking out of his remembered Winnebago sense of his father. The next moment he seems to be speaking

out of his Peyotist/Christian/Carlisle/Pan-Indian sense of his father. According to this uneasy constellation of values, his father
would be "bad" if only for being a long-hair, a *Winnebago*. Hensley's
determination to distance himself from such a tribal conception of
himself is perhaps most strikingly evident in his attempts (with
John Rave) to affiliate their peyote church with a local Protestant
church (whose clergyman rebuffed them: Hertzberg, 1981
[1971]:248). Again, the conception of himself that Hensley wishes
to convey in the 1908 narrative is like Sam Blowsnake's conception
of *him*self as we find it in *Crashing Thunder*. Both Hensley and
Blowsnake are convinced that their conversion to peyote has opened
a huge gulf between their Peyotist present and their wicked, wan-
dering, Winnebago-tribal past. But both autobiographies in fact
seem to *us* clearly to have been composed by men with their feet
planted in at least two cultures. The watery peyote infusion with
which these men were baptized may have washed away their sins;
their tribal past seems to have been more nearly indelible.

The 1916 autobiography was written, not oral. And perhaps the
leisure for reflection and revision which writing allows is largely
responsible for the more controlled idea of himself that this autobiography conveys. But there has also been the passage of time.
Hensley has had some years to settle into his new way(s) of life.
In the 1916 autobiography it is as though Hensley has managed to
conform his conception of himself to a nontribal ideal. No loose
pieces dangle outside the mold. To all outward appearances at
least, Hensley is a Carlisle Success Story. If the 1908 autobiography
seems to us to be richer, more alive, we may be sensing some of
what Hensley struggled to give up over the long course of his
"melting."

Two autobiographies, two conceptions of self, each tailored for
a particular audience and occasion—all this Hensley manages
within the spacious boundaries of the Winnebago *oral* traditions of
these years. In order to tell the first life story, Hensley, like Sam
Blowsnake, need not have read a single autobiography. In writing
the second he could have been prompted by oral and/or written
Carlisle Success Stories. Hensley's narratives, then, offer a nice
indication of just how early in their acculturation Indians could
make use of autobiographical forms for their own purposes. Hensley
shows us that an Indian who had begun to conceive of an indi-

vidual—as opposed to a tribal—self at all was quite capable of
conceiving of more than one self, and of suiting the autobiographical self, and thus the whole pattern of his life, to a particular
audience and occasion. Hensley has left a record of just two of the
ways in which he imagined himself; but he must have imagined
himself in other ways as well. And we must guess that this man
had a lively, perhaps a painful, awareness of yet other selves that
might have been.

7

CHARLES ALEXANDER EASTMAN'S
INDIAN BOYHOOD:
ROMANCE, NOSTALGIA, AND
SOCIAL DARWINISM

Charles Alexander Eastman must claim a prominent position in any historical treatment of American Indian autobiography. He was more fully acculturated than any of the autobiographers we have thus far discussed. And he was a man who achieved some fame by his writings. Eastman is the first Indian author who tried self-consciously to write autobiography after the modern, Western fashion (aside from the few Indians like George Copway, Samson Occom, and William and Mary Apes who wrote pious accounts of their conversion to Christianity). His first volume of autobiography, *Indian Boyhood* (1916), begins in this way:

> The North American Indian was the highest type of pagan and un-civilized man. He possessed not only a superb physique but a remark-able mind. But the Indian no longer exists as a natural and free man. Those remnants which now dwell upon the reservations present only a sort of tableau—a fictional copy of the past.

This is a rather remarkable passage. For the first fifteen years of his life, Eastman lived according to the ancient tribal ways of the Santee Sioux. He was raised up to be a hunter and a warrior. He was taught never to spare a white enemy. Then, at the age of fifteen, he was abruptly taken out of this life and brought to Flandreau, South Dakota, to learn to live in the white man's way. Soon he outgrew the local school; he went on to Santee Normal School, in Nebraska, then to Beloit College, Knox College, Dartmouth College, and finally to the Boston University Medical School, where he took his degree in 1890. He had long since decided that he wanted to serve his people; and so, degree in hand, he went off to begin his work as Government Physician to the Sioux at Pine Ridge, South Dakota. He arrived one cold and windy day in November. Just one month later he was binding wounds and counting frozen corpses at Wounded Knee.

How could a Sioux Indian who had had such an experience, how could a man who came to know so many of the reservation Indians during his years as a reservation doctor, how could *Eastman* have written so dismissively of the Indians on the reservations? It is not surprising that those who write about Eastman either ignore this passage or agree with Arlene Hirschfelder that these sentiments are "unworthy of the rest of the book" (1973:37).

But the passage is not an aberration, really. The passage serves, in fact, as a perfectly apt introduction to some of the book's main concerns and themes. And it springs from Romantic Racialist and Social Darwinist assumptions fundamental to Eastman's thinking during these years—and fundamental as well to some other Indian autobiographies in the first decades of this century. *Indian Boyhood* can best be understood in the light of these assumptions and the feelings to which they gave rise.

Eastman was born in 1858, a year before the publication of *The Origin of Species*. But even in his mother's day, white-American attitudes toward race were undergoing a profound change.[1] By the mid-nineteenth century, scientific and popular opinion had moved decisively away from the eightenth-century ideas about the essential unity of the human race that had inspired the Jeffersonian declaration that "all men are created equal." The differences between savages and Americans, for Jefferson, could be explained in terms of environmental differences. Savages were deprived (or degenerate) humans.[2] But by the time Eastman was fingering his first bow, environmental differences were no longer thought to be sufficient to explain human diversity. In 1847 the eminent craniologist S. G. Morton had proved to his own satisfaction that separate races were separate species. This was no mean feat, since scientists at this time assumed that the fertility of offspring was *the* test for species distinctions—and mulattos, after all, were obviously, indeed disturbingly, fertile. Morton argued that since hybrids—and he cited examples of hybrids among species of birds, fish, mammals, insects—are sometimes fertile, one can account for interracial fertility as a case of hybridity. Some species, Morton argued, are simply endowed with more capacity for hybridization than others, and none more than the several species of man.

And there were as well the separate creationists, those who believed, with Josiah Clark Nott, that all men could not have descended from Adam and Eve; not even God's mark on Cain could suffice to explain such great mental, moral, and physical differences. Racial variations could be scientifically explained only by positing separate acts of creation.

Obviously, such scientific theories often worked to justify deeply felt prejudices. But it is well to remember that even abolitionists could assume that blacks and Indians, because of their inherent inferiority or (more kindly) their inherent weakness, were unlikely long to survive. In 1863, for example, the Reverend J. M. Sturtevant wrote on "The Destiny of the African Race in the United States." He concluded that the direct competition with the white race, which would be the immediate result of emancipation, will have "inevitable" consequences for the Negro:

> He will either never marry, or he will, in the attempt to support a family, struggle in vain against the laws of nature, and his children, many of them at least, die in infancy. . . . Like his brother the Indian of the forest, he must melt away and disappear forever from the midst of us. (In Fredrickson, 1971:159)

As George Fredrickson has written, Sturtevant's "racial Malthusianism" anticipates Darwin's idea of the struggle between the species—"as well as the 'social Darwinist' justification of a *laissez-faire* economy as the arena for a biological competition resulting in the 'survival of the fittest'" (1971:159).

Such ideas were at the peak of their influence when Eastman entered Darmouth College in 1883. Just ten years earlier Whitelaw Reid, sometime influential Assistant Editor of the New York *Tribune* under Horace Greeley, had addressed the college, speaking about how quickly the new scientific ideas were winning acceptance:

> Ten or fifteen years ago the staple subject here for reading and talk, outside study hours, was English poetry and fiction. Now it is English science. Herbert Spencer, John Stuart Mill, Huxley, Darwin, Tyndall, have usurped the places of Tennyson and Browning, and Matthew Arnold and Dickens.
>
> (In Hofstadter, 1969:21)

And in the year of Eastman's matriculation, for another example, *The New Englander,* an important periodical for Yankee clergymen, reversed itself and began to publish editorials to justify the ways of Darwin to man (Hofstadter, 1969:28). Sizeable pockets of resistance remained, of course; but still it may be said that evolution had won the high ground in its battle with religion by the time Eastman began college. Much of the success of these ideas was due to Herbert Spencer. It was he who coined the phrase "survival of the fittest." It was Spencer who worked out most completely the social and racial implications of evolutionist ideas. Spencer managed, as well, much of the popularization of Social Darwinism. By the time Eastman published *Indian Boyhood,* Spencer's books had sold well over 300,000 copies—a figure probably unmatched by any other author dealing with subjects as difficult as sociology and philosophy (Hofstadter, 1969:34).

It was largely to Spencer, then, that white Americans owed thanks for ideas that must have seemed divine compensation for the awkward religious choices forced upon them by Darwinian evolution. It was Spencer who did most to teach Americans that what was happening to the Indians was the inevitable—sad, of course, but certainly inevitable—working out of the laws of nature. And such ideas powerfully influenced those who concerned themselves with Indian affairs during these years. They provided the intellectual underpinnings of the Dawes Severalty Act of 1887— "the political expression of American thought about the Indian" (Krupat, 1985:59) throughout Eastman's adult years. This Act, which caused land to be taken from the tribes and allotted to individual Indians, assumed that the tribes were bound to die out. This was perfect Spencerism, perfect Social Darwinism. Societies, or races (it was so difficult, really, to distinguish between the two), were fundamentally like organisms. They had their span of life, and then they died, sooner if they were weaker than competing societies/ races, later if they were strong of tooth and claw and intellect. The Indians, then, simply could not survive as *Indians.* Eastman was officially consulted about the provisions of the Dawes Act. And he was consulted precisely because he was rather famous proof that an individual Indian could compete with Americans (Miller, 1978: 61). He approved of the Act and urged his Indian friends to embrace it (Wilson, 1983:33). He and his fellow Indians could compete as *individuals,* each with his separate allotment; the tribes must, of course, inevitably vanish.

This kind of thinking produced a curious blend of fatalism and nostalgia. Indians are vanishing—and let us cherish our remembrances of real Indians. The Bureau of Indian Affairs even arranged an official farewell. With Joseph K. Dixon as prime mover, the Bureau arranged the Last Council, a meeting of chiefs and aging warriors from several of the Western tribes. This meeting took place in the Valley of the Little Bighorn in 1909. The record of that meeting was Dixon's *The Vanishing Race* (1913). In this book Dixon collected narratives (mostly autobiographical) from twenty-one Indians from fifteen tribes. The book was illustrated with Rodman Wanamaker's gorgeous sepia photographs. Dixon explained the Last Council and his book in this way:

> The preservation of this record in abiding form is all the more significant because all serious students of Indian life and lore are deeply convinced of the insistent fact that the Indian, as a race, is . . . soon destined to pass completely away. . . . These original Americans *Deserve a Monument.* (1913:5–6)

It is important to realize that Dixon is no champion of Anglo domination. He does not think of the Indians as morally inferior:

> The ruthless tread of cruel forces—we call them civilization . . . have in cruel fashion borne down upon the Indian until he had to give up all that was his and all that was dear to him—to make himself over or die. He would not yield. He died. (1913:4)

Dixon is certainly sympathetic; he feels a very personal sense of loss: "The door of the Indian's yesterdays opens to a new world—a world unpeopled with red men, but whose population fills the sky, the plains, with sad and spectre-like memories" (1913:4). He is thinking in social-Darwinist terms. "The white is the conquering race," he says; the Indians are "ancient forerunners" (1913:5). He is not as happy as Andrew Carnegie or Teddy Roosevelt was about the consequences of evolutionary forces, but he is every bit as certain that what has happened was inevitable. What he feels he can do now is to preserve as much of what is *really* Indian as he can. And so he gives us Red Whip's story of his fight with the

Sioux—eleven against a hundred and thirty; he gives us Pretty Voice Eagle's remembrances of a time when there were no white men along the upper reaches of the Missouri; he gives us Mountain Chief's recollections of his boyhood sports. He also includes Wanamaker's photographs. And just as Dixon asked the questions that elicited the narratives, so Wanamaker posed the Indians for the photographs. The next-to-last photograph in the book shows the old warriors in their best buckskins and feathers riding in single file down a treeless hill toward the camera. This is captioned "Down the Western Slope." And in case we should miss the point, the last photograph in the book shows a huddle of riderless horses: "The Empty Saddle."

Memories of this glorious people will be preserved, their stories collected, their spears carefully laid by in our museums. But the race itself will vanish—inevitably, tragically, but quite naturally. The "forerunner" race will be supplanted by the more vigorous (if less glorious), the stronger white race.

Dixon expected his Indians to hover over the American West, in fact, just as Richard Wagner's Valhallians were to hover over Germany during these years. It is no coincidence that one of the most striking examples of Romantic Racialism in American Indian autobiography comes to us from a German. Edgar von Schmidt-Pauli elicited and edited *We Indians: The Passing of a Great Race,* the autobiography of White Horse Eagle, an Osage. Von Schmidt-Pauli was a Nazi historian who wrote history in such a way as to demonstrate the inevitability of the rise of the German race in general, and Adolf Hitler in particular.[3] Why should such a scholar interest himself in Indians? According to von Schmidt-Pauli, White Horse Eagle was capable of sensing the presence of gold, silver, or water in the earth beneath his feet. White Horse Eagle, again according to von Schmidt-Pauli, was capable of reading Egyptian hieroglyphics. And White Horse Eagle and von Schmidt-Pauli were, of course, in agreement that the only reason the Indians allowed the whites to land in the first place was that the whites had the good sense to greet the Indians with ancient cabalistic signs. All of this von Schmidt-Pauli's Indians could do because of their *race;* White Horse Eagle and the Indians in general are living—or rather dying—evidence of inborn racial characteristics.

When all of this is taken into account, we may see that the

opening epigraph in *Indian Boyhood* is not heartless. There is no failure of compassion here. The passage is a verbal equivalent of Wanamaker's "The Empty Saddle." The "real" Indians had been a glorious race; but it was a race that could not compete with the whites, and so it was dying out. Eastman saw upon the reservations the sad survivors of the Darwinian struggle. In his assessment of these people Eastman was agreeing with Spencer that contemporary primitive societies were sometimes retrograde.[4] And he was agreeing with Dr. Carlos Montezuma, who was known as "the fiery Apache." Montezuma had been stolen from his family by raiding Pimas when he was four years old; he was then purchased and adopted by a Mexican-American reporter. Eventually, he worked his way through Chicago Medical College. He went on to serve as a physician on the reservations. And it was there, he said, that he "saw in full what deterioration is for the Indians" (Hertzberg, 1981 [1971]:43). Montezuma bridled at the suggestion that he ought to live "among his people":

> Not that I do not revere my race, but I think if I had remained there on the reservation and not have been captured years and years ago, I would not be standing here defending my race. . . . I find that the only, the best thing for the good of the Indian is to be thrown on the world. . . . Better send every Indian away. Get hold and send them to Germany, France, China, Alaska, Cuba, if you please, and then when they *come back* 15 or 20 years from now you will find them strong, a credit to the country, a help and an ornament to this race. (In Hertzberg, 1981 [1971]:87)

This was a view widely held by progressive Indians looking at the misery and poverty on the reservations. The pan-Indian and progressive Society of the American Indian argued that the BIA was very much mistaken to permit—let alone encourage—Indians to retain such vestiges of tribal life as the reservation system allowed. The Indians needed to be forced out of the tribes, off the reservation. The tribes must vanish as social institutions, for it was the tribe that kept individual Indians from achieving all that Eastman and Montezuma had achieved as individuals, away from their tribes.

Elaine Goodale, the woman who was to become Eastman's wife, provides another interesting case in point. She went to work in the

Indian schools before she was twenty years old; she soon came to the attention of General Richard Henry Pratt, the founder of the Carlisle Indian School, and other prominent figures in the Indian reform movement. Her memoirs make fascinating reading for anyone interested in the enlightened attitude toward Indians in these years. Goodale steeped herself in the customs of the Dakota. She herself learned Sioux and thoroughly enjoyed her knowledge of the language. But utility and not sentiment, she was convinced, must rule in matters of education; and she saw no reason why teachers should know Sioux, since instruction was, quite rightly in her view, in English only. She was proud of her knowledge of Sioux customs, and observed them fairly punctiliously in her intercourse with her neighbors. The whole business, then, of Americanizing the Indians had for her and her progressive friends nothing to do with abhorrence of their ways. She had an explicitly romantic love of their ways. But the Americanizing was necessary, inevitable; consequently, sentiment had to be set aside (Elaine G. Eastman, 1978:34–38).

The tribes must vanish, but they were important as memories. The glory of the tribe must be remembered. Goodale worked very hard and very ingeniously to turn Indians into civilized Americans. And yet she could write with real fondness of Indians as they were before their civilizing:

> Dear, lovable, intensely feminine Sioux women of days gone by! How affectionately I recall their devotion to their families, their innocent love of finery and gossip, eager curiosity and patient endurance. (Elaine G. Eastman, 1978:34)

It is in just this way, with the same limitations, that Montezuma can "revere" his race. And it is in this same way that Eastman hopes to convey a sense of the glory of his people, for most of the same reasons that von Schmidt-Pauli is interested to purvey the glories of White Horse Eagle's Osage past, *and* the glories of the German Folk. All that Eastman can do now is try to record what he remembers of the old ways. What he can do is set down for his Anglo audience the nobility of the "real" Indians. Like Dixon and the Bureau, Eastman wants to set it all down before it vanishes. He would have agreed with Dixon that at least this much is owed to the vanquished race:

Men are fast coming to recognize the high claim of a moral obligation to study the yesterdays of this imperial and imperious race. . . .

It is little short of solemn justice to these vanishing red men that students, explorers, artists, poets, men of letters, genius, generosity, and industry, strive to make known to future generations what manner of men and women were these whom we have displaced and despoiled. (Dixon, 1913:5)

There are other ways as well in which *Indian Boyhood* reflects evolutionist ideas. The book assumes, for example, that the races may be ordered, that some are higher, some lower. We should not be surprised, then, when we find Eastman telling us that the Indians were a "primitive people" (49). But for Eastman there were also distinctions—gradations—to be found among primitive peoples. As we have seen, Eastman began *Indian Boyhood* with the assertion that "The North American Indian was the highest type of pagan and uncivilized man." And if the North American Indians were "higher" than the South American Indians and the Africans, and the other primitive peoples, there are also gradations even among the Indians. Consider, for example, Eastman's comparison of the woodland Indians, like Eastman's Santee Sioux, and the Plains Indians:

There was almost as much difference between the Indian boys who were brought up on the open prairies and those of the woods, as between city and country boys. The hunting of the prairie boys was limited and their knowledge of natural history imperfect. They were, as a rule, good riders, but in all-around physical development much inferior to the red men of the forest. (87)

Environment alone could not account for such differences. Eastman believed that differing races have differing instincts. For example, Indians in general have an instinct for the hunt. Eastman's idea of Santee instincts is less patently absurd than von Schmidt-Pauli's idea of Osage instincts for gold, silver, water, and hieroglyphics; but both ideas spring from common Romantic Racialist assumptions. So it is that when hunting, Eastman's Indian moves with an "inborn dignity" and "native caution" (87). Eastman can even recall for his readers the moment when he first felt these native stirrings:

> I was scarcely three years old when I stood one morning . . . with my
> little bow and arrow in my hand, and gazed up among the trees.
> Suddenly the instinct to chase and kill seized me powerfully. Just then
> a bird flew over my head and then another caught my eye. . . . Every-
> thing else was forgotten and in that moment I had taken my first step
> as a hunter. (87)

Eastman considered himself, then, to have inherited the blood
of a superior tribe of the "highest" type of pagan people. And
Eastman's family, it seems, was remarkable too—even among the
Santee Sioux. His mother, Eastman wrote, was "sometimes called
the 'Demi-Goddess' of the Sioux, who tradition says had every
feature of a Caucasian descent with the exception of her luxuriant
black hair and deep black eyes" (5). His uncle "was known . . . as
one of the best hunters and bravest warriors among the Sioux in
British America" (19). It was, however, his grandmother who was
largely responsible for raising Eastman:

> It was not long before I began to realize her superiority to most of her
> contemporaries. This idea was not gained entirely from my own obser-
> vation, but also from a knowledge of the high regard in which she was
> held by other women. (21)

In some measure, of course, Eastman's sense of his tribe's and
his family's superiority is quite traditional. It is well known that in
some tribes the word for a member of the tribe was the same as
the word for human being. And Eastman's pride in his family could
have been matched by Achilles as readily as by other nonliterate
people whose sense of self-definition was shaped by ancient attitudes toward tribe and family. But ideas about the stages of human
development are at work in Eastman's book as well, ideas that were
central to much of social evolutionist thought. In 1877 Lewis Henry
Morgan offered up a scientific rendering of Romantic conceptions
of "national character" (such as we find, for example, in Carlyle
and in Emerson's *English Traits*).[5] He theorized that human history
could be divided into three main "ethnical periods": Savagery,
Barbarism, and Civilization. And these could further be broken
down as follows:

Lower Savagery: from "the infancy of the human race" up to the time of the discovery of fire; fruit and nut gathering; beginnings of language.

Middle Savagery: fishing and use of fire; spread of mankind over the globe (examples: Australians and Polynesians).

Upper Savagery: bow and arrow (examples: northern Atapascan tribes).

Lower Barbarism: pottery making (examples: tribes east of the Missouri River).

Middle Barbarism: in the Old World, the domestication of animals; in the New World, farming with irrigation and building with adobe and stone (examples: "Village Indians of New Mexico . . . and Peru").

Upper Barbarism: commences with the smelting of iron (examples: Homeric Greeks)

Civilization: from the time of the first use of phonetic alphabet up to present time.[6]

Eastman did not see the history of the human race in quite the same way as Morgan did. For Eastman the North American Indian was "the highest type of pagan and uncivilized man," while Morgan would have graded Eastman's Santees no higher than the bow-and-arrow Upper Savagery stage. But it is quite clear that Eastman did assume, like Morgan and Spencer and others, that societies could be ranked in terms of their stage of evolution. And so, even though he considered his people, and especially his own family, to have been remarkably close to the Caucasian ideal, Eastman did realize that his family still was not fully evolved. His uncle, for example, was "a typical Indian—not handsome, but truthful and brave" (21). The Santees in general were a "primitive people" (49) and "superstitious" (38).

Eastman saw himself as an embodiment of Social Darwinist notions about the evolution of the races. He had "evolved" from the woodland life of the Santee Sioux to the heights of white culture. And he was not alone in conceiving of his life in this way. This is the unifying assumption, as well, of Joseph K. Griffis's autobiography, *Tahan: Out of Savagery, into Civilization* (1915). Griffis recalls that the Kiowas were morally the equals of civilized people:

The Indian woman is careful to guard her little girl from evil and to train her in virtue and modesty and industry. . . . We children loved each other as well as do those of any well-regulated, civilized family. (26–27)

But they were as rough in their play "as little brother-bears" (27). Indeed, the Kiowas were in many ways like the animals:

> Obedience is the first law of the savage Indian. He believes it as vital to his existence as to that of animal creation. As the buffalo, the deer, the beaver and the turkey trained their young to obey, so did our parents train us. (27)

The "savages," then, were closer to the animals than were "civilized" people. Griffis's book is the story of his progression from this state of (benevolent) animal savagery to civilization. In his introduction to the book Arthur C. Parker[7] makes all this explicit:

> Tahan is a man who has passed through a series of transitions that have led him up from savagery, through the experiences of an Indian warrior . . . to the state of broad culture that fits him for his association and friendship with scientists, statesmen and leaders of world-thought. (7)

He has progressed from being a leader of savages to being "the friend of the scientist and the literary critic" (8).

Griffis, Eastman, Montezuma, and Parker were all prominent early members in the Society of the American Indians (SAI). Small wonder then that the influence of evolutionary thinking at the first SAI meeting in 1911 was pervasive. The founders of the SAI, according to Hazel Hertzberg, conceived social evolution to be "a mighty and inexorable force." The Indians who attended the SAI's first conference in 1911 "viewed 'the face' as in the process of working itself up the evolutionary ladder." Hertzberg writes that "In spite of the nostalgia expressed for aboriginal life, 'evolution' and 'progress' tended to be equated" (1981 [1971]:73–74).

In *Indian Boyhood*, then, Eastman provides an explanation for just why it was that he was able to compete so successfully with the white man in Spencer's laissez-faire world. He could compete because he was a member of perhaps the best family of the best tribe of the "highest type of pagan and uncivilized man." This idea of competition is central to *Indian Boyhood*—just as it is central to Social Darwinism. Andrew Carnegie, for example, one of the best at the *practice* of Social Darwinism, was convinced by his reading of Darwin and Spencer that the "law" of competition was fundamentally biological. In an article for the *North American Review* Carnegie argued that although we may object to what seems the harshness of this law,

> It is here; we cannot evade it; no substitutes for it have been found; and while the law may sometimes be hard for the individual, it is best for the race, because it assures the survival of the fittest in every department. (1889:655)

There is much in *Indian Boyhood* for Carnegie to applaud. "There was always keen competition among us," Eastman wrote. "We felt very much as our fathers did in hunting and war—each one strove to excel all the others" (63). After hunting he and his mates would compare their kills: "We . . . kept strict account of our game, and thus learned who were the best shots among the boys" (89). He remembers that the adult hunters "started before sunrise, and the brave who was announced throughout the camp as the first one to return with a deer on his back, was a man to be envied" (214–215). There were even prizes for the young men who could hull rice the fastest (237). Because his mother died shortly after he was born, Eastman recalled, he "had to bear the humiliating name 'Hakadah,' meaning 'the pitiful last'" (4). *Indian Boyhood* is, among other things, the story of how he earned—and how he continued through life to deserve—the name Ohiyesa, "winner."

This is certainly not to suggest that the Santee knew nothing of competition before Darwin, Spencer, and Carnegie whispered to them upon the wind. One has only to read *Two Leggings: The Autobiography of a Crow Warrior* to realize how intensely competitive a warrior society could be. But as he wrote about competition, as he thought about all the ways in which he had himself competed, Eastman must have been influenced by what he had learned about competition in the classroom and on the playing fields of Dartmouth. And Eastman was captain of athletic teams at Dartmouth.

Another striking feature of the book is its emphasis on childhood: the book is about an Indian boyhood, and the book was written for children.[8] This, too, I think, is related to Eastman's Social

Evolutionist assumptions. Notions about the childhood and the maturity of races were the common coin of Social Evolutionist explanations. The following passage from Spencer's *Principles of Sociology* is typical. I quote at length in order to demonstrate how rich the metaphor seemed to the Social Evolutionist:[9]

> The intellectual traits of the uncivilized . . . are traits recurring in the children of the civilized.
>
> Infancy shows us an absorption in sensations and perceptions akin to that which characterizes the savage. In pulling to pieces its toys, in making mud-pies . . . the child exhibits great tendency to observe with little tendency to reflect. There is, again, an obvious parallelism in the mimetic propensity. Children are ever dramatizing the lives of adults; and savages, along with their other mimicries, similarly dramatize the actions of their civilized visitors.

The reader may be spared Spencer's examples of the marvels of mimicry (the primary art of childhood, according to Spencer) achieved by Negroes, New Zealanders, Dyaks, Chinese, Nootkas, Snake Indians, Brazilian Indians, Patagonians, and other primitive peoples (1897 [1876–1896]:I, 83–84). But note that according to Eastman the Santee children were "good mimics. . . . We watched the men of our people," he writes, "and represented them in our play" (3).

Spencer continues:

> Want of power to discriminate between useless and useful facts, characterizes the juvenile mind, as it does the mind of the primitive man. . . . Again, we see in the young of our own races a similar inability to concentrate the attention on anything complex or abstract. From feebleness of the higher intellectual faculties comes, in both cases, an absence, or a paucity, of ideas grasped by those faculties. The child, like the savage, has few words of even a low grade of abstractedness. . . . Unsupplied as its mind is with general truths . . . the civilized child when quite young, like the savage throughout life, shows but little rational surprise or rational curiosity.

And, of course, just as there are stages of childhood, so there are stages along the way to civilization:

> After a time . . . when the higher intellectual powers [the civilized child] inherits are beginning to act . . . its stage of mental development represents that of such semi-civilized races as the Malayo-Polynesians. (1897 [1876–1896]:I, 91–92)

There was a time, then, when their enemies *and* friends could refer to Indians and blacks as "childlike" with the full authority of science. In her memoirs Elaine Goodale, for example, refers to the Sioux as being childlike, even though she could be infuriated by the official government statements that so often "were patronizing in tone, addressing the Indians as if they were children incapable of reason" (90). There is no real inconsistency here, for Goodale wanted Indians to be treated like other Americans; she wanted them off the reservation, out of the reservation schools. Since she wanted them to become "adults," she wanted them to be treated like adults. And so in *Indian Boyhood* we find that the Santees were "children of the wilderness" (3). When he was very young, Eastman conversed with squirrels and birds in "an unknown dialect" (7)—he was, then, a child of Nature. As he was in years, so were his people in spirit:

> They are children of Nature, and occasionally she whips them with the lashes of experience, yet they are forgetful and careless. Much of their suffering could have been prevented by a little calculation. (17)

But "calculation" is just what Spencer would not expect of savages, for "Lacking the ability to think, and the accompanying desire to know, the savage is without tendency to speculate" (1897 [1876–1896]:I, 89). Eastman's formulation is a bit less brutal, but he is in fundamental agreement with Spencer. Eastman quite freely explains some of his people's behavior, for example, by speaking in terms of their "superstitions" (e.g., 31). And he devotes a whole chapter to making a distinction between the medicine men and women who worked upon the people's credulity and the herbal healers, whose remedies were real remedies. Eastman's grandmother was one of the latter, and so we see again that Eastman is descended from the best, most nearly rational, most fully evolved family of the best, most fully evolved tribe of the "highest type of pagan and uncivilized man."

There is, then, something quite consciously appropriate in Eastman's addressing *Indian Boyhood* to children. "I have put together these fragmentary recollections of my thrilling wild life," Eastman wrote in the dedication, "expressly for the little son who came too late to behold for himself the drama of savage existence." The hope would seem to be that his son, and his other youthful readers, might derive vicariously some of the benefits of a savage childhood:

> What boy would not be an Indian for a while when he thinks of the freest life in the world? This life was mine. Every day there was a real hunt. There was real game. Occasionally there was a medicine dance away off in the woods where no one could disturb us, in which the boys impersonated their elders, Brave Bull, Standing Elk, High Hawk, Medicine Bear, and the rest. (3)

Much that Tom Sawyer urged his band to imagine, Eastman lived in fact. Eastman was very active in the Boy Scouts of America, and he wrote extensively for them. After he gave up doctoring, he ran for a time a woodsy camp for young women. He taught them archery and other Indian lore as being peculiarly appropriate to their formative years. In one book he described Indian life as the prototype for the Boy Scouts and the Campfire Girls (Wilson, 1983:135). He considers his own remembrances of Indian ways, then, to be naturally well suited for children. It is no coincidence that *Indian Boyhood* should end with Eastman's passage into the adult world *and* the white world. The passage into the white world *is* the passage into adulthood for the Indian.

Eastman was not alone in assuming that Indian life—the life of *real* Indians—provided good stories for children. Much of what was published about Indians during the first three decades of this century was intended for children. James Willard Schultz wrote many of his stories about his life among the Black-feet for *Youth's Companion* and *American Boy*. But among many examples, Luther Standing Bear provides probably the closest analogy. Standing Bear, like Eastman, was brought up in the old ways; he learned all that an Oglala boy ought to learn. He describes himself as having been precisely of an age to allow him the traditional Oglala education, but none of its application. This will say that he, too, conceives of himself as having been taken away from his people and brought to school just as he was entering upon the life of an adult. Soon after he killed his first and only buffalo he was whisked off to be a student in the first class at Carlisle Indian School. Standing Bear described his Indian life in *My Indian Boyhood*. He inscribed the book to children, "with the hope that the hearts of the white boys and girls . . . will be made kinder toward the little Indian boys and girls."

Standing Bear is like Eastman, too, in having written more than one volume of autobiography. Standing Bear went on to write *My People the Sioux* in 1928. And Eastman wrote *From the Deep Woods to Civilization* in 1916. Both were written for adults. But there are interesting differences between the adult books and Eastman's boyhood book that cannot be explained simply by the change of audience. For example, neither Standing Bear nor Eastman in their "adult" autobiographies is willing to dismiss Indian spiritualism as "superstition," the way Eastman had done in *Indian Boyhood*. Now, a good deal had happened since the publication of *Indian Boyhood* in 1902. By the time they wrote their adult autobiographies, both Standing Bear and Eastman had lived long enough in civilization to have felt some pangs of disillusionment. But it must also be remembered that the vogue for Social Darwinism had faded by this time. Boasian, particularist anthropology was in the ascendancy. The bright promise of the Dawes Act had faded, and Indian tribes were demonstrating a remarkable staying power. They were neither vanishing nor melting with quite the alacrity Social Darwinists had anticipated. The older he became, the more Eastman allowed himself to conceive of himself as a Santee, the more eager he was to return to the lakes and the woods and find there some of what he had left behind.[10]

But *Indian Boyhood*, as we have seen, is driven by earlier, Social Darwinist assumptions. And so, at the end of the book, Eastman recalls his preparations for initiation into Santee manhood. When his Santee elders feel that he is ready to become a warrior, when they feel that he is ready to become an adult, they give him his first gun, the white man's "mysterious iron" (285). This image of the first gun is full of meaning: it is symbolic of the rite of passage; it looks forward to the white world Eastman will soon enter; it implies white dominance; it suggests the imminent breakup of the old ways. It is "mysterious," and so it is suggestive, too, of the rationality of white civilization and the credulity of the Indians.

It is a powerfully ambivalent image. And it sums up a good deal of *Indian Boyhood*'s Social Darwinist thinking. Eastman encourages his readers to consider his bow-and-arrow childhood as something like the ideal, or at least the quintessential, childhood. How painful it must have been for Eastman to leave off such a childhood, such a time of freedom, of racing, hunting, swimming—all out in the woods, in the company of birds, deer, and rabbits. How could he remember trading this childhood for the fears and the hard, scarred desks of a cramped schoolhouse in Flandreau without feeling nostalgia for those secure years of childhood? But when Eastman's father sent him off to school, he said, "Remember, my boy, it is the same as if I sent you on your first war-path. I shall expect you to conquer" (*From the Deep Woods to Civilization*, 31–32). Childhood must pass. There is obviously something sad in this. But then puberty rituals were not always entirely joyous occasions among the Indians. Childhood must pass. So, too, Eastman insists, must the Indian pass into the white world, lest he remain a pathetic kind of aging child, a ward of the state—"a fictitious copy of the past." There is very real power in the gun, a kind of power that it can do no good to deny. If he is to evolve, the Indian must leave the old ways, however fondly tribal glories, like the glorious summers of childhood, may be remembered.

8

N. SCOTT MOMADAY: ORAL TO WRITTEN TRADITION

The Indian autobiographers differ in interesting ways from the black autobiographers. Black autobiographers characteristically write about their attempts to enter into the promised land, a land flowing with milk and honey and freedom, a land peopled with new Canaanites determined to forbid them the fords of the Jordan. Indian autobiography looks back to Eden. Like the Ghost Dancers, most Indian autobiographers want to return. Two Leggings's sense of himself has entirely to do with the stories that keep his past vital. White Bull has taught himself to glory in later deeds as though they were coups. Sanapia, Beetus, Maxidiwiac, Black Elk, Benjamin Calf Robe, and many others want to pass on their knowledge of the old ways to a younger generation, so that the old ways might flourish again, or that at least the old ways might not utterly pass away. Beverly Hungry Wolf's autobiography records her attempt to leave "civilization" and return in the most literal sense to the "ways of her grandmothers."

Some Indian progressives, like Thomas Wildcat Alford and the early Charles Eastman, speak with conviction about the superiority of new ways to old. But Alford and Eastman, and even the most devout Christian Indian autobiographers seem never to be far from a sense of loss. Sometimes this rises bitterly to the surface, as it does in the case of Gertrude Bonnin, Jimmie Durham, Jim Barnes, Thrasher, and Bobbi Lee. Sometimes we sense it despite the autobiographers' own assertions that all is well, as in the case of Blowsnake and Hensley. Often it is an ache at the back of the throat, nostalgia fused sometimes with conviction, sometimes with despair. The editors, of course, played their part in all this, but in some way, in some sense most Indian autobiographers seek to return—if only by the workings of the memory, if only by mounting a memorial in words.

N. Scott Momaday certainly participates in this tradition. But for Momaday this notion of a return to the old ways is more than a subject, more than an organizing principle; it has determined the form of his autobiographical books. The choice of archaizing forms was quite self-conscious on Momaday's part, for when Momaday set out upon his autobiographical project, he had a much wider awareness of autobiographical forms and traditions than any of the other autobiographers we have discussed. This autobiographer occasionally teaches a course in autobiography at the University of Arizona. He has his students read such books as Isak Dinesen's *Out of Africa,* Robert Graves's *Goodbye to All That,* and Nabokov's *Speak, Memory* (interview, 1985). The reading list reflects the range one might expect of a man who earned his Ph.D. from Stanford at a time when literature Ph.D.s still read more literature than literary theory. But he chose none of these moderns for his model. In his two published volumes of autobiography, *The Way to Rainy Mountain* (1969) and *The Names* (1976),[1] he chose to write autobiography after the fashion of the nonliterate, oral Indian storytellers: "In general," Momaday wrote on the first page of *The Names,*

> my narrative is an autobiographical account. Specifically, it is an act of the imagination. . . . When Pohd-lohk told a story he began by being quiet. Then he said *Ah-keah-de,* "They were camping," and he said it every time. I have tried to write in the same way, in the same spirit. Imagine: They were camping.

Momaday, then, will *write* autobiography after the fashion of an *oral* storyteller. This was to attempt something quite new.[2] His method produces something that in many ways is like what we have found in White Bull's *Personal Narrative* and like what we can see through Wildschut's editorial veil in *Two Leggings.* In neither *The Way to Rainy Mountain* nor *The Names,* for example, do we find continuous, chronologically ordered narrative. *The Way to Rainy Mountain* contains twenty-four sections. Each section is three pages long and consists of three related accounts, one from Kiowa myth or folklore, one from Kiowa recorded history, and one from Momaday's personal or family history—"the mythical, the historical, and the immediate," as Momaday put it in his own commentary on *The*

Way to Rainy Mountain.[3] There are drawings, images, throughout. None of these sections is longer than about three hundred words. Momaday tells the story of the twins and the giant in just two hundred words; the story of the arrow maker and his enemy in about the same space; he tells about the image of *tai-me*, central to the Kiowa Sun Dance, in about a hundred and fifty words.

Momaday has called this "staccato-like narrative," one brief story after another. He wrote with such studied compression in order to convey in writing a sense of oral storytelling (interview, 1985). Oral narratives can, of course, achieve epic length.[4] But Momaday's autobiographical narratives are meant to recall the kinds of stories he himself heard as a child. It is for this reason too that Momaday only rarely makes explicit connections between one story and the next—just as no explicit connections would have been made for the boy Momaday when his grandmother would tell him a story about the emergence of the Kiowas from a hollow log, and then the next night, before bedtime, tell him a story about his grandfather—just as there is no explicit connection when I tell my own children the story of Jack and the beanstalk one night, and a story about some one of my schoolyard triumphs the next. Clearly, Momaday wanted his readers to experience something like his own experience of listening to his mother and father and his Kiowa relatives telling stories.

In *The Names* Momaday's plan remained essentially the same. He writes in short units (although not as short as in *The Way to Rainy Mountain*), and very few explicit connections are made between this story and that. Again, there are images, family photographs this time.

That Momaday is attempting to write after the fashion of oral storytellers explains, too, why *The Names* and *The Way to Rainy Mountain* lack literary allusions. In his 1966 novel, *House Made of Dawn*, by contrast, an Indian named *Abel* kills an evil man, who is an albino. Most readers have recognized in Abel a reference to the story in Genesis and in the albino an allusion to Melville's whale and to Melville's reasons for painting evil white (and Momaday has himself confirmed this reading [Velie, 1982:57]). But he wrote nothing like this in either of his autobiographical works. Again, in these books Momaday is writing in a way as nearly like that of the old oral storytellers as possible. And so he writes without literary allusions.

No literary allusions and brief, unconnected narrative: such features of preliterate storytelling are relatively easy to imitate. It is rather more difficult to imagine how such a man as Pohd-lohk, who could have been acquainted with no tradition of modern, written autobiography, might have gone about the task of describing his self and its development. I think Momaday responded to this problem by including tribal and personal history and myth in his autobiographical books.

Certainly just such a mix is one of the striking features of many of the Indian autobiographies. Geronimo's autobiography,[5] for example, includes the following:

> In the beginning the world was covered with darkness. There was no sun, no day. The perpetual night had no moon or stars.
> There were, however, all manner of beasts and birds. Among the beasts were many hideous, nameless monsters. . . . Mankind could not prosper under such conditions, for the beasts and serpents destroyed all human offspring.

And Geronimo also spoke of the history of the tribe:

> The Apache Indians are divided into six subtribes. To one of these, the Be-don-ko-he, I belong. Our tribe inhabited that region of mountainous country which lies west from the line of Arizona, and south from the headwaters of the Gila River.

Of course, he also tells about his own life. Myth, tribal, and personal history—"the mythical, the historical, and the immediate," in Momaday's phrase. *Black Elk Speaks* includes these same three components of identity. The boundaries between the three are not as sharply drawn in *Black Elk Speaks;* but myth, tribal history, and personal history are at least as important here as in *Geronimo*. Early in the first chapter, for example, we read Black Elk's story of how the holy pipe came to the Oglalas.[6] A sacred woman came to the Oglalas:

> And after a while she came, very beautiful and singing, and as she went into the tepee this is what she sang:

> "With visible breath I am walking.
> A voice I am sending as I walk.

In a sacred manner I am walking.
With visible tracks I am walking.
In a sacred manner I walk."

. . . Then she gave something to the chief, and it was a pipe with a
bison calf carved on one side. . . . "Behold!" she said. "With this you
shall multiply and be a good nation." (3–4)

As to tribal history, Black Elk's narrative is never far from this;
almost everything that he tells us about himself is explicitly or
implicitly related to the history of the tribe. Black Elk tells about
how things were for his tribe before the coming of the white man,
about the great herds of buffalo before the railroad cut the herd in
two. Even the Great Vision, which dominates the book just as it
dominated Black Elk's life, has to do with Black Elk's relation to
the tribe and its well-being.

Patencio, for another example, a Cahuilla Indian born about
1860, had his life story taken down by Kate Collins in the late
1930s. The book preserves much of the flavor of oral storytelling,
and it moves quite unpretentiously back and forth from tribal
history, to myth, and personal reminiscences.[7] In 1923 Edward
Sapir took down autobiographical narratives that work in much
the same way from John Fredson, in the Gwich'in Athabaskan
language of Alaska.

This conception of how one may tell the story of one's life is not
confined to the as-told-to autobiographies taken down from nonliterate Indians. Simon Pokagon (1830–1899), for example, was considered during his lifetime to be the best-educated Indian of his
generation. He attended Notre Dame, Oberlin, and a school in
Twinsburg, Ohio (Clements, 1986:237). In 1898 he wrote an account of "Indian Superstitions and Legends." He began with a
brief autobiography, telling about his early fear and loathing of the
white man, then about his conversion and education. And most of
the legends and superstitions he relates in some way to some fragment of autobiography or tribal history. Indeed, his whole account
of Indian superstitions and legends is told within the framework of
his own changing attitude toward these beliefs, from his initial
native trust in them, to his church-inspired skepticism, and finally,
late in his life, to his conviction that such beliefs are the essence of
Christian *and* Indian spirituality.[8]

Even the most literate of the Indian autobiographies before Momaday's, Joseph Mathews's *Talking to the Moon,* includes tribal history, Osage myth, and personal reminiscences. This is remarkable in the case of Mathews, by the way, since he clearly has Thoreau's *Walden* as his primary model. Dan Kennedy's *Recollections of an Assiniboine Chief* is much less sophisticated than Mathews's book, but here too we find autobiographical detail intermixed with tribal history and myth. Examples could be multiplied: James Paytiamo's *Flaming Arrow's People: By an Acoma Indian,* Don Talayesva's *Sun Chief,* Alma Greene's *Forbidden Voice: Reflections of a Mohawk Indian,* and the brief autobiography of Hastiin Biyo'. But I think that enough has been said to make the point that personal history is often mixed with myth and tribal history in the Indian autobiographies.

Given his academic training and his work in Indian Studies programs,[9] and given the number of Indian autobiographies that combine tribal with personal history, one might assume that Momaday went to work as he did because of his reading. In fact, however, Momaday had read virtually none of these narratives when he was at work on his own autobiographies: "Until quite recently I really knew very little about Indian autobiography as such," Momaday said in 1985. "I came very late to *Sun Chief* and *Black Elk Speaks* and other such books":

> I was working pretty much with oral tradition exclusively when I wrote *The Names.* . . . I loved hearing people talk about their experiences—my father especially, to whom I was very close. And he told me stories from the first time I could first deal with language. And I loved just to be around when he was recalling something from his childhood. And I think that it was that kind of immediacy, that kind of personal involvement. I wasn't thinking about Indian biography as a classification; I was simply thinking of it as a recounting of experience, very personal. (Interview, 1985)

Momaday combined tribal and personal history, then, largely because of his own childhood immersion in oral narrative traditions, traditions that were not far removed from those which guided Two Leggings, Geronimo, Patencio, and many other unacculturated Indians in their autobiographical labors. And we should not forget White Bull, for, like White Bull, Momaday brings a calendar history into his personal narrative. Pohd-lohk, it seems, kept a calendar history of the Kiowas in an old ledger book.[10] Momaday writes:

> Now that he was old, Pohd-lohk liked to look backwards in time, and though he could neither read nor write, this book was his means. It was an instrument with which he could reckon his place in the world. . . . The calendar . . . began a hundred years in the past. Beyond that, beyond the notion of a moment in 1833, there was only the unknown, a kind of prehistoric and impenetrable genesis, a realm of no particular shape, duration, or meaning. (*The Names:* 48)

The time beyond 1833 was only in a special sense the "unknown," for Pohd-lohk and other Kiowa storytellers and oral historians certainly did tell stories about this time, this "realm of no particular shape, duration, or meaning." How did a man like Pohd-lohk conceive of the difference between mythic stories and the stories that the calendars were designed to recall? Momaday has said that for Pohd-lohk what we call the mythic stories,

> are like all other stories, with one exception. And that is that they cannot be attached or connected to any particular time—the origin myth being one of them. Where that story originated, no one knows; how old it is, no one knows; but since it is an origin myth, it is bound to be ancient. Other stories you can date with some accuracy. (Interview, 1985)

Momaday added that there may even have been some special conventions that governed the telling of mythic history:

> I had the impression in talking to some of the older people in the tribe, . . . especially when I was putting *Rainy Mountain* together, that there was a kind of convention which was it was incumbent upon the storyteller to observe, a kind of silence. I remember, for example, . . . interviewing the old woman, Ko-sahn, whom I mention at the end of *Rainy Mountain.* I . . . was struck by the fact that when I asked her a question [about mythic times], she would immediately . . . have a disclaimer ready. She would say, "Oh, that—don't ask me that question, because very little is known about *that.* That is so far back in time." And then having observed that convention, she would answer the question. She would tell me in great detail. (Interview, 1985)

When we read the book of Genesis, we must be struck by the chasm that yawns between the mythic stories and the story of Abraham. On the one side lie the stories of the creation, of the Serpent in Eden, of Titans, of a flood which covered the earth, and a story of men who could build a tower reaching up into the heavens. This is history before the stars fell, history before 1833. "Oh, that," says Ko-sahn, "don't ask me that question, because very little is known about *that*. That is so far back in time." And yet it may be told by a special act of mythic grace. On the near side of the chasm is the story of Abraham, which leads toward the stories of Isaac and Jacob and Samuel, and of David, who killed a giant of human, not mythic, proportions. This is the history of the calendar histories.

The time before the first event in Pohd-lohk's calendar is "so far back in time," the time of myth; the concrete, "datable" remembrances of his people begin with the first entry in the calendar, in 1833. To these two kinds of history must be added a third, that which grows out of personal remembrances. It is Momaday's sense, then, that the Kiowas tell three distinct kinds of "historical" stories, giving expression to three kinds of tribal memories: the myths, the remembered, "datable" history, and personal remembrances— three kinds of history, three kinds of memories, at once distinct and interpenetrating, all essentially tribal. In both *The Names* and *The Way to Rainy Mountain* Momaday tries to work according to this ancient, tribal sense of history.

In *The Way to Rainy Mountain*, for example, Momaday tells a story about the mythic grandmother spider, of her tender care for the sun's child. Momaday juxtaposes this story with a fragment of history: in 1874 the Kiowas were being driven by the army toward the Staked Plains. The people were "bone weary and afraid," and then the people saw what must have seemed to them a sign of promise, of welcome: "the earth was suddenly crawling with spiders, great black tarantulas." Next come Momaday's own remembrances of spiders: "I know of spiders," he writes. "Now and then there comes a tarantula, at evening, always larger than you imagine" (32–34). In the same way and for the same reasons, Momaday gives us mythic, historical, and personal remembrances of horses, for example, and of buffalo, and of rain. Momaday's feelings about the spider and his feelings about horses are affected by his people's remembrances, and his people's history lives and achieves new form in his remembrances.

For Momaday this is, I think, the quintessential difference between "Indian autobiography" and modern, Western autobiography. Momaday has suggested, for example, that the oral characteristics of *Two Leggings* are recognizable through all the layers of editing:

> I don't think that [Two Leggings] is recounting, in the way that we think of that as an *activity,* but he is creating. . . . He is really creating something. He is carrying the whole process forward. It is not dead matter that he is dealing with. He does not think of it in that way. Nor does the Indian within the oral tradition think of the story as dead matter. It is something that is to be carried on. And it seems to me that this is the most exciting and the most salient part of the oral tradition in *Two Leggings.* . . . Set it beside *The Autobiography of Benjamin Franklin:* on the one hand you have the story that is being carried on, as opposed to the story that exists in the past and has an ending somewhere in the past. (Interview, 1985)

Momaday, then, stands in relation to Pohd-lohk as Pohd-lohk does to his calendar history—and White Bull to his calendar history. Momaday's memories of Pohd-lohk cannot be anything but scattered images. Indeed, since Pohd-lohk died when Momaday was quite young, Momaday must be relying largely on other people's memories of Pohd-lohk, really. But he "remembers" Pohd-lohk in detail; he is able to remember Pohd-lohk in the same way that Ko-sahn is able to remember mythic events "far back in time." He is able, for example, to follow Pohd-lohk throughout the morning of the day on which the old man conferred upon the six-month-old Momaday his Kiowa name, Tsoai-talee. He is able to remember Pohd-lohk in detail by an act of what Momaday has called "the racial memory."[11]

Momaday's phrasing is unfortunate, I believe. Especially with his fondness for Isak Dinesen, the laureate of racialism-in-gossamer, the notion of "racial memory" must give us pause. Does Momaday really want to claim all allegiance to racialist ideas? If ideas can be determined by race, then perhaps levels of intelligence can as well. Is Momaday really in agreement with Eastman and such academically respectable racial determinists as Arthur Jensen?

I am certain that Eastman (to say nothing of Jensen) meant what he said about race literally. But for Momaday, I think, "race" and "blood" are evocative synonyms for "culture." We must remember that for Momaday, "We are what we imagine" (1970:103). Memory and imagination shape Momaday and his characters, not genes. For Momaday "an Indian is an idea which a given man has of himself" (1970:97). As we read in *The Names* even Momaday's mother, who was only one-eighth Cherokee, could become Indian by *imagining* "herself as an Indian. That dim native heritage became a fascination and a cause for her. . . . She imagined who she was" (25). Even as a child "she imagined herself audaciously" (*The Names:* 20). Like his mother, Momaday himself, at a certain period in his life, began to imagine himself in a new way. He made the journey of which we read in *The Way to Rainy Mountain;* he began to imagine himself as an Indian. This is not racial determinism.

"Racial memory" is not in Momaday's genes. Some of his mother's memories, for example, have become his own, not because of anything like racial memories in Jung's sense, but more simply because she has told him some of her stories: "This is the real burden of the blood" (*The Names:* 22). "Racial memory," then, is an act of the imagination, imagination shaped by memory and culture. "I remember," all this allows him to write: "my mother was very young, four or five years old . . . " (*The Names:* 22).

In the same way, Pohd-lohk and White Bull include in their calendar histories events which are well beyond the scope of what *we* would consider to be their memory. Momaday wants us to see that he is like Pohd-lohk, that for them there is no such sharp distinction between the tribe's memories and their own. The images are all there in the calendar, one image per year. Pohd-lohk would have discussed the images with the old tribal historians just as White Bull did. Each image calls forth a whole range of associations, a whole year's worth of other memories. The first image in Pohd-lohk's calendar, for example, recalls a day we know to have been November 13, 1833, when just before dawn there was a remarkable meteor shower. Momaday "remembers" that on the morning of his naming, Pohd-lohk opened up his book to the first page:

. . . it was *Da-pegya-de Sai* . . . and the stars were falling. He closed his eyes, the better to see them. They were everywhere in the darkness, so numerous and bright indeed that the night was shattered. (48)

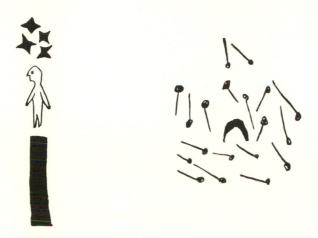

Figure 3. The meteor shower of 1833, the year the stars fell. *Left*, from a Kiowa calendar; *right* from a Dakota calendar. (By permission of the Smithsonian Institution Press from *Calendar History of the Kiowa Indians* by James Mooney. © Smithsonian Institution, 1979.)

The guiding principle of Momaday's autobiographical writing, then, is that his sense of himself is determined not only by his own remembrances but also by all that his tribe (and his family, Kiowa *and* Anglo)[12] remembers in its myths and its history. This is how he imagined he might write autobiography after the fashion of nonliterate Kiowas. Insofar as we have seen White Bull and Geronimo and other Indians include tribal history and myth along with the recounting of their own deeds, we may see that Momaday's solution is traditional. Indeed, when Momaday tells us in *The Way to Rainy Mountain* and in *The Names* that his sense of himself is intimately related to the movement of his Kiowa ancestors down out of the Rocky Mountain forests onto the Plains, that he is who he is because of his mother's people's relation to the hills of Kentucky, that his sense of self is shaped by the Kiowa's genesis, their coming forth out of a log—in all of this and in the very form of his autobiographies, Momaday encourages us to see in his personal development the analogue of the effects of oral transmission on preliterate societies. I quote the philosopher/anthropologist Robin Horton:

> In considering oral transmission, we must stress that its most distinctive effects depend upon the use of human memory as a storage device. On the one hand, memory tends to remould the past in the image of the present, and hence to minimize the amount of change that has taken place down through the ages. On the other hand, memory tends, over the generations, to ascribe all innovations, whether sociocultural or intellectual, to an initial "time of the beginnings." Oral transmission, therefore, encourages a view of the past which sees the main outlines of one's society as having been shaped long ago and as having undergone little essential change since then.[13]

This, then, is Momaday's solution. The ancients did not write autobiography; neither did they conceive of themselves in a way that would have led them to compose autobiography-as-self-discovery even if they had been literate. But, says Momaday, their idea of themselves was a product or a creation of the free interplay of imagination and three kinds of memory: the mythical, the historical, and the immediate. For Momaday, "an Indian is an idea which a given man has of himself."[14] An unlettered, traditional Indian such as Pohd-lohk may never have given explicit utterance to any such single idea of the self, but the constituents of the idea were there nonetheless. And so Momaday can write autobiography after the fashion of the ancients by setting down all the fragments that make up the unuttered whole.

Momaday leaves to his readers the task of constituting a self out of all these stories, just as White Bull and Two Leggings tell their coup tales in the expectation that their hearers will add all the stories up and *so* understand just who it is that has recounted these coups. Just as the Miniconjou must come to understand White Bull anew each time he adds a new coup tale, so, too, must Momaday continue to constitute *his* self out of all the stories he has heard, all the images he has seen, out of all the experiences that have become stories for him in the free interplay of his memory and imagination. For White Bull, Two Leggings, *and* Momaday, autobiography is dynamic, a project that has no end. One thinks yet again of how literally we here may take Roy Pascal's dictum that the making of autobiography recreates the autobiographer (1960:182–183).

Of course, other influences also worked on Momaday. He would not, for example, have worked as he did with limited point of view, nor would he have asked his readers to piece together his stories on their own had he not read Faulkner and Joyce.[15] But, still, I think it may be said that Momaday set for himself the task of writing autobiography according to the conventions of an autobiographical tradition that had never before been considered to be a tradition.

Now, it is worthy of note that since the appearance of *The Way to Rainy Mountain* more and more Indian autobiographers have written (or collaborated) with an awareness of other Indian autobiographers before them: John Lame Deer, for example, and Frank Fools Crow, both Sioux medicine men, knew enough about *Black Elk Speaks* to allow the book to influence their own autobiographies and their sense of themselves as autobiographers and medicine men; and, of course, their collaborators, John Erdoes and Thomas Mails, respectively, also knew *Black Elk Speaks*. Mails in particular seems to see himself as Neihardt *redux*. Belle Highwalking mentions in the course of her autobiography that her reasons for doing autobiography are the same as those that motivated her brother, John Stands in Timber, to do his book. Albert Yava had read *Sun Chief*, and Yava's reserve in his autobiography seems in part to be a response to Talayesva's un-Hopi willingness to tell all. And we now even have autobiographical narratives by Asa Daklugie, Geronimo's nephew, the man who served as interpreter for Geronimo and Barrett.

Momaday certainly did not influence Fools Crow, Yava, Lame Deer, Highwalking, or Daklugie. But Momaday did begin upon his autobiographical labors at just the time that Indians—even Indians like Fools Crow who were not themselves fully literate—were coming to know *literary* Indian autobiography and its uses. Momaday's work, then, may be seen as a kind of embodiment of a particular moment in the history of American Indian autobiography. He is also a force in this transition from oral to written traditions. And Momaday is quite self-conscious about this. His plan here is in keeping with his sense of the history of literature in the largest sense. In 1970 Momaday wrote that he had for "three or four years" been interested "in the matter of 'oral tradition'":

Specifically, I began to wonder about the way in which myths, legends, and lore evolve into that mature condition of expression which we call "literature." For indeed literature is, I believe, the end-product of an evolutionary process, and the so-called "oral tradition" is primarily a stage within that process, a stage that is indispensable and perhaps original as well. (1970:105)

Momaday is speaking in general of the transformation of oral literature into a written literature. But I think that Momaday's aims here are particularly important to the history and development of American Indian autobiography. Before Momaday, these narratives were regarded as a miscellaneous if fascinating assortment of anthropological, historical, psychological, and literary documents. Momaday's self-conscious attempt to write autobiography after the fashion of the oral storytellers has done much to make this miscellany into a literary tradition. No Indian autobiographer before Momaday, I think, tried to imagine the literate equivalent of preliterate autobiography.[16]

One has only to see how closely Leslie Silko's *Storyteller* (1981), for example, is modeled upon *The Way to Rainy Mountain* and *The Names* to realize that Momaday has transformed this miscellany into a *living* literary tradition. Silko, for example, wants to convey a sense of herself as a story*teller,* just as Momaday tries to write his stories in such a way as to allow his readers some sense of oral storytelling. Some sections of *Storyteller* are in verse; and often the verse forms seem designed to render—or at least suggest—oral performance in written form. This may be seen most clearly, perhaps, in Silko's Coyote stories:

Toe'osh: A Laguna Coyote Story

In the wintertime
At night
we tell coyote stories
              and drink Spañada by the stove.
How coyote got his
ratty old fur coat
              bits of old fur
              the sparrows stuck on him
              with dabs of pitch.

That was after he lost his proud original one in a poker game.
anyhow things like that
are always happening to him,
that's what he said anyway. (236–237)

The diction in *Storyteller* is like the diction in *The Names*. It is often familiar, intimate, especially in the stories having to do with family, with Grandpa and Grandma and Dad, and thus, suggestive of informal, oral storytelling.

Momaday includes graphic as well as verbal images; in *The Names* the graphic images are family photographs. Silko also includes family photographs. Momaday presents in his autobiography the mythic, the historical and the personal. Silko has all this, too. But most strikingly, *Storyteller* is discontinuous. Just as Momaday expects his readers to synthesize a conception of just who he is by reading the stories that continue to form him, so Silko expects us to constitute a sense of *her* self out the many, brief, discontinuous stories in *Storyteller*. Like Momaday she expects us to see her as the sum total of the experiences that have become her stories. Like Momaday, Silko is trying to write autobiography in something like the way her Indian ancestors might have carried out such a project.

We see this same influence at work in at least half of the eighteen autobiographies collected in *I Tell You Now: Autobiographical Essays by Native American Authors*. The editors, Brian Swann and Arnold Krupat, have long been interested not only in Indian literature but specifically in the problems of translating oral into written forms. They left their Indian authors free, then, to shape their autobiographical narratives as they would. Jack Forbes, for example, Diane Glancy, and Maurice Kenny each chose to write autobiography in some variation on Momaday's discontinuous form.

We may see Momaday's influence at work, too, in some of the recent autobiographies coming to us out of Alaska (see chapter 3). The autobiographies of Henry Beatus, Joe Beetus, Roger Dayton, John Honea, Oscar Nictune, Edwin Simon, Madeline Solomon, Chief Henry, Frank Tobuk, and Belle Herbert each appears as a collection of separate stories. As Ray Barnhardt put it, *The Way to Rainy Mountain* appeared in "the first round, when native [American] oral forms were first being recognized and articulated."[17] Momaday is certainly not the most important influence here, but

we do see Momaday's assumptions reflected especially in Bill Pfisterer's work with Herbert and Eliza Jones's work with Henry. They
have tried to preserve not just the words and sentences of their
narrators, but their narrators' own sense of the order of the tales,
even the breaks between units that become lines upon the printed
page. They neither feel obliged to provide for us narrative transitions nor to comply with the demands of the Chronological Imperative. And so we are put in something like the same position as were
the Teton Sioux who heard White Bull deliver his coup tales: we
are left by the editors to piece together from the stories of their
deeds a sense of who these people are.

Momaday has placed his autobiographical project squarely on
the divide between oral and literate traditions. The work of Jack
Goody (1963, 1977), Albert Lord (1981 [1960]), Dennis Tedlock
(1983), Dell Hymes (1977, 1981), and others is making us ever
more aware of the consequences of literacy, of the special nature
of oral forms and performance. And here, ready to hand, are *The
Way to Rainy Mountain* and *The Names*, embodying much of what
these scholars have to say about such differences. Momaday's autobiographical books are unpretentious recreations of one of the wonders of Genesis and Homer—the transformation there before us
upon the page of oral traditions into literature. Momaday has
devised a form in which editors may set down in writing the lives
of tribal-minded Indian informants without forcing the Indians
themselves or their stories into modern, individualizing, Westerniz-
ing molds. Think for a moment how different *Sun Chief* would have
been had Simmons been as nondirective with Talayesva as Pfisterer
and his colleagues were with Belle Herbert; think how different *Sun
Chief* would have been had Talayesva's stories been set down, each
by the other, in the order Talayesva had told them, had they been
set down without transitions, connections, had we been asked to
read as Faulkner and Joyce have taught us to read.

Momaday's form and method serves as well to allow such modern, literate Indians as Silko, Forbes, Glancy, and Kenny to convey
a sense of themselves in something like a tribal way, perhaps even
an ancient way. Put another way, Momaday has found comfortable
old wineskins for the new wine of Indian autobiography. And so
we have come full circle or if not full circle, we have returned at
least to a point where the beginnings may once again be seen.

Concluding Postscript

Recently, in Israel, I attended a lecture by Kamal Mansour, the Advisor to the President of Israel on Minority Affairs. He was to tell us something about the Druse people. He is himself a Druse, and I was eager to hear him speak. In the event, he told us about the Druse in three sentences: the Druse don't drink; the Druse are monogamous; and his father lived to a great age by following the tenets of the Druse religion. He went on to talk about other things. I was puzzled and a bit annoyed. I had wanted to learn about the Druse. Later, I found that one of the principles of the Druse is that they are not to talk about their religion. In his silence, then, I have come to recognize something essential to his sense of his religion. I have come to know Belle Herbert, White Bull, and Maxidiwiac, I think, in something like the same way.

Roy Pascal has written that one of the signal attractions of autobiographies is that they "offer an unparalleled insight into the mode of consciousness of other men. Even if what they tell us is not true, or only partly true, it is always true evidence of their personality" (1960:1). Surely Pascal is right in this. We read autobiography because we are interested in seeing things with the eye of the other; we are interested in seeing how people represent their lives, how they understand their lives; we are interested in seeing another personality from the inside. But if a Sioux warrior tells about his life by describing his deeds, if he tells us nothing about how his personality developed, I hope that we can now recognize that, still, he *is* telling us something essential about his personality, that we *are* being allowed a glimpse of the way this man sees himself. If Maxidiwiac makes nothing explicit about just how it was that she came to be the person she is; if she tells us about her farming, about her plants, about the time she spent on the platforms in the fields, singing songs and frightening away the birds, keeping watch for the boys who loved to prey on the sweet corn of the unwary, if she does all this, why should we lament that she has not told us about the "turning points" in her life? We should realize

that in all her talk of fields and plants and her deeds, we may catch
a glimpse of self very different from our own. We should recognize
that Eagle-ribs, White Bull, Maxidiwiac, and Two Leggings are by
their silences providing us with "true evidence of their personality"—precisely by telling us nothing about their personality.

Perhaps we should return, then, to the problem of defining autobiography. Philippe Lejeune has provided one of the best known
definitions of autobiography: it is a "retrospective account that an
actual person makes in prose of his own existence, stressing his
individual life and particularly the history of his personality"
(1975:14). Maxidiwiac, Eagle-ribs, and the rest have nothing to say
about the history of their personality. Pascal insists that in "true"
autobiography we must find some "coherent shaping of the past"
(1960:5). There is no coherent shaping of the past in White Bull's
Personal Narrative; there are only the stories of deeds. But autobiographers who thus "restrict themselves to *res gestae,*" according to
Pascal, "fail to realize the potentialities of the genre" (1960:9).
Pascal's definition of autobiography would exclude Eagle-ribs's
coup tales, then, despite his assertion that what interests him in
autobiography is the chance it offers to come to know another from
the inside.

Now I am certainly not the first to notice how confining are such
generic definitions (e.g., Olney, 1980:12, 18). But narrow definitions are more crippling in the consideration of Indian autobiography, I think, than they are in considerations of autobiography in
general. Neither Lejeune nor Pascal would consider the *res gestae*
inscribed on the Egyptian tombs as "true" autobiography. But,
then, no one would claim that the tomb inscriptions are essential
to an understanding of Franklin's autobiography. I hope that I
have demonstrated that with Indian autobiography the case is
different. We need to know the coup tales in order to understand
Winnemucca. We need to know the preliterate autobiographical
traditions if we want to learn to make distinctions between the work
of the editors and that of the Indian autobiographers. Oral traditions are vital to a proper understanding of Momaday and Silko.

But the oral, as-told-to autobiographies warrant attention not
only for what they can tell us about later, literate autobiographers.
Read without a culture-bound insistence that the autobiographer
speak to us as would Henry Adams or Rousseau, the hundreds of

Indian autobiographers—speaking to us from three centuries, from well over a hundred different tribes—can show us an immense range of human ground. Comock, a Stone Age Eskimo, tells us how he lost half his family out upon the open ice, when the ice split right through their igloo in the middle of the night. He tells about starting life anew on an uninhabited island, with nothing but a few dogs, an ivory knife, and his "fire stones." Chris was taken off to the East with the other Apaches after the surrender of Geronimo. His autobiography provides a classic example of the Indian caught between two cultures. Mark Hanna tells about his life as a Havasupai in a deep canyon in northeastern Arizona. The Saayaachapis narratives allow us to see the remarkable complexity of Nootka life from the point of view of an accomplished Nootka storyteller.

Perhaps this book will aid others to explore this ground systematically. But my best hope is that it will, quite simply, win new readers for these remarkable narratives, readers interested in seeing the world from a new point of view, readers willing to read—in their imagination to hear—lives told in other ways.

Appendix
Lévi-Strauss's
Unmentioned Sorcerer

The introduction to this book discusses the use Claude Lévi-Strauss makes of a narrative by a Kwakiutl sorcerer, George Hunt, or Quesalid. Hunt wrote that narrative himself, after he was taught to write Kwakiutl by Franz Boas. What follows here is a narrative by another Kwakiutl shaman, Fool, the man who taught Hunt the ways of the shamans. It is, I think, worth quoting in its entirety, first so that Lévi-Strauss's argument may be evaluated in the light of the narrative he chose not to mention, and second, because it is a good example of a preliterate Shaman's Life (see Chapter 1). Hunt took this narrative down from Fool's dictation. Both narratives were edited and published by Boas (1930:1–46). Where Boas has names in phonetic notation, I have provided approximate equivalents in English orthography.

> I am (literally: this is) a hunter of all kinds of animals, I always go paddling about, for this is what I desire, seals, for I try out the oil from the blubber, to be bought by my tribe for gravy. I always get many hair seals; and so I am never poor. I was the principal one who does not believe in the shamans, when they speak about taking out sickness from sick people, and when they say that they see the souls of men; and formerly I did not believe in shamans, for I used to tell them aloud that they were lying when they were curing the sick; for I would sit down among them when they were beating time for the shamans when curing those who were very sick, and therefore I was really hated by the shamans of the Năkwăchdăĕchoo. I just wish to talk about this first.
>
> One fine day I paddled on the sea shooting seals with the one who was always my steersman, whose name was Lălămādĕnōl, for he was courageous. Nothing frightened him, neither gales nor all the bad animals, or the bad fishes, or the sea monsters which are often seen by the hunters when they hunt game at night. Therefore hunters ask courageous men to be their steersmen.
>
> Now I was paddling along at Achōlēs. Then I saw a wolf sitting on

a rock, rolling about on the rock, scratching with his forepaws both sides of his mouth. When I came near he saw us. He whined. He was never afraid of us and I stepped out of my small canoe and went to where he was sitting on the rock. When I came up to him the wolf was whining and I saw that his mouth was bleeding. I looked into his mouth and saw a deer bone crossways in his mouth, stuck between the teeth on both sides of his mouth, and it was really firmly (imbedded). The wolf was sitting on a rock watching me and evidently expected me to do something; to kill him or help him out of his trouble. I sat down on the rock close to him and I spoke to him, as he was sitting still, looking at me. I said to him, "You are in trouble, friend. Now I shall be like a great shaman and cure you, friend. I will take out your great trouble and cure you, friend. Now reward me, friend, that I will be able, like you, to get everything easily, all that is taken by you on account of your fame as a harpooneer and of your supernatural power. Now reward my kindness to you, friend. Go on! Sit still on the rock and let me get my means of taking out that bone," said I to him, as I went and took cedar twigs from a cedar tree inland from me. I twisted the cedar twigs and now they were a good rope. After I had done so, I went to where the wolf was sitting on the rock, just always keeping his mouth open. I took hold of the back of his head and put the thin end of the cedar rope into his mouth and I tied it to the middle part of the bone in his mouth and I pulled at it. Then the bone came out after that. (The wolf) only stared at me and I spoke to him and said, "O, friend your trouble has gone. Now take care of your mind and reward me for what I have done to you," said I to him. After I had said so to him the wolf turned around to the right and trotted away, not fast. He did not go far before he stopped and turned his face. Then he howled. Once he spoke and howled and went into the woods. I stepped into my small traveling canoe and paddled with my steersman Lālămādĕnōl. Now we never talked about the wolf as we paddled along.

Now night came and I wished to anchor inside of Foam-Receptacle (Awătsā), for no wind ever blows there. Now we lay down in our small traveling canoe, floating on the water; but really my eyes went to sleep. Lālămādĕnōl also did the same. His eyes also really went to sleep, for we had risen early when we started before nearly daylight came in the morning; and so we were very sleepy.

Now I dreamed of a man who came to me in a dream speaking to me in a dream. In my dream he said to me, "Why do you stay here? There are many seals lying on this island, friend. Take care, friend, I am Harpooneer-Body on whom you took pity today, and now I reward you for your kindness to me, friend. There is nothing hereafter that you will not obtain, whatever you wish to get. This also, do not lie down with your wife for four years, to pass through all that you will have to do," thus he said in my dream, Harpooneer-Body to Fool (Něnōlō). Then in my dream he disappeared.

I woke up and called Lālǎmāděnōl. When he awoke he hauled up the anchor. We went ashore and I washed in the sea. After I had done so I went aboard our small traveling canoe. I wished to see whether my dream would come true regarding the words that Harpooneer-Body had said in my dream, that there were many seals lying on the rocks on the island, for I did not believe in dreams and shamans and all the sayings of the people, for I only believed in my own mind. Then we paddled away before daylight came and we arrived at the island without trees. Now I saw that it was really covered with seals that were tight asleep. I took my yew wood seal club, stepped out of my small canoe and clubbed four large seals. Then a great number of seals tumbled into the water. Then I put the four large seals aboard my small canoe and we went home.

Now there was one thing I believed, namely the words of Harpooneer-Body, that he had said in my dream. Now it was really easy for me to get seals when I went out hunting and also all kinds of animals. Two years later, beginning at the time that I took out the bone from the wolf I went to Victoria with my late nephews Hǎmālělǎsěmāě and his late younger brothers Quǎnǎs and Owner-of-Throwing-away-(Property) (Tsěchěǎd), and also their late wives and their late children. I was with my wife the late Māchmǎkōdǎlǎōgwǎ. It was in the summer of 1871. We came home now traveling in the large canoe. We came to Rock Bay, at the north side of Seymour Narrows. We went ashore there. After we had stepped out of our canoe the late Hǎmālělǎsěmāě saw much clothing and four nice boxes full of very good clothing on the beach; and also two flour bags and all kinds of food. We did not see any man who owned them. Then we took them aboard and went away. When we came to Beaver Cove a northeast wind sprang up. We stayed there for six days. It was ten days after we had left from where we had found the boxes. Now my whole crew became sick and we started in the morning and it was calm. We arrived at Achōlēs. We unloaded our cargo there. Now we all were sick with the great smallpox. We got it where the boxes were found by us. We all lay in bed in our tent. I was lying among them. Now I saw that all our bodies swelled and were dark red. Our skins burst open and I did not know that they were all dead and I was lying among them. Then I thought that I also was dead. I was as in a sleep and I awoke on account of many wolves who came whining and others howling. Two of them were licking my body and I saw two wolves vomit up foam and putting it on my body. The two wolves tried hard to put the foam all over my body. They did not treat me well when they turned over my body. Now my body was quickly getting stronger and also my mind. The two wolves kept on licking my body. After they had licked off all they had vomited, they vomited foam again and put it on my body. Again they licked it off and then I saw that they had taken the scabs from the sores on my body. Now I saw that I was lying among my dead past nephews.

Now it was evening and the two wolves took a rest. I must have been afraid, being the only one who was still alive, therefore I crawled away and went to the shelter of a thick spruce tree. And so I lay down that night. Now I had no bedding; only a shirt which I had on. Then it was as though the two wolves came and lay down on each side of me. When daylight came in the morning the two wolves got up and again licked my body. They licked it for a long time and vomited white foam and put it on my body, my face and my head. Then they licked the foam off again. Now I was getting strong. I was strong enough to stand up and now I recognized that the one wolf was the one that had been in trouble with the bone which I had taken out of the mouth of the wolf. Then the many wolves did not leave me. Indeed, I walked among them. Indeed I became well and I lay down when the other wolf came, the one of whom I had dreamed at Foam-Receptacle and who had told me his name was Harpooneer-Body. He sat down seaward from me and nudged me with his nose that I should lie on his back, and he vomited and pushed his nose against the lower end of my sternum. He vomited the magic power into me. After he had done so he sat down. I was getting sleepy and I went to sleep. Then I dreamed of the wolf who was still sitting there. In my dream he became a man. In my dream he laughed and spoke and said, "Now take care, friend, now this shaman-maker has gone into you. Now you will cure the sick and you will catch the souls of the sick and you will throw sickness into anyone whom you wish to die among your tribe. Now they will be afraid of you," said he to me in my dream. Then I woke up and my body was trembling and my mind was different after this, for all the wolves had left me. Now I was a shaman. Now I walked and went to Fern-Point (Săgŭmbălă). Then I met Gwāsălălēs there. I told him that my whole crew was dead, killed by the smallpox. Then Gwāsălălēs was afraid of me, and he left me and went home to Tāgŭchstā. I stayed for a long time in a house at Fern-Point. I did not mind it, for I stayed in one of the houses and there was much food in the seven houses which are at Fern-Point. There were also two canoes there. I was never depressed and I kept on singing my sacred songs every evening, the four sacred songs of the wolf, for I was just like drunk all the time and I was always happy. More than one moon I stayed at Fern-Point, then Spearing-Dance (Săkĕlăl) paddled along in the evenning [sic] going toward Tăgŭchstă. He heard me singing my sacred song and he reported to the Năkwăchdăĕchoo at Tăguchstă. Immediately the Năkwăchdăĕchoo wished to come for the new shaman that was heard singing his sacred songs at Fern-Point, to cure the chief, Causing-to-be-well (Hălămăs).

Now the wolf came in my dream and warned me to be ready for the chief, Causing-to-be-well, who was very sick. "Now you will suck out his sickness and throw upward his sickness. Do not apply your mouth more than four times when you treat him," said in my dream the wolf to me. Then I woke up after that. At once began to tremble my body and my stomach. I sang my sacred song and, when it had been day for a long time, I stopped singing. Then I heard many men talking outside my house and Endeavoring-to-invite spoke and said, "We come to ask you, great treasured one, to take pity, to bring back to life our friend, chief Causing-to-be-well, with your water of life, friend," said he. Then all the men went aboard their traveling canoe, a large canoe. Endeavoring-to-Invite came into my house and begged me to go aboard with them. I followed him and we went aboard the traveling canoe. We arrived at Tăgŭchstă. When we arrived at the beach of the house of Causing-to-be-well all the men stepped out of our traveling-canoe and they all went into the house of Causing-to-be-well. They made a fire in the middle of the house. As soon as the fire blazed up four shamans went to call all the men and all the women and all the children that all should come and watch the new shaman. When they had all come in the four shamans called me, for I was still sitting in the canoe. I walked among the four shamans and we entered the house where they were beating time for me. When I went in I saw Causing-to-be-well sitting on a new mat in the rear of the house. As soon as all the men had seen me I went with the four shamans and they all beat fast time with the batons on the boards. Then my body and my belly began to tremble and I sang my sacred song while I was still standing in the doorway of the house with the four shamans. Then I went to the place where Causing-to-be-well was sitting and the four shamans followed me. Then I treated him, and I followed the instructions given by the wolf what I should do, and now I have the name Fool as a shaman's name. It is ended after this.

Notes

INTRODUCTION

1. Much of the scholarly interest in the concept of the self may be traced back to a 1938 essay by Marcel Mauss. Working along lines established some forty years earlier by Durkheim (his uncle and teacher), Mauss argued that the conception of ourselves, which seems so natural to us as to count as one of the constants of human nature, is in fact culturally determined—has in fact evolved over millennia of social history. Misch (1951) and Weintraub (1975, 1978) may be understood as attempts to give definition to the history Mauss posited by writing the history of autobiography. Dumont (1985), too, is concerned with the history of modern individual conceptions of the self, while most of the other essays collected by Carrithers, et al. (1985) are devoted to the concept of the self as it varies across cultures. Langness and Frank (1981:90–91) discuss the problem of the self in relation to the collection by anthropologists of autobiographies and other personal documents. See also Ullman, 1967; Raju and Castell, 1968; Mischel, 1977; Lakoff and Johnson, 1980; Benton, 1982; Rosen, 1985; Wong, 1985; and Heller, et al., 1986.

For an immediate sense of some of the consequences of differing conceptions of the self, see Fabrega and Mezzich (1986), who rely on such scholarship as is mentioned above in order to discuss psychological adjustment disorders in cross-cultural terms. They hypothesize, for example, that culturally determined conceptions of self may largely influence "the content of psychopathology and perhaps, also, its structure."

2. See Horton (1982) for a careful discussion of the theoretical grounding of this method, the comparison of contemporary "traditional" societies and ancient societies. The method is not without its perils. But carefully applied, it has produced some outstanding work. Among the anthropologists, see especially the work of Jack Goody. Goody used what he learned from his fieldwork in North Ghana to understand the role of literacy in the explosion of learning in ancient Greece (Goody and Watt, 1963; Goody, 1977). The outstanding example among literary scholars must be the work of Albert Lord. Building on the work of Milman Parry, Lord used what he called "the laboratory of the living epic tradition of the Yugoslavs" (1981 [1960]:3) to explain the consequences of oral composition on the Homeric poems.

3. Emphasis mine.

4. At least this was one of his reasons; he also wanted to preserve some examples of Kwakiutl-language narratives for linguistic analysis. He provides the narratives in Kwakiutl and in English translation.

5. See, e.g., Mandel (1968).

6. O'Brien (1973:7). The problem had long before been recognized by the anthropologists; see e.g., Kluckhohn (1945:81–82).

7. See Brumble (1981:1–5) for an overview of such problems; see also Brumble (1985a, 1985b, 1986; revisions of these appear herein as chapters 5, 6, and 4, respectively). Although their work is fraught with problems, Bataille and Sands (1984) do include chapters on the work of Ruth Underhill with Maria Chona and that of Nancy O. Lurie with Mountain Wolf Woman. Literary scholars, then, are coming to concern themselves with such problems of investigator/informant "interference" as have concerned anthropologists for many years. See, e.g., Kluckhohn (1945), Langness (1965), and Langness and Frank (1981).

8. John Ellis (1974) makes just this point in the course of his argument against defining literature by "features"; see his chapter on "The Definition of Literature."

9. See, e.g., David G. Mandelbaum's influential 1973 article, "The Study of Life History: Gandhi." What Mandelbaum calls "turnings" are important to his understanding of how autobiography may be analyzed.

10. Theodora Kroeber's two biographies of Ishi provide an interesting case in point. Ishi was the last of the Yahi Indians, almost certainly the last Stone Age man in the United States. In 1911 Ishi came down out of the mountains where he had for some years been living utterly alone. He was found one morning in a cattle pen, sick and still wearing the short hair of Yahi mourning. Soon the anthropologist A. L. Kroeber took him under his wing and gave him board and room in the anthropological museum in Berkeley. As Theodora Kroeber (A. L. Kroeber's wife) tells this remarkable story in *Ishi in Two Worlds* (1971 [1961]), there is very little sense that Ishi himself conceived of his life in terms of climactic moments or turning points. Later, Theodora Kroeber wrote *Ishi, Last of His Tribe* (1973 [1964]). This book was a fictionalized version of Ishi's life, intended for adolescents. Here she puts into Ishi's mind a clear sense of building toward a climactic experience, a life's work. Here Ishi—the fictionalized, Westernized Ishi—does think about his life in terms of turning points (Brumble, 1983).

11. Sands herself edited one of the very good Indian autobiographies, Refugio Savala's *Autobiography of a Yaqui Poet*.

12. Since 1981 Momaday has been a member of the Native American Studies faculty at the University of Arizona.

13. Generally, literary scholars are strict in their exclusion of as-told-to autobiographies from discussions of autobiography. For example, the first of Elizabeth Bruss's three "rules" for autobiography is that the autobiographer be the source of the subject matter *and* the structure of the text (1976:10–11; cf. Olney, 1980:3–27). But one wonders just how much this has to do with how bad the (non-Indian) as-told-to's tend to be. When a powerful, well-written as-told-to does appear, the critics can be nearly unanimous in ignoring the editor. I am thinking in particular of the response to *The Autobiography of Malcolm X*. Albert Stone wrote, for example, that this book is "the most impressive of recent autobiographies" (1972:23). For similar praise, see, e.g., Paul Eakin (1980), Ross Miller (1972), Barrett Mandell (1972), Warner Berthoff (1971), and Carol Ohmann (1970). It will be interesting to see how *The Autobiography of Malcolm X* will be treated now that Alex Haley himself has become much more widely known.

14. See O'Brien (1973) and Revard (1980). See also Bataille and Sands (1984:52–62).

1: PRELITERATE TRADITIONS OF AUTOBIOGRAPHY

1. For accounts of the nature of the collaboration of each of the Indian autobiographies, see Brumble, *Annotated Bibliography* (1981), and the "Supplement" to the *Bibliography* below.

2. Roy Harvey Pearce provides perhaps the best antidote to such seductive habits of mind with his *Savagism and Civilization: A Study of the Indian and the American Mind* (1965). See also Paulin Hountondji's disdainful dismissal of "the myth of primitive unanimity" (1976:chapter 3).

3. See Marian W. Smith (1938) for a good introduction to the differences among tribes about what might count as a coup. This article is also valuable for its extensive bibliography.

4. Grinnell (1960:245) and Grinnell (1960 [1910]).

5. The curious will find the Sarsi-language original, along with an awkwardly literal translation, in Goddard (1915:268–273).

6. Grinnell (1960 [1910]:301) describes the Cheyenne assumption that to lie about coups was to court death. But warriors did, of course, make the occasional fraudulent claim. See, e.g., *Two Leggings:* 14–15, 200. Some tribes were evidently less concerned about exaggeration than others. See, e.g., Robert Jefferson's eyewitness account of coup tales among the Plains Cree:

> It has often been remarked by old Indians that the tales told by braves during the sun dance, are, to say the least, outrageous exaggerations. Each event

narrated has been witnessed by someone in the audience, so the truth of each
is well known. So, it may safely be taken that these stories have merely a
foundation of truth; interwoven with this, are all the embellishments that the
imagination and oratorical powers of the narrator allow.

(In Goddard, 1919b:309)

But note that even here each deed has its witness—however much the
deed may be embroidered upon.

7. There are numerous other examples. Plenty-coups usually had what
we may recognize as witnesses present while he worked with Frank B.
Linderman; see also the example of Black Elk cited below.

8. Krupat (1985:120–121) has recognized that Yellow Wolf's reasons
for so arranging the sessions with McWhorter derive from the customs
for the telling of coup tales.

9. See, e.g., Grinnell (1960:250).

10. See Mishkin (1940:35–56). According to Mishkin, one could also
rise from rank to rank according to one's prowess as an arrowmaker, a
shaman, a horse-breaker—even as a lover. "But to compare [such] social
standing with the kind related to war honors is analogous to setting intellectual distinctions against financial achievement in our own society" (35).

11. See chapter 2, n. 5.

12. For a sense of the problems involved in the translations of Indian
materials, see, e.g., Hymes (1977, 1981) and Tedlock (1972, 1977, 1983).

13. See, e.g., Lowie (1915:31), Wissler (1918:236, 256), Wallis
(1919:326).

14. See also Llewellyn and Hoebel (1967 [1941]:82–86), where we find
Little Wolf, a Cheyenne, examining his conscience; see also Grinnell (1962
[1926]:6).

15. See Grinnell (1962 [1926]):6. Thomas Sanchez, by the way, makes
use of exactly such notions to tie together the generations of Washo
Indians who people his remarkable first novel, *Rabbit Boss* (1972).

16. Stevenson was remarkably energetic and resourceful. She managed
to get from the Zunis so many artifacts that shipping became a real
problem. Eventually she convinced General Sherman ("The only good
Indian is a dead Indian") to send his army wagons to carry her prizes to
the railhead at Las Vegas, New Mexico. See Brumble (1981b). One
anthropologist (who prefers anonymity in this matter) with a wide acquaintance at Zuni going back many years has suggested to me that
Sherman provided more than wagons, that when Stevenson ran into
trouble at Zuni, his troops were there with guns.

17. I have perhaps underestimated Black Elk's initiative in working
with Neihardt (1981:28–30). See Holler (1984) for a corrective.

18. See Nabokov's account of his editing of Wildschut's manuscript (*Two Leggings:* 213–217).

19. In his own autobiographical narrative, Geronimo's nephew and interpreter, Asa Daklugie, has provided a fascinating account of Geronimo's collaboration with Barrett (173–174).

20. See also *Sun Chief:* 77.

21. Wilson later put together an autobiography out of all the material he had collected from Maxidiwiac from 1908 to 1918: *Wa-Hee-Nee: An Indian Girl's Story, Told by Herself* (1921). Some of the material from *Agriculture of the Hidatsa Culture* is repeated here, but *Wa-Hee-Nee* also includes a good deal that is not published elsewhere. Bataille and Sands (1984:169) mistake themselves, then, in asserting that Maxidiwiac narrated *Wa-Hee-Nee* in 1921. Indeed, some of what appears in *Wa-Hee-Nee* comes from some of Wilson's other Hidatsa informants (including Maxidiwiac's brother, Wolf-chief).

22. Generally speaking, Indians of tribes west of the Rockies were not expected to seek out the help of the spirits. Among these tribes it was thought that such help, if it were to come, should come at the initiative of the spirit. But the Indians of these tribes could still tell about the acquisition of their powers. See, e.g., Gregorio's "Life Story," *Geronimo,* and Fool's narrative, in the Appendix above.

Halifax (1979) reprints a number of these narratives of the acquisition of shamanic power, although her insistently credulous commentary is more than a little cloying.

23. The buying and selling of certain kinds of narratives was not uncommon. White Bull (see chapter 2) had to purchase his calendar history, for example, which should suggest some exceptions to recent characterizations of the essential differences between modern, Western authorship and Indian storytelling. Krupat argues, for example, that the Indians understood stories to be without individual "authors," to arise from the community; and so they did not hope to profit from storytelling as do Western writers, who consider themselves to be the originators of their stories (1985:9–16). See also John Bierhorst, who argues that "the Indian does not consider himself the originator of his material but merely the conveyer" (1971:4).

24. See Eliade (1974 [1964]:104) for some of the ways in which the warrior's quests are like those of the shamans.

25. Under what circumstances a vision was to be kept secret is a vexing question—at least to my mind. It is possible to find in the autobiographical narratives counter instances for virtually all the generalizations one reads about this matter. For present purposes, however, it is sufficient to see that there were occasions when it was necessary and fitting to tell about visions, dreams, and quests.

2: PRELITERATE TRADITIONS AT WORK

1. Winnemucca actually published her autobiography under her married name, Sarah Winnemucca Hopkins. The marriage did not last long, however, and it was much troubled by L. H. Hopkins' imbibing and spendthrift ways.

2. James Howard entitles his edition of the pictographic autobiography *The Warrior Who Killed Custer: The Personal Narrative of Chief Joseph White Bull,* following Vestal (1957:4–9, 90–91), who asserted that it was White Bull who had killed the General. But DeMallie (1984*b*:xx–xxii) has found no evidence to support this claim in the transcripts of Vestal's interviews of White Bull. And so I have chosen to refer to Howard's book by its subtitle.

3. My sense is that the women were less reluctant to speak of childhood; but it is difficult to know, since there are many fewer early as-told-to autobiographies by Indian women.

4. Howard is evidently wrong in assuming that four of the pictographs show White Bull killing Custer. See n. 2, above.

5. Usually a year, but the period recalled by a single pictograph did vary from calendar to calendar. In some there would be a pictograph for each month; in others, one per year or season. The best introduction to the calendars is still Mooney (1979 [1898]).

The calendar histories are very like the Date Lists which Butterfield describes among the ancient Egyptians and Babylonians. Here, for example, is an excerpt from a Babylonian Date List for the fourteen years of the reign of Sumu-abu:

> 4. The year in which the temple of Nin-sinna was built.
> 9. The year in which the wall of the city of Bilbat was built.
> 12. The year in which the plantation of the gods was made.
> 13. The year in which the city of Kasallu was laid waste.
>
> (In Butterfield, 1981:27)

Indeed, Butterfield suggests that the making of lists seems "to represent the earliest gropings towards a classification of data. When [such lists] concern the succession of things in time they can be taken as representing in a certain sense the beginning of historical science" (23).

Neither were Indians alone among *pre*literate peoples in recalling their history in this way. Jan Yoors—to choose an example far removed from White Bull in time and geography—has recently written about his boyhood travels with the gypsies. He wrote as follows of their sense of remembered time:

> Unaware of the historical years recording the Christian era, they designated the passing of time only by referring to "the summer Pipish died," "the winter

we almost perished of cold and hunger and were attacked by wolves," or "the year Zurka was born and we sold the three stallions." (1983 [1967]:29)

6. Revard (1980:84–97). I hope it is clear that in disputing this point I am simply providing better reasons for agreeing with the main lines of Revard's argument. For more discussion of tribal history in relation to Indian autobiography, see Brumble (1981), nos. 186, 204, 265, 318, 344, 385; and chapter 8, below.

7. See Krupat (1985:54–74) for the best account of Barrett's collaboration with Geronimo.

8. Butterfield (1981) suggests that virtually all civilizations pass through a stage in which the making of lists is common. "When the lists are concerned with objects in the natural world we regard them as in a sense the beginnings of natural science, because they seem to represent the earliest gropings towards a classification of data. When they concern the succession of things in time they can be taken as representing in a certain sense the beginning of historical science" (1981:23). See 23–28 for more on lists, some of which were remarkably like the Winter Counts in ancient societies.

9. For the influence of Boasian assumptions on early as-told-to autobiographies, see Langness and Frank (1981:18–20) and Krupat (1985:54–105).

10. See, e.g., Nabokov's introduction: xxi; see also O'Brien (1973:20). Other Indians expressed a similar reluctance to tell stories about reservation times. See, e.g., *Plenty-coups* (311) and Linderman's foreword to *Prettyshield:*

> Like the old men Pretty-shield would not talk at any length of the days when her people were readjusting themselves to the changed conditions brought on by the disappearance of the buffalo, so that her story is largely of her youth and early maturity. "There is nothing to tell, because we did nothing," she insisted when pressed for stories of her middle life. "There were no buffalo. We stayed in one place, and grew lazy." (10)

11. Canfield's (1983) biography of Sarah Winnemucca is essential reading for anyone interested in *Life among the Piutes.* Fowler (1978) is also helpful, especially for her arguments about the authorship and style of the book.

12. While I do take issue with some of what Ruoff has to say about Winnemucca, her essay is a very helpful introduction to three early autobiographers who have otherwise received scant attention. Ruoff places Apes in relation to early American pietistic autobiography, and she is able to tell us a great deal about the life of Copway, who seems to have been

a more deeply troubled man than his autobiographical writings would suggest.

13. Canfield (1983:88, 164) includes a good sampling of these.

14. Canfield and Fowler both warn us that it is difficult to know just how literate Winnemucca was. One newspaper man reported in 1891 that Winnemucca "spent a goodly portion of her meager earnings on books" (Fowler, 1978:58). See also the manuscript letter reproduced in Canfield (1983:66) that is virtually free of errors. But it is not at all difficult to imagine Winnemucca seeking out assistance from friendly whites when she had an important letter to write—just as she had Mann's help in writing her book.

15. N. Scott Momaday has written so evocatively about landscape and self-definition that he has inspired a good deal of nonsense. Bataille and Sands, for example, go so far as to assert that one of the "basic characteristics" oral Indian literature "shares" with American Indian women's autobiography is the "concern with landscape" (1984:3). In fact, of course, one could easily find many autobiographical narratives by Indian men *and* women and hundreds of transcriptions of oral performances by Indians which do not mention landscape at all.

16. See, e.g., *Life among the Piutes:* 142, 166, 190–191, 235.

17. All that follows relating to Winnemucca's stage career comes from Canfield (1983).

18. She probably had already set some of her stories down in writing, in letters to supporters and in letters written to appeal to various authorities. See, e.g., the passage where Bannock Jack, realizing that Winnemucca "can talk on paper," asks her to write down all that he will tell her about certain injustices that his band has suffered. He then asks her to send it to "our Great Father in Washington" (142–143).

3: EDITORS, GHOSTS, AND AMANUENSES

1. Kluckhohn (1945:81–82) suggests that some Indian informants appreciated the anthropologists' interest because it seemed in some measure to make up for the white rejection that was more the norm.

2. Some, perhaps, might want to gain a sense of day-to-day life in the field, of the dust, the damp, and the sweat, a sense of the habits of mind and the problems of the anthropologists who spent hours and days collecting words, myths, tales, syntax, and autobiographies from American Indians during the first half of this century. Here are some suggestions for those who would like to meet four anthropologists with widely differing temperaments but a single passion. Ronald Rohner's fine edition (1963) of Franz Boas's letters and diaries allows us to see the feisty father of

modern anthropology at work in the Northwest (1886–1931). Carobeth Laird's *Encounter with an Angry God* (1975) tells about her life with, and her reasons for leaving, John Peabody Harrington. Harrington was a brilliant man whose career began to come apart as his paranoia increased. He published very little—but his field notes, preserved in the Anthropological Archives of the Smithsonian Museum of Natural History, run to well over a million pages.

Two books by Theodora Kroeber (1970, 1971 [1961]) and one by the anthropologist Julian Steward (1973) provide affectionate accounts of the work of A. L. Kroeber. Kroeber was immensely productive. He may be said to have inherited the mantle of leadership in the discipline from his teacher, Franz Boas. Robert Lowie, the master of Plains Indian anthropology, has written a self-effacing autobiography (1959).

3. Those interested to witness phenomenology, hermeneutics, and existentialism all drawn up, wheeled about, and aimed at the life histories should consult Lawrence Watson and Maria-Barbara Watson-Franke's *Interpreting Life Histories* (1985).

4. Robert Sayre (1971) was the first to compare—albeit very briefly— the Black Elk–Neihardt transcripts with *Black Elk Speaks*. Soon thereafter Sally McClusky (1972) interviewed Neihardt about his work with Black Elk. And in 1979 Michael Castro reported on his systematic comparison of transcript and book; this work was published in expanded form in Castro (1983).

5. Krupat (1985) treats Radin's work with Sam Blowsnake and Barrett's with Geronimo; Bataille and Sands (1984) include a chapter on Underhill's work with Maria Chona. For an early survey of editorial strategies, see R. D. Theisz (1981).

6. Wilson also fleshed out Maxidiwiac's accounts of certain events with information he had collected from her brother, Wolf-chief, and other Hidatsa informants.

7. And even here we must have doubts, if we take into account some of what Underhill remembered in a 1981 interview. Bataille and Sands (1984:58) report that Underhill "herself says that she put things into her own words but tried to keep things 'vivid' like Old Testament writing."

8. This does not, of course, take into account the modern as-told-to autobiographies of such Indians as Iron Eyes Cody, where we are left with about as much faith in the collaboration as we have in the autobiographies of illiterate and nearly illiterate sports heroes. Completely off the scale is Cash Asher's synthetic and partially plagiarized "edition" of Red Fox; see William Hodge (1976:159) for the plagiarism charge.

9. See Krupat (1985:54–74) for an account of Barrett's shaping of Geronimo's autobiography.

10. Seele notes a single exception in his introduction to his edition of Schultz's *Blackfeet and Buffalo: Memories of Life among the Indians* (1962). Most of the what I have to say about Schultz's life comes from Seele and Schultz's *My Life as an Indian* (n.d. [1907]). See also Jessie Donaldson Schultz (1960), Schultz's second wife, for more biographical information. For a less favorable appraisal of Schultz's work, see Bedford (1974).

11. It should be noted that Charles Alexander Eastman published a brief as-told-to autobiography by Chief Rain-in-the-Face as early as 1906, and Eastman set the scene for the narrative in very much the way Schultz does. I would not argue, however, that either Linderman or McWhorter would have been aware of the piece.

12. Adolph Hungry Wolf has put together a booklet of Fine Day material, *My Cree People*. He worked from Mandelbaum's field notes, which are preserved at the New York Museum of Natural History. Hungry Wolf includes a good deal that does not appear in *The Plains Cree*, but much of this is Fine Day telling about Cree customs and material culture. Finally, we get a better sense of Fine Day by reading the passages in Mandelbaum, since Hungry Wolf, with his characteristic emphasis on the homely and the sacred, leaves out virtually everything Fine Day had to say about his war deeds. Clearly, these deeds seem central to Fine Day's own sense of himself.

13. Dennison Nash and Ronald Wintrob (1972) describe the emergence of self-consciousness in anthropologists after World War II. They argue that this self-consciousness came about because of "(1) an increasing personal involvement of ethnographers with their subjects, (2) the 'democratization' of anthropology, (3) multiple field studies of the same culture, and (4) assertions of independence by native peoples" (1972:533).

14. This and the quotations that follow are actually from the foreword to *The Fifth World of Forster Bennett: Portrait of a Navaho* (1972:v–vi). Forster Bennett's *Fifth World* turns out to be virtually identical to Enoch Maloney's *Fifth World!* In fact, the only differences would seem to be the substitution of one set of pseudonyms for another, a few footnote changes, and the addition of the brief foreword. One wonders what could have led Viking Press and such a moralist as Crapanzano to publish the book without the slightest reference to the previous Random House edition. My own university's library was probably not alone in assuming that these were two different books—and so buying both.

15. But not *quite* full disclosure; see n. 14.

16. Crapanzano cannot even be credited with being the first to employ this method. In 1966 Richard Lancaster worked in essentially the same way with a Piegan Indian named White Calf. His *Piegan: A Look from within at the Life, Times, and Legacy of an American Indian*, like Crapanzano's

"portrait" of Maloney, takes the form of a smoothly edited journal. White Calf is more nearly at the center of this book, however, than is Crapanzano's Maloney.

17. Crapanzano (1987) himself sees—with approval—the connection between his conception of anthropology and the deconstructionist literary critics. See Louch (1986) and Crews (1986:115–181) for appraisals of the self-contradictory and self-aggrandizing theories of the deconstructionists.

18. The autobiographers are Frank Tobuk, Madeline Solomon, Joe Beetus, Edwin Simon, Oscar Nictune, Henry Beatus, John Honea, Roger Dayton, and Moses Henzie.

19. Most of this communication has been personal and informal. Those who would like to gain a sense of what passed may consult Scollon and Scollon (1979, 1981). I am indebted to William Pfisterer, Ronald Scollon, and Ray Barnhardt (personal communications) for information about these editors and how they came to work as they did.

20. Pfisterer says (personal communication) that Moses is not Herbert's biological grandchild; Herbert calls her "grandchild," then, in the larger sense common among Indians. All the information about the work with Herbert comes either from the introduction to the book or from conversations with Pfisterer, Ronald Scollon, and Ray Barnhardt.

21. For an explanation of the assumptions behind this method, see Scollon and Scollon (1979:15–81).

4: DON TALAYESVA AND GREGORIO

1. Of course life histories were collected from nonliterate peoples other than the Indians. See, e.g., Du Bois (1960 [1944]).

2. When anthropologists discuss these autobiographies, they almost always lament this lack of analysis. See, e.g., Kluckhohn (1945:103) and Langness (1965:20).

3. See, e.g., Butterfield (1981:46–79).

4. One finds this tendency to conceive of autobiography as a list of deeds even quite late. Peter Le Claire, born in 1883, wrote a brief life history in 1949. It is, essentially, just such a list of deeds as White Bull and Gregorio and the rest might prepare us to understand.

5. The interdisciplinary mood did not long survive. "Then things changed," Leighton recalled. "William James Hall . . . was no sooner built than the Department of Social Relations which it was supposed to house . . . fell apart" into separate disciplines (interview, 1985).

6. The raw data was to have been preserved at Yale. I have been unable, however, to locate this material. Probably, according to the chairman of Yale's Anthropology Department, Frank Hole (who was so kind

as to have spent considerable effort trying to track it down for me), it was destroyed or lost by Simmons's family after his death in 1978 (personal communication).

7. Kluckhohn (1945) is littered with references to the Leightons, and Kluckhohn's huge Ramah Navajo project "crystallized during discussions" with them, according to Kluckhohn's introduction to the Leightons' *Gregorio* (v).

8. See Leighton and Leighton (1944:119).

9. Some of this information about the collaboration is available in *Gregorio* (7–8, 46), and Leighton and Leighton (1944:95–96). For the rest, I am indebted to Dr. Alexander Leighton (interview, 1985).

10. Gregorio had done a little work with anthropologists before the Leightons met him.

11. The autobiographies of Left Handed (another Navajo) could prove to be massive exceptions to this claim, but little is known about the degree to which Walter Dyk guided Left Handed with questions. Left Handed discusses sexual matters, for example, with remarkable frankness and in considerable detail. But, as Kluckhohn (1945:92) cautions, this candor may tell us less about Left Handed's lack of inhibitions than about the insistence of Dyk's questioning.

12. For another example, V. S. Naipaul's account (1981:315–316) of the Indonesian poet Sitor closely parallels much of what I have to say in this chapter. Sitor was born into a preliterate society in North Sumatra and was snatched away from the tribe to be educated by the Dutch, eventually to become a poet of some local renown. In late middle age he took it upon himself to write his autobiography. But he had great difficulties; he could not get beyond the episodes of his life—until he began to work as an interpreter for an anthropologist. The anthropologist, then, began to aid him in his autobiographical labors, asking him the kinds of questions that finally allowed him to conceive of his life and his relation to his people and their past in a unified, Western way.

13. It is not uncommon to find preliterate Indians thinking of themselves as unusual, especially some of the fiercely competitive Plains warriors. See especially the early chapters of *Two Leggings*. What is unusual in *Sun Chief* is the range of experience that Talayesva unifies by thinking of himself in this way.

5: SAM BLOWSNAKE

1. For the early history of Western autobiography see Weintraub (1975, 1978) and Georg Misch (1951).

2. See, e.g., those collected by O. G. Libby (1973 [1920]).

3. What follows is the working out of an idea first suggested in Brumble (1981*b*:267–268).

4. The 1983 reprint includes an introduction and afterword by Arnold Krupat. Krupat provides a good account of the nature of Radin's work as editor.

5. For more on Underhill's editorial assumptions, see chapter 3. Underhill, by the way, would have come by her positivistic conception of facts and objectivity—like Radin—in the course of her Boasian training. See Harris (1969:250–318).

6. See also Copway's *Life, History, and Travels of Kah-ge-ga-gah-bowh* (1847).

7. Blowsnake himself said that he had only attended school for one "winter" (*Crashing Thunder:* 89–90).

8. While he has nothing to say about the Indian autobiographers in particular, Shea's *Spiritual Autobiography in Early America* (1968) provides a good introduction to the kind of narratives Occom, Apes, and Jones wrote.

9. For an example of the way anthropological training can swell what is essentially a preliterate autobiographical form, see chapter 3 for the case of Quesalid/George Hunt.

10. Albert Hensley, Blowsnake's fellow Peyotist, composed not one but two autobiographies at about this same time, but Hensley's narratives are quite brief, just a few pages each; and Hensley had had a Carlisle Indian School education (see chapter 6).

11. See, e.g., La Barre (1971 [1959]:163–166). The Russellites (later to be known as Jehovah's Witnesses) and the Mormons were important influences on the Winnebago Peyote Cult. Both churches were actively proselytizing among the Winnebago in these years. The Russellites appealed to the Peyotists not least because of their refusal to subject themselves to any "earthly" government, at a time when the earthly government of the United States was actively persecuting the Peyotists. John Rave's brother once said (quoting another Peyotist), "My friend we must organize a church and run it like the Mormon church," and one of the eventual founders of the Native American Church, Jonathan Koshiway, was for a time a missionary among the Indians for the Mormons (La Barre, 1971 [1959]:167–169). Both the Mormons and the Russellites incorporated public confession and bearing of testimonies into their services.

12. This is, then, contrary to the view of Bataille and Sands (1984:5) that "The urge toward spiritual introspection fostered by Puritan doctrine . . . has consistently influenced written autobiographies by Indians converted to Christianity," while "this form of writing does not have any significant effect on oral autobiography by American Indians." The In-

dian converts to several Christian sects besides the Peyote Cult—the Mormons, e.g., and the Episcopalians—would have regarded conversion stories and confessions as quite a common part of their church-going experience. Whether they could read or not, then, many Indians were hearing and delivering oral, spiritually introspective autobiographies quite regularly during these years.

13. For a Peyotist autobiography by Hensley, see chapter 6. See also the Peyotist autobiographical narrative by Sam Blowsnake's elder brother, Jasper Blowsnake (whose Indian name really was Crashing Thunder), which Radin edited as "Personal Reminiscences of a Winnebago Indian."

14. See also Goody (1977). Goody and Watt (1963) argue that there are psychological as well as cultural consequences of literacy. This is controversial: see Scribner and Cole (1981); see also Frake (1983).

15. See, e.g., *On Christian Doctrine*, II, 40.

6: ALBERT HENSLEY

1. Nancy Ostereich Lurie elicited an autobiography from Mountain Wolf Woman. There have been published, then, autobiographies by the two brothers, Sam and Jasper, and this sister.

2. See La Barre (1971 [1969]:73–74). La Barre's is still the best history of the Peyote Cult. See also Hertzberg (1981 [1971]:274). See also fellow peyotist Oliver Lamere's remembrances of Hensley in Radin (1970 [1923]:347).

3. John Rave's brief autobiography may be added to those mentioned in n. 2.

4. See, e.g., Krupat (1985:28–29); Brumble (1981:1–2); O'Brien (1973:5); Kluckhohn (1945).

5. It is reprinted with the kind permission of the University of Nebraska Press.

6. I would like to thank Mr. Robert Kvasnicka, of the General Services Administration, National Archives and Records Service, in Washington, D.C., for locating these Hensley documents and making them available to me. The originals may be consulted in the National Archives, as Records of the Bureau of Indian Affairs, RG 75, Carlisle Indian School Records, 2144. I am indebted to Hertzberg (1981 [1971]:340), for bringing the Hensley letter to my attention.

7. Hensley's daughters' names were Agnes and Esther Hensley; the nieces were Alice and Margaret Irwin (Carlisle Indian School Records, 2144).

8. Alice Cunningham Fletcher (1838–1923) was an anthropologist as well as an Allotting Agent. In collaboration with the Omaha anthropologist Francis La Flesche, Fletcher produced a number of studies of Omaha

music and rituals. Hensley was not alone in trusting this remarkable woman. She was well known among the Omahas, Winnebagos, and Poncas for her philanthropic work. Those interested in how she might have come to know such a boy as Hensley might be interested to read her account of a companionable evening (c. 1883) with Omaha friends and storytellers (Clements, 1986:155–161). For biographical material, see Lurie, 1966:31–81.

9. This is a reference to the Carlisle Outing System. Carlisle had as its goal during these years the quick assimilation of its Indian charges into American society. Individual students, then, were sent to live with approved families in nearby communities, where they worked and attended school. They were visited periodically by the Carlisle Outing Agent. See Hertzberg (1981 [1971]:16).

10. Hensley worked for E. V. Barr of Gladwyne, Montgomery Co., Pa., from April to Sept., 1891 (Carlisle Indian School Records, 2144).

11. Hensley worked for A. Kruesen of Newton, Montgomery Co., Pa., from March to Sept., 1894 (ibid.).

12. Weintraub (1978:2–4). For one of many anthropologists who make essentially the same point, see Kluckhohn (1945:119). Revard (1980:84–87) makes this distinction, too, in the course of his insightful comparison of Geronimo's autobiography and the autobiography of a younger, "civilized" Apache, Jason Betzinez.

13. Krupat (1985:63–64) argues that there is little emphasis on the self and personal agency in *Geronimo* because of the assumptions of the editor, Barrett. Krupat reminds us that *Geronimo* was edited during the age of Thomas Hardy, when heroes were out of fashion and at a time when Boas was insisting upon the importance of gathering culture data. It seems, then, that Geronimo's own disinclination to concentrate on the self was neatly, if coincidentally, in conjunction with the assumptions of his editor. Later anthropologists were much more interested than Boas and Barrett in individual psychology (see chapter 4).

14. Hertzberg (1981 [1971]:15–19) provides a good introduction to the history and principles of Carlisle.

15. There is even a possibility that Hensley wrote the narrative himself in *Winnebago*. Radin explained in his preface to *The Winnebago Tribe:*

> Owing to the fact that the Winnebago have for some time been accustomed to the use of a syllabic alphabet borrowed from the Sauk and the Fox, it was a comparatively easy task to induce them to write down their mythology and, at times, their ceremonies. (1970 [1923]:xv)

He later wrote, however, that ninety percent of his texts in the syllabary came from one man, Sam Blowsnake (1949:4). (Blowsnake wrote his autobiography, for example, in the syllabary.) Given the mass of material

which Radin collected from many different Winnebago informants, it is
not likely that Hensley's little autobiography would happen to be one of
the few syllabary texts not written by Blowsnake.

16. See Radin's footnote, *Autobiography of a Winnebago Indian*, 67.

7: CHARLES EASTMAN's *INDIAN BOYHOOD*

1. What follows is, of course, no more than a sketch of the development
of ideas about race, evolution, and romantic racialism as they pertain,
according to my view, to Eastman. This account necessarily leaves out
many of the variants and counter arguments that enlivened contemporary
discussion of these ideas. See Hofstadter (1969) for what is still the best
treatment of Social Darwinism in American thought; for discussions of
scientific and religious ideas about race in America, see Stanton (1960)
for the years 1815–1859 and Fredrickson (1971) for the years 1817–1914.
Pearce (1965) deals specifically with American ideas about the Indian,
1609–1851. See also the invaluable Marvin Harris (1969:80–211).

2. Pearce argues that in "Jefferson's analysis there are the essential
outlines of an American theory of savagism" (1965:94).

3. See, e.g., von Schmidt-Pauli's *Adolf Hitler: Ein Weg aus eigner Kraft*
(1933*b*); see also his *Hitler's Kampf um die Macht* (1933*a*), where we read
that on the night Hitler was made Chancellor, "Nicht nur die Fackeln
brennen—es brennen auch die Herzen." The people sing "Lied nach Lied
in die Nacht . . . Das Deutschlandlied, das Horst-Wessel-Lied, die Wacht
am Rhein und wieder das Deutschlandlied." The people are united.
Bourgeois and worker alike "werden nicht mude, der inneren Bewegung
ihrer deutschen Herzen Luft zu machen" (201–202).

4. See, e.g., *Principles of Sociology:*

> It is possible, and I believe probable, that retrogression has been as frequent
> as progression.
>
> Evolution is commonly conceived to imply in everything an *intrinsic* tendency
> to become something higher. This is an erroneous conception of it (1897
> [1876–1896]:I, 95).

5. The scientific community's all-too-eager acceptance of Piltdown
Man arose, in part, out of these same ethnic enthusiasms. Virtually no
trace of ancient man had been found in England. "France, on the other
hand, had been blessed with a superabundance of Neanderthals, Cro-
Magnons and their associated art and tools. French anthropologists delighted in rubbing English noses with this marked disparity of evidence"
(Gould, 1980:116). Piltdown Man redressed this disparity with a vengeance. It seemed to predate Cro-Magnon by a wide margin, and it had

a brainpan of modern dimensions! And so the French Cro-Magnons could be regarded as no more than degenerate offshoots of the true line of descent, represented by the brainy Piltdown Man, orangutan jaw and all. See the inimitable Steven J. Gould (1980:108–124).

6. See Morgan (1964 [1877]: chapter 1). Leslie White's introduction to this edition is also a good introduction to Morgan and his place in the history of anthropological thought.

7. Parker (1881–1955), a Seneca, was an ethnologist, archeologist, museum director, and scholarly editor. He was the great-nephew of Civil War General Ely Parker (Seneca, 1828–1895), for whose autobiography, see the Bibliography.

8. In developing the following argument, I was aided by a discussion with LaVonne Ruoff and Daniel Littlefield.

9. Of course theoreticians of other persuasions had also made use of childhood. For one of many examples—this one brought to my attention by Michael West—the English Saxonist enthusiasts in the 1840s and 1850s were convinced that, in cultural terms, childhood ontogeny recapitulates phylogeny. And so they were eager that their children learn Anglo-Saxon, the language of the childhood of the race.

10. See Raymond Wilson's (1983) account of Eastman's later years.

8: N. SCOTT MOMADAY

1. Strictly speaking, Momaday has written three volumes of autobiography. *The Journey of Tai-me* (privately printed, 100 copies, 1967) is an early version of *The Way to Rainy Mountain*. I have not seen *The Journey of Tai-me*, but Schubnell (1985:145) reports that it includes all the traditional material that we find in *The Way to Rainy Mountain,* along with six stories that Momaday later published separately as "Kiowa Legends from *The Journey of Tai-me*" (1976). The introduction, prologue, epilogue, and the two framing poems are unique to *The Way to Rainy Mountain*.

2. Momaday has written about "Oral Tradition and the American Indian" (1976b) and about how Indian oral literature may enter into a written tradition in "The Man Made of Words" (1970). For Momaday's relation to oral traditions, see Evers (1977) and Brumble (1983).

3. See Momaday (1970:107). McAllister (1978) provides the best account of the structure of *The Way to Rainy Mountain*.

4. Momaday mentioned to me the Kiowa Twin Cycle as an example of oral epic (interview, 1985). See also Radin's edition of *Winnebago Hero Cycles* (1948) and Lord's (1981 [1960]) study of oral epic.

5. For the "Indianness" of Geronimo's use of myth, tribal, and personal history, see Revard (1980) and chapter 2, above.

6. For an account of the specific function of the pipe and this origin myth in *Black Elk Speaks,* see Holler (1984:22–23).

7. A second volume of Patencio's reminiscences, *Desert Hours with Chief Patencio,* was published in 1971.

8. Pokagon also wrote a fictionalized, romanticized autobiography: *O-Gi-Maw-Kwe Mit-I-Gwa-Ki (Queene of the Woods)* (1899). Dickason's (1961) brief biography of Pokagon helps to sort fact from fiction; see Larson (1978:37–46) for a discussion of *O-Gi-Maw-Kwe Mit-I-Gwa-Ki.*

9. Momaday established the Native American Studies Program at Stanford, and since 1981 he has been a member of the Native American Studies faculty at the University of Arizona.

10. Momaday tells us that Pohd-lohk obtained this ledger book "from the Supply Office at Fort Sill" during the time of his service there as a "private in L. Troop, Seventh Cavalry, under the command of Hugh Scott" (*The Names:* 47). According to James Mooney's wonderful *Calendar History of the Kiowa Indians,* Captain Scott was himself interested in the calendar histories of the Kiowa. It seems likely to me that Pohd-lohk would have seen the important Kiowa calendar that Scott had in his possession, the one kept by chief Doha'san until his death in 1866. This was continued by Doha'san's nephew until it passed into the hands of Scott. This was, according to Mooney, the oldest calendar history known to the Kiowas (1979 [1898]:144).

For more on the calendar histories, see chapter 2, n. 5.

11. Momaday (1970:102); Momaday also speaks of "blood memory" and "memory of the blood."

12. Momaday is careful, by the way, to make it clear in *The Names* that he has Anglo family as well as Kiowa family. Momaday's mother was just one eighth Indian (Cherokee); and he devotes a chapter in *The Names* to his mother's family, just as he devotes a chapter to his father's Kiowa family. Schubnell (1985) is a welcome corrective to the commentary on Momaday that seems to assume that his Indian heritage was the only shaping influence at work upon him.

13. Horton (1982:251) is drawing here on ideas first put forward by Goody and Watt (1963) on the social consequences of literacy.

14. Momaday (1970:97). What Momaday is content to do largely in his imagination, others are doing in fact. See Beverly Hungry Wolf's autobiography, *The Ways of My Grandmothers* (1980), for a good example of a young white-educated Indian leaving off white ways to learn and self-consciously practice an approximation of the old ways. She accomplished this transformation under the tutelage of her Swiss husband, a convert to Blood Indian ways: "It was not until I married my husband, Adolf Hungry Wolf, that I began to learn the ways of my grandmothers. Al-

though he was born in Europe, my husband knew more about being a traditional Indian than I or any of my generation at that time. He encouraged me to find pride and meaning in my ancestry" (16).

15. Schubnell (1985) provides the best and most extended treatment of Momaday's debt to Faulkner, Lawrence, Joyce, and other modern authors. But this debt was recognized, e.g., by Evers (1977:297–298) and Velie (1982:42–43, 53).

16. Some editors did attempt something like this, as chapter 3 has suggested. Some editors have drawn attention to some of the radical differences between Western and oral/Indian autobiography. Linderman, for example, describes a scene, sets a stage, and then allows his Indian autobiographer to speak upon that stage. But Momaday can speak to us directly, translating oral forms into written forms.

17. Interview, 1986. Barnhardt has worked extensively with the group of editors, linguists, educators, Eskimos, and Indians discussed at the end of chapter 3.

The Autobiographies

What follows is a list of the American Indian autobiographies mentioned in this book. The numbering corresponds to the numbering in my *Annotated Bibliography of American Indian and Eskimo Autobiographies* (1981), where may be found a description of each narrative and an account of how each was produced. Some autobiographies have appeared since the publication of the *Bibliography*, and these, along with those I missed in the *Bibliography*, are included and annotated below. The first name in each listing is that of the Indian autobiographer; where a second name is given, it is the name of the editor-anthropologist-amanuensis. The name in caps is the one most likely to be found in card catalogs and indices. Where names leave any doubt about gender, a M/F designation is provided.

2-M   Ahlooloo (M). SUSAN COWAN. *We Don't Live in Snow Houses Anymore: Reflections of Arctic Bay.* N.p.: Canadian Producers Ltd., 1976. 194 pp.

      Born, 1908; interviewed, 1975. Arctic Bay Eskimo. This book contains many autobiographical narratives by the artists of Arctic Bay, for the most part, stone carvers whose work has come to be widely admired. The avowed intent of the editor, Cowan, is to acquaint those who are interested in this art with the artists. Most of these narratives have to do with "How I came to be a carver" or "How I feel about my carving." But some tell us more. Ahlooloo (25–30), for example, recalls a time before the coming of Christianity when many shamans were at work, and he recalls one in particular who had a harpoon thrust into himself as a part of a ritual. He remembers, too, a murderer, and thoroughly harrowing experiences out upon the ice, experiences which bring to mind the adventures of Comock (no. 122) and some of the Eskimos to whom Rasmussen introduces us (for example, nos. 50, 237, 330, 364, 478).

      This book contains brief narratives by some forty-three Eskimos, in addition to Ahlooloo. Most of those who speak to us in these pages were interviewed in Inuktitut, and the texts as we have them were translated from tape recordings of those interviews. The Inuktitut text appears on facing pages with the translation. Besides editing out the interviewer's questions, Cowan has edited in such a way as "to group together all the references to a particular subject or event, made during the same conversation" (9).

3-M   Aitsan, Lucius. *The Story of My Life.* Chicago: Women's Baptist Home Mission Society, n.d. [c. 1905]. 12 pp.

Born, c. 1863; wrote, 1905. Kiowa. Aitsan tells here about his passage from the old ways—"my father prayed that I might be a great man on the war path, steal horses, and kill and scalp people" (4)—through the halls of Captain Pratt's Carlisle School to the new way, as illuminated by the Baptists. The most interesting part of this brief autobiography is Aitsan's recollection of his childhood during the Kiowas' early years on the reservation:

> Up to this time the Kiowas had never done any work except hunt. Government tried to make them, but they wouldn't, and when sheep were issued to them they ate them. Charlie Galibein . . . and I were shepherd boys and lots of times we would kill a sheep and eat it while out herding. At least the government got some of the men to plough and plant a field, but most of the Kiowas stood around watching and giving "funny talk." When the corn and melons came up everybody was so surprised and they ate a whole lot before the things were ripe and ever so many got sick and died. (4)

6   ALFORD, THOMAS WILDCAT. Florence Drake. *Civilization, as Told to Florence Drake.* Norman: University of Oklahoma Press, 1936. 203 pp.

1860–1938; collaborated, shortly before 1936. Shawnee.

8-M   Allen, Paula Gunn. BRIAN SWANN and ARNOLD KRUPAT. "The Autobiography of a Confluence, in Swann and Krupat, *I Tell You Now: Autobiographical Essays by Native American Writers.* Lincoln: University of Nebraska Press, 1987.

Born, 1939: wrote, 1985. Laguna Pueblo. Swann and Krupat have been interested in American Indian literature for some time (see, e.g., Swann, 1983, Krupat, 1985, and Swann and Krupat, 1987a). In 1984 it occurred to them to solicit autobiographies from American Indian authors. A remarkable range of authors cooperated. In addition to Allen's, then, there are narratives here by Jim Barnes (27-M), Joseph Bruchac (83-M), Barney Bush (93-M), Elizabeth Cook-Lynn (123-M), Jimmie Durham (153-M), Jack Forbes (179-M), Diane Glancy (188-M), Joy Harjo (214-S), Linda Hogan (226-M), Maurice Kenny (265-M), Duane Niatum (363-

G), Simon Ortiz (379-M), Carter Revard (424-M), Wendy Rose (431-M), Ralph Salisbury (436-S), Mary Tallmountain (483-M), and Gerald Vizenor (512-M). Swann and Krupat also provide a good brief introduction to American Indian autobiography, bibliographical references to much of the published work of these authors, and a helpful list of the small presses that have been particularly active in publishing American Indian poetry and prose.

While suggestions for revisions were made in some cases, in general Swann and Krupat were careful to allow these authors wide latitude; there is considerable diversity here, then, in form and content. Their editing was also minimal, in accord with their belief "that Native American autobiographies—if not texts by Native Americans generally—have been more often over-edited than under-edited." The result must be required reading for anyone interested in any of these authors in particular, or in Indian autobiography, or in Indian literature in general.

Allen is best known as a poet, but she is also a novelist (*The Woman Who Owned the Shadows* [San Francisco: Spinsters Ink, 1983]), scholar (editor, *Studies in American Indian Literature* [New York: MLA, 1983]), and essayist (*The Sacred Hoop: Recovering the Feminine in American Indian Traditions* [Boston: Beacon, 1986]). Allen here tells about her life and her art by talking about places, allowing a journey down Highway 66 to recall people and events, while the Rio Puerco calls up its set of associations, Tucson others. Thus she gives us a sense of the consequences for herself of all these places and their memories.

12   Apauk (M). JAMES WILLARD SCHULTZ. *Apauk, Caller of Buffalo*. Boston: Houghton Mifflin, 1916. 227 pp.
      1822– c. 1882; interviewed in the winter of 1879–1880. Piegan.

14   Apes, William. *A Son of the Forest. The Experience of William Apes, a Native of the Forest. Comprising a Notice of the Pequot Tribe of Indians. Written by Himself.* New York: published by the author, 1829. 216 pp.
      Born, 1798; wrote 1829. Pequod. See Ruoff (forthcoming) for an introduction to Apes's autobiography.

14-K   Apess, Mary. WILLIAM APESS (Variant spelling of Apes, nos. 14, 14-M). "Experience of the Missionary's Consort, Written by Herself," in the book cited in no. 14-M, pp. 21–34.

Born, 1788; wrote, c. 1833. Pequod. See no. 14-M for other autobiographies in this little book. After a few words about her orphaned childhood, and the ill-nature of her foster parents, Apess devotes this narrative entirely to her conversion to Methodism.

14-M   Apess, William (variant spelling of William Apes, no. 14). *Experience of Five Christian Indians of the Pequod Tribe.* Boston: published by the author, 1837 [1833]. 47 pp.

Born, 1798; wrote, c. 1833. Pequod. Apes here publishes four brief autobiographies—his own and three others (see nos. 13-M, 97-E, and 187-M)—and one brief biography. Apes's narrative (pp. 3–20) is a briefer version of his 1829 autobiography, *A Son of the Forest* (no. 14). This is very much a conversion narrative, but Apes's insistence on the ill effects of white prejudice and interference stand out here perhaps even more starkly than they do in the earlier work.

23   Aua (M). KNUD JOHAN VICTOR RASMUSSEN. "Aua Is Consecrated to the Spirits," in *Intellectual Culture of the Hudson Bay Eskimos, Report of the Fifth Thule Expedition, 1921–24,* 7, no. 2, Copenhagen: Gyldendalske Boghandel, 1930:115–120.

Born, probably c. 1870; interviewed, c. 1922. Iglulik Eskimo.

23-M   AUPAUMUT, HENDRICK. B. H. Coates. *A Narrative of an Embassy to the Western Indians, from the Original Manuscript of Hendrick Aupaumut, with Prefatory Remarks by Dr. B. H. Coates. Pennsylvania Historical Society Memoirs,* 2, pt. 1 (1827), 61–131. Aupaumut's original manuscript, *Journal of a Mission to the Western Tribes of Indians,* is in the collection of the Library of the Historical Society of Pennsylvania, Philadelphia.

1757 (?)–1830; wrote 1792.[1] Mahican. I have compared the original manuscript of the *Journal* with the published *Narrative.* Coates seems to have done no editing beyond altering some punctuation, turning "Grand Fathers" into "grandfathers" and the like. For the most part, he allowed Aupaumut's occasionally idiosyncratic grammar and spelling to stand.

This is the second oldest extended Indian autobiographical narrative of which I am aware. (For the oldest, see Samson Occom, no. 370-M; see also the letters of some early Christian Indian converts and missionaries, nos. 18, 99, 180, 250, and 447.) Indeed, it predates the next oldest by nearly forty years. For the writer, the Six Nations were a living reality, and he himself was the chief of the Stockbridge, Massachusetts, remnant of the Mahicans. And he was convinced that he could better convey to the western tribes the intentions (and the armed might) of the United States than could any white man. After considerable argument he was granted his commission, and so in 1792 he travelled for eleven months among the Senecas, Ottawas, Shawnees, Onondagas, the Wyandots, and others. Sometimes he travelled in a birch-bark canoe. Quite apart, then, from the remarkable sense this narrative provides of Aupaumut's feeling for his mission and the western tribes' responses, it also tells us about the customs of the tribes he visited, about their speech making, their gifts of wampum, and a good deal more.

25-M   Austin, Buck. ROBERT W. YOUNG and WILLIAM MOR-GAN. "The One with Magic Power," as found in Young and Morgan, eds., *Navaho Historical Selections, Navaho Historical Series,* 3, Phoenix: Phoenix Indian School Print Shop, 1954, 34–38, 108–111.

This book contains many narratives by Navajos, and several of these are autobiographical. The editors tell us nothing about their informants and nothing about how these narratives were elicited. Texts are printed in Navajo and in English translation. All of these narratives were collected, I presume, c. 1953; all the narrators are Navajos.

Austin, Buck. Born, 1909. Austin tells about the good life before the government's Livestock Reduction Program and about the poverty that followed, essentially the same story, then, as he tells in no. 24.

Blind Man's Daughter. Born, probably before 1915. "The Special Grazing Regulations," pp. 74, 145–146. Remembrances of the bitter times that followed upon the Livestock Reduction Program.

Claw, John C. Born, probably before 1915. "A Childhood Tale," pp. 51–54, 123–127. Shepherding at the age of eight and other childhood anecdotes.

Nez, Teddy. Born, probably before 1920. "My Wife Was Struck and Killed," 77–80, 151–154. In response to the terrible blizzard of 1949, the government air-dropped supplies in Navajo country. Nez recalls how his wife was killed by one of these falling packages.

Phillips, Dan. Born, probably before 1905. "Our Abuse," pp. 65–68, 138–141. Phillips recalls injustices, including the Livestock Reduction program, visited upon the Navajos by the government.

Son of Red House Clansman. Born, probably before 1915. Recalls the trouble attendant upon some early attempts to convince Navajo parents to send their children away to school. Phillips ends with a lament that, as a result of this strife, he himself was never educated.

Woodman, Nancy. Born, c. 1892. "The Story of an Orphan," pp. 65–68, 138–141. This has been reprinted, complete with Navajo-language text, in Evers (1981:77–88). Brief as this narrative is, it covers a wide range of experience: Woodman's mistreatment at the hands of her grandmother, the Livestock Reduction Program, her rug weaving and the associated difficulties with the traders—even a bit about her mixed Christian and Navajo religion.

Yazzie, Tim. Born, probably before 1915. "I Flew over Navajo Land," pp. 81–83, 155–157. Because of his knowledge of the terrain, Yazzie flew in the planes that dropped supplies to those stranded in the blizzard of 1949.

25-T Autaruta (M). KNUD JOHAN VICTOR RASMUSSEN. A narrative is to be found in *The People of the Polar North,* trans. G. Herring, New York: AMS Press, 1976 [1908]:107–110.

Born, probably before 1855; narrated, probably c. 1907. Eskimo, East Greenland. For the details of the collaboration, see no. 50. This is Autaruta's account of the acquisition of his shamanic powers.

27-M Barnes, Jim. BRIAN SWANN and ARNOLD KRUPAT. "On Native Ground," in the book cited in no. 8-M.

Born, 1933; wrote, 1984. Choctaw/Welsh. For more information about the collaboration and a list of the other Indian authors whose autobiographies are collected in this book, see no. 8-M. Barnes is a professor, translator, editor (*The Chariton Review*), and he has published four volumes of poetry. His autobiography proceeds largely by comparing the poisoned land he sees today with the land he knew as a child: he remembers the scream of a mountain lion, the rivers flowing free, and Choctaw commonly spoken in eastern Oklahoma. The land he sees today has been made safe by defacing most of what was sacred in the earth and the rivers. He also talks about his conception of himself as a poet, his reluctance to be thought of merely as a regional or Native American poet.

29-M Bear, John. "How John Bear Got Here." *Southern Workman,* 17 (July, 1988):80.

Born, c. 1864; wrote, 1888. Winnebago. Bear writes a very brief account of how he wanted to go to school, how he earned the money for his own tuition by purchasing sweets in Sioux City and selling them back on the reservation at payment time. His aim in all of this was to enroll at Carlisle. His piece ends with an account of how he came to change his mind. This is worth quoting:

> So I thought I go to Carlisle School but not very long that Julia St. Cyr went back from this school [i.e., Hampton]. So I went to see her about this school, asked her all about it. She said everything good except corn bread and she want me come out here. So I did.

31   Bear Head (M). JAMES WILLARD SCHULTZ. "The Baker Massacre (Told by Bear Head, a Survivor)," in *Blackfeet and Buffalo: Memories of Life among the Indians*, ed. Keith Seele. Norman: University of Oklahoma Press, 1962:282–305.
     Born, c. 1856; narrated, c. 1935. Piegan.

31-M   Bears Arm (M). ALFRED E. BOWERS. Narratives by Bears Arm and others are to be found in Bowers, *Mandan Social and Ceremonial Organization*. Chicago: University of Chicago Press, 1950.
     Bowers makes use of substantial Mandan and Hidatsa narratives for illustrative purposes. Not all of these narratives are autobiographical, but those who seek this book out for the autobiographical passages will also want to read, for example, the several myths that describe the origins of the ceremonies, sacred bundle transfers, and eagle-trapping upon which the autobiographical narratives center. Bowers worked through an interpreter, but internal evidence—the lack of concern for chronological order in some of the narratives, for example—suggests that little cutting or rearranging was done.
     Bears Arm, pp. 385–393 (M). Born, c. 1864; narrated, sometime in the years 1930–1933. Hidatsa. Bears Arm recounts his eagle-trapping experiences, the earliest of which took place in 1888. He describes, among other things, the building of the eagle-trapping lodge, the digging and the camouflaging of the trapping pit, and the ritual self-torture—"suffering for the birds"—that was a part of the complicated business of Mandan and Hidatsa eagle trapping.
     Crows Heart, pp. 169–173, 256–259 (M). Born, c. 1858; narrated in the years 1930–1933. Mandan. There is a good deal said in this book, both by Bowers and his informants, about ritual

self-torture, but Crows Heart's account of his own experiences is far the most remarkable; indeed, his is the most complete, and the most gruesome, first-person account of such matters I have read. At one point, for example, he drops himself off the edge of a bluff, to have his fall arrested by skewers tied to thongs that had been pushed through the flesh of his chest. He also tells of visions, scavenging behind Custer's troops (1876), hunting, and catfish trapping.

Wolf Chief, pp. 137–144, 228–231 (M). Born, 1849;[2] narrated, sometime in the years 1930–1933. Hidatsa. In the first of the two narratives cited Wolf Chief recalls his participation in an Okipa Ceremony, "an elaborate and complicated affair . . . a dramatization of the creation of the earth, its people, plants, and animals, together with the struggles the Mandan endured to attain its present position" (111). In the second narrative, Wolf Chief recalls the transfer of a sacred bundle, a story, he says, which "by custom I should not tell; but, since I have changed my ways, I will" (228). For other narratives by Wolf Chief, see nos. 540, 541, 542.

31-P   Bears Heart. JAMAKE HIGHWATER. Autobiographical narratives are to be found in *Song from the Earth: American Indian Painting*, Boston: New York Graphic Society, 1976, pp. 137–185.

Highwater devotes one section of this book on American Indian painting to autobiographical narratives by the painters. Bears Heart's narrative was delivered as a speech before his fellow students at Hampton Normal and Agricultural Institute in Virginia in 1880. Highwater reprints the speech as it was published in the school's newspaper. All the rest of these narratives are edited versions of Highwater's own interviews (1975) with the artists.

Bears Heart. Born, c. 1846. Some tribe of the southern plains. Brief as it is, this is a complete autobiographical statement, first hunting, then fighting, imprisonment (Fort Marion, Florida), and his transfer from prison to Hampton. Bears Heart's nonstandard English is preserved.

The rest of the narratives have largely to do with the narrators' artistic careers: Fred Beaver (born, 1911; Creek/Seminole), Archie Blackowl (born, 1911; Cheyenne), Blackbear Bosin (born, 1921; Kiowa), T. C. Cannon (born, 1946; Caddo/Kiowa), R. C. Gorman (born, 1932; Navajo), Allan Houser (born, 1915; Chiricahua Apache), Oscar Howe (born, 1915; Yanktonai Sioux), Fred

Kabotie (born, 1900; Hopi), Fritz Scholder (born, 1937; Mission-Luiseño).

31-R BEATUS, HENRY, SR. Kurt Madison and Yvonne Yarber. *Henry Beatus, Sr.* Surrey, B.C.: Hancock House, 1980. 72 pp.

Born, 1932; narrated, 1980. Athabaskan. This is one of a series of nine autobiographies collected and edited by Madison and Yarber. (See nos. 33-M, 140-M, 220-M, 228-M, 363-M, 453-M, 463-M, and 497-M.) The series was designed for school children, to give them a sense of local, oral history. The editors have tried to retain insofar as possible the rhythms and nuances of the oral narrations. They have not edited their material, then, into seamless narratives; and they have allowed their autobiographers' English to remain nonstandard. For the influences that led Yarber and Madison to their editorial method, see no. 220-F.

Beatus tells about his life in Hughes, Alaska, about his hunting and fishing and other labors within miles of the Arctic Circle. He also tells how to build fish traps; but Beatus is mostly interested in talking about his sled dogs, training them, caring for them, and racing them.

31-T Beaver, Fred. See no. 31-P.

33-M BEETUS, JOE. Kurt Madison and Yvonne Yarber. *Joe Beetus*. Surrey, B.C.: Hancock House, 1980. 72 pp.

Born, 1915; narrated, 1978. Athabaskan. For the other volumes in this series and the details of the collaboration, see no. 31-R. This is one of the most interesting of the autobiographies in this series, mainly because Beetus has his own clearly defined sense of purpose in collaborating in this work. He sees himself as passing on to young people the stories of how to live in this cold and fruitful land, just as his elders had told him stories that allowed him to learn how to hunt, trap, and survive at sixty below. Beetus recalls a life working in the mines and on river boats, but most fondly he tells his stories of hunting and trapping.

52 BETZINEZ, JASON (born, c. 1860; Apache). Wilbur Sturtevant Nye. *I Fought with Geronimo*. Harrisburg, Pa.: Stackpole, 1959. 214 pp.

Born, c. 1860; wrote, shortly before 1959. Apache.

54   Big Brave. JAMES WILLARD SCHULTZ. "Gros Ventre
        Slaughter," in the book cited in no. 31, 271–281.
            Born, c. 1853; narrated, c. 1938. Blackfeet.

66   Black Elk. JOHN G. NEIHARDT. *Black Elk Speaks,* with an
        introduction by Vine Deloria, Jr. Lincoln: University of Nebraska
        Press, 1979 [1932]. xix + 299 pp.
            1863–1950; narrated, 1931. Oglala Sioux.

66-M   ———. DeMALLIE, RAYMOND. *The Sixth Grandfather: Black
        Elk's Teachings Given to John G. Neihardt.* Lincoln: University of
        Nebraska Press, 1984. xxix + 452 pp.

68   BLACK HAWK. Antoine LeClaire and John B. Patterson. *Black
        Hawk: An Autobiography,* ed. Donald Jackson. Urbana: University
        of Illinois Press, 1955 [1833]. 206 pp.
            1767–1838; narrated, 1833. Sauk.

68-M   Blackowl, Archie. See no. 31-P.

69   Black-Wolf. A. L. KROEBER. "Black-Wolf's Narrative," in
        *Ethnology of the Gros Ventre, Anthropological Papers of the American
        Museum of Natural History,* 1, no. 4 (1908):197–204.
            Born, c. 1840; interviewed, 1901. Gros Ventre.

72-M   Blowsnake, Jasper (Crashing Thunder). See no. 129.

73   Blowsnake, Sam (pseudonym: Crashing Thunder). PAUL
        RADIN. *The Autobiography of a Winnebago Indian.* New York: Dover,
        1963 [1920]. 91 pp.
            Born, 1875; wrote, c. 1913. Winnebago.

74   ———. ———. *Crashing Thunder,* with an introduction and after-
        word by Arnold Krupat. Lincoln: University of Nebraska Press,
        1983 [1926]. xxxv + 215 pp.

77   Bonnin, Gertrude. See no. 562.

77-M   Bosin, Blackbear. See no. 31-P.

79   Brown, Catherine. RUFUS ANDERSON. *Memoirs of Katherine
        Brown, a Christian Indian of the Cherokee Nation.* Philadelphia: Amer-
        ican Sunday School Union, 1832 [1824]. 183 pp.

I cite this book again because in the *Bibliography* I failed to notice that the book was first published in 1824. It was in fact already in its third edition in 1828!

83-M Bruchac, Joseph. BRIAN SWANN and ARNOLD KRUPAT. "Notes of a Translator's Son," in the book cited in no. 8-M.
   Born, 1942; wrote, 1985. Abenaki (St. Francis-Sokoki branch). For information about the collaboration and a list of the other Indian authors whose autobiographies are collected in this book, see no. 8-M. Bruchac is a poet, fiction writer, and editor. His narrative begins with an emphasis on his physical accomplishments: "my arms and hands are strong—as strong as anyone's I've met." But Bruchac goes on to describe his years of growing up in the care of his Indian grandfather in such a way as to prepare us to understand why he likes to use the term *métis* to describe himself. It is a term he learned from the Lakota: "In English [the word] becomes 'Translator's son.' It is not an insult, like *half-breed*. It means that you are able to understand the language of both sides, to help them understand each other."

85 Buck, Neil. GRENVILLE GOODWIN. Narratives are to be found in *The Social Organization of the Western Apache*, Tucson: University of Arizona Press, 1969:206, 467, 486–496, 550.
   Born, c. 1863; interviewed, 1930s. Apache.

93-M Bush, Barney. BRIAN SWANN and ARNOLD KRUPAT. "The Personal Statement of Barney Bush," in the book cited in no. 8-M.
   Born, c. 1945; wrote, 1984. Shawnee. For information about the collaboration and a list of the other Indian authors whose autobiographies are collected in this book, see no. 8-M. Bush is a poet (e.g., *Petroglyphs* [Greenfield Center, N.Y.: Greenfield Review Press, 1982]). He is presently at work on a volume of short stories, *Running the Gauntlet*. In his "Personal Statement" he proceeds by alternating his memories with some of the poems those experiences inspired. The early memories have especially to do with his remembrance of racist feelings in the Ohio River valley where he spent his youth. The narrative is never far from the critique of American life that is so important to his conception of himself as poet, person, and Indian.

97-E Caleb, Hannah. WILLIAM APESS (variant spelling of Apes, nos. 14, 14-M). "Experience of Hannah Caleb," in the book cited in no. 14-M, pp. 35–39.

Born, probably before 1785; wrote, c. 1833. Pequod. See no. 14-M for other autobiographies in this little book. This has to do almost entirely with Caleb's conversion to Christianity (the Free-Will Baptists), partly due to the urging of her white foster parents.

97-M   Calico (M). CLARK WISSLER. "The Heyoka," as found in *Societies and Ceremonial Associations in the Oglala Division of the Teton-Dakota, Anthropological Papers of the American Museum of Natural History*, 11, no. 1 (1912), 83.

Born, c. 1844; narrated, c. 1910. Oglala Sioux. Wissler worked here through an interpreter. This is a brief account of a vision and consequent Heyoka (sacred clown) ceremony which, as Paul Olson (1982:25) suggests, can be usefully compared with Black Elk's (no. 66) account of his own conversion of vision to ritual.

101-M   Cannon, T. C. See no. 31-P.

101-P   Carius, Helen Slwooko. *Sevukakmet: Ways of Life on St. Lawrence Island*, illustrated by the author, with foreword by Priscilla Tyler and Maree Brooks. Anchorage: Alaska Pacific University Press, 1979. xi + 45 pp.

Born, c. 1945; wrote, c. 1978. Sevukakmet Eskimo. Carius wrote her book in three parts: brief histories of pre- and postcontact life on St. Lawrence Island and a personal history (33–45). This is, then, yet another American Indian autobiography that juxtaposes personal and tribal history (see, for example, nos. 186, 204, 344, 345, 385). Carius's book is perhaps most interesting, however, for the sense it provides of the happy isolation that was still possible for her family in the mid-twentieth century. When she was a child, she says, she thought that her immediate family "were the only people in the world." Carius's remembrances of the ways in which her family coped with her crippling case of polio are as warming as they are unsentimental. For the rest, we read about her play, her schooling, her feelings about her family, and there is a fair amount about the material culture as well. The text retains features of Carius's nonstandard English.

102-M   Carter, Forrest (Little Tree). *The Education of Little Tree.* New York: Delacourte Press/Eleanor Frieda, 1976. 216 pp.

Born, 1925; wrote, c. 1976. Cherokee mother. Carter, the author of *Gone to Texas* (filmed as *The Outlaw—Josey Wales*), writes here about his childhood and his coming of age, all under the tutelage of his Cherokee grandparents in some unnamed tract of eastern mountains. He learns to live according to "the Way": kill, eat, own no more than is needful—but savor colors, sounds, tastes, and friends to the full. To say this, however, is to make this book seem much more nearly a solemn tract than it is. Carter is a master of down-home English—"I learned right off that when you walked behind granpa, you trotted"—and the associated knack of seeming wiser than he seems. Doubtless, some of Carter's stories even Huck Finn might have regarded as stretchers, and this book is certainly sentimental in its evocation of granpa and granma and life in the mountains, but Carter is a gifted storyteller.

112   Chona, Maria. RUTH UNDERHILL. *The Autobiography of a Papago Woman, Memoirs of the American Anthropological Association,* no. 64 (1936), 64 pp.; reprinted as pt. 2 of Underhill, *Papago Woman,* New York: Holt, Rinehart and Winston, 1979. xiii + 98 pp.
        Born, c. 1846; interviewed, 1931–1935. Papago.

115   Chris (pseudonym). MORRIS EDWARD OPLER. *Apache Odyssey: A Journey between Two Worlds.* New York: Holt, Rinehart and Winston, 1969. xvi + 301 pp.
        Born, c. 1880; interviewed, 1933–1936. Chiricahua Apache, Mescalero Apache upbringing.

121   COCHISE, CIYE "NINO." A. Kinney Griffith. *The First Hundred Years of Nino Cochise.* London: Abelard-Schuman, 1971. 346 pp.
        Born, 1874 (according to Cochise's own claim); collaborated, 1969. Chiricahua Apache ("Some authorities, however, regard this book as spurious. . . . some will not even grant that [Nino Cochise] is an Apache" [Melody, 1977:15–16]).

121-M   CODY, IRON EYES (M). Collin Perry. *Iron Eyes Cody: My Life as a Hollywood Indian.* New York: Everest House, 1982. 290 pp.
        Born, 1904; collaborated, c. 1980. Cherokee. Perry tape recorded his interviews with Cody, and then worked up this book. No account is given of the nature of his editing, but this book has the feel of the standard fairly-famous-person as-told-to autobiography. Lots of insider-in-Hollywood sort of talk here. Gary Cooper is "Coop," and we are given the inside scoop on just how it was that Marion Morrison became John Wayne (86). But the book does attempt to convey one man's sense of what it meant to be a Hollywood Indian.

122   Comock (M). ROBERT FLAHERTY. *The Story of Comock the Eskimo,* ed. Edmund Carpenter. New York: Simon and Schuster, 1968. 95 pp.
        Born, probably c. 1870; narrated, 1912. Eskimo, from the northeastern shores of Hudson's Bay.

123-M Cook-Lynn, Elizabeth. BRIAN SWANN and ARNOLD KRUPAT. "You May Consider Speaking about Your Art," in the book cited in no. 8-M.
        Born, 1930; wrote, 1984. Sioux. For information about the collaboration and a list of the other Indian authors whose autobiographies are collected in this book, see no. 8-M. Cook-Lynn is a poet, essayist, fiction writer, and English Professor (Eastern Washington University). Her best-known work is a collection of poems, *Then Badger Said This* (New York: Vantage, 1978). Cook-Lynn's talks about her life in such a way as to reflect upon what might be the relation of Indian poet to tribe. For more of her thoughts about her work as a poet, see Cook-Lynn (1985).

124   Copway, George (Kah-ge-ga-gah-bowh). *Life, History, and Travels of Kah-ge-ga-gah-bowh.* Albany: Weed and Parsons, 1847. vii + 224 pp.
        1816–1863; wrote, 1846. Ojibwa. See Ruoff (forthcoming) for a welcome introduction to Copway's autobiography.

124-M ———. *The Life, Letters, and Speeches of Kah-ge-ga-gah-bowh.* New York, 1850.
        The *Bibliography* mentions this book as simply a later edition of *The Life, History, and Travels of Kah-ge-ga-bowh* (no. 124). Actually the 1850 edition differs in that it adds letters, speeches, and press notices; otherwise the editions are the same.

124-Q ———. *Running Sketches of Men and Places, in England, France, Germany, Belgium, and Scotland.* New York: Riker, 1851. 346 pp.
        Wrote, 1850. Copway was sent as a representative of the Christian Indians of America to the Third General Peace Congress, held in Frankfort-on-the-Main in August of 1850. He was able, however, to see a good deal of Europe along his way, speaking before various church gatherings and temperance organizations. This volume is a journal of his travels, his accounts of his speeches, his meetings with such famous people as the Baron DeRothschild, and his impressions of famous places.

125-M ————. Unpublished letters are outside the scope of the *Bibliography*, but Copway is so early a figure in the history of American Indian autobiography that I make bold to mention here that six of Copway's letters are available in the Library of the Pennsylvania Historical Society, Philadelphia. (None of these letters is included in Copway's *The Life, Letters, and Speeches of Kah-ge-ga-gah-bowh* [no. 124-M].)

Jan. 12, 1846, Albany. To Mr. W., relating an anecdote to demonstrate the Indian's "superstitious" belief in the "Bad Spirit."

April 28, 1848, Washington. To Isaiah Hacker, concerning a meeting of the Committee for Welfare of Indians.

Oct. 4, 1848, n.p. To Col. Gardiner. Copway mentions seeing an advertisement for him in the papers on Oct. 1 and asks Gardiner to send letters and other material to him at the Norfolk Post Office.

June 18, 1852, Concord. To Benj. Silliman, about a lecture Copway is to deliver.

Jan. 8, 1854, Albany. To Mr. Paralee, with directions about sending his letters.

Jan. 24, 1860, n.p. To Erastus Corning, about a lecture tour Copway expects to make to England.

129 Crashing Thunder (Jasper Blowsnake). PAUL RADIN. "Personal Reminiscences of a Winnebago Indian," *Journal of American Folklore*, 26 (1913):293–318.

Born, c. 1865; narrated, c. 1913. Winnebago. For the confusion in the names of the Two Blowsnake brothers and the two Crashing Thunders, see the *Bibliography*, no. 73.

132-H Crow Wing (M). ELSIE CLEWS PARSONS. *A Pueblo Indian Journal 1920–1921. Memoirs of the American Anthropological Association*, 32 (1925):123 pp.

Born, c. 1875; dictated, 1920–1921. Hopi. Crow Wing dictated his journal entries to Parsons in English; the material is published here with little alteration, aside from cutting. Parsons provides copious ethnographic notes. Crow Wing talks about corn planting, preparation for ceremonies, relations with other villages, dealings with the Indian agent, clan doings, ball games—all the stuff of daily life in Sichumovi, on First Mesa. There is very little that is personal here, but this is not surprising given the intensely tribal, nonindividualistic ways of the Hopis. We see something very like the same reticence as late as 1971 in the autobiography of Albert Yava, a Tewa-Hopi (see no 547).

132-M Crows Heart (M). See no. 31-M.

138   Daklugie, Asa. EVE BALL. Narratives are to be found in *Indeh: An Apache Odyssey*. Provo, Utah: Brigham Young Univ. Press, 1980. Passim.
         C. 1870–1955; narrated, c. 1954–1955. Nednhi Apache.

140-M DAYTON, ROGER. Kurt Madison and Yvonne Yarber. *Roger Dayton*. Surrey, B.C.: Hancock House, 1981. 85 pp.
         Born, 1921; narrated, 1978. Athabaskan. For the other volumes in this series and the details of the collaboration, see no. 31-R. Dayton did get three years of schooling from the Holy Cross Mission Brothers, but for the most part his life was spent trapping and fishing in the northern woods, and most of what he remembers for us in these pages has to do with this outdoor life.

140-T DeCora, Angel. "Angel DeCora—An Autobiography." *The Red Man*, 3 (March, 1911):279–285.
         Born, probably c. 1875; wrote, c. 1911. Winnebago. DeCora was raised as the daughter of the son of the hereditary chief of the Winnebagos. This is one of a number of autobiographical narratives that were published in Indian school magazines in order to show what Indians had achieved by virtue of their own Indian school education. DeCora does describe her eventual successes in the world of art and Indian art education, but her path into the white world was not strewn with roses. Her account of her conscription is worth quoting at length:

> In all my childhood I never received a cross word from anyone, but nevertheless my training was incessant. About as early as I can remember, I was lulled to sleep night after night by my father's or my grandparents' recital of laws and customs that had regulated the daily life of my grandsires for generations and generations. . . .
>
> A very promising career must have been laid out for me by my grandparents, but a strange white man interrupted it.
>
> I had been entered in the Reservation school but a few days when a strange white man appeared there. He asked me through an interpreter if I would like to ride in a steam car. I had never seen one, and six of the other children seemed enthusiastic about it, so I decided to join them, too. We did get the promised ride. We rode three days and three nights until we reached Hampton, Va.
>
> My parents found it out, but too late. (279–280)

141-M DEER, ADA. R. E. Simon, Jr. *Speaking Out*. Chicago: Children's Press, 1970. 63 pp.

Born, probably c. 1938. Menominee father, white mother. Simon evidently functioned in some way as editor, but the nature and extent of his work are not specified. This is an autobiography written for children, designed to show what good things can happen when one works hard, believes in oneself, and "speaks out." We follow Deer from childhood to her work in government for her people.

153-M Durham, Jimmie. BRIAN SWANN and ARNOLD KRUPAT. "Those Dead Guys for a Hundred Years," in the book cited in no. 8-M.

Born, 1940; wrote, 1984. Wolf Clan Cherokee. For information about the collaboration and a list of the other Indian authors whose autobiographies are collected in this book, see no. 8-M. Durham is a poet, editor, and founding director of the International Indian Treaty Council of the American Indian Movement. His narrative is a lament, linking his brother's early death, his father's death, the dissolution of the Cherokees brought about by the Dawes Severalty Act, the poisoning of the land, the decline of the American Indian movement, and his own physical problems (at age forty-four, the average life expectancy for an Indian male). The narrative is driven by rising anger, anger directed at whites and Indians alike.

159 Eagle-ribs. PLINY EARLE GODDARD. Three coup tales are to be found in "Notes on the Sun Dance of the Sarsi," *Anthropological Papers of the American Museum of Natural History* 16, no. 4 (1919):281–282.

Born, c. 1840; interviewed, 1905. Sarsi.

161 Eastman, Charles Alexander. *Indian Boyhood*. Boston: Little, Brown and Co., 1922 [1902].

1858–1939; wrote, 1902. Santee Sioux. viii + 289 pp.

162 ———. *From the Deep Woods to Civilization: Chapters in the Autobiography of an Indian*, with an introduction by Raymond Wilson. Lincoln: Univ. of Nebraska Press, 1977 [1916]. xxii + 206 pp.

165 En-me-gah-bowh (John Johnson). *En-me-gah-bowh's Story*. Min-

neapolis: Women's Auxiliary, St. Barnabas Hospital, 1904. 56 pp.
1816–1902; wrote, 1902. Ojibwa.

174-M   Fine Day (M). DAVID G. MANDELBAUM. Narratives are to
be found in *The Plains Cree, Anthropological Papers of the American
Museum of Natural History*, 37, pt. 2 (1940):198, 224–226, 253, 256,
278, 301–306, 313–316.
Born, c. 1853; interviewed, 1934. Cree. Much of this material
reappears in no. 175.

175   FINE DAY. Adolph Hungry Wolf. *My Cree People*. Invermere,
B.C.: Good Medicine Books, 1973. 63 pp.
Hungry Wolf is working from Mandelbaum's field notes. Much
of the material in this pamphlet appears in no. 174-M.

177-M   Fool. See 234-M.

178   FOOLS CROW, FRANK. Thomas E. Mails. *Fools Crow*. Garden
City, N.Y.: Doubleday, 1979. 278 pp.
Born, c. 1891; collaborated, beginning 1974. Teton Sioux.

179-M   Forbes, Jack. BRIAN SWANN and ARNOLD KRUPAT.
"Shouting Back to the Geese: Autobiographical Statement of Jack
D. Forbes," in the book cited in no. 8-M.
Born, 1934; wrote, 1984. Powhatan/Delaware/Saponi. For information about the collaboration and a list of the other Indian
authors whose autobiographies are collected in this book, see no.
8-M. After some twenty years in academia—he is now a Professor
of Native American Studies at the University of California,
Davis—he began writing poetry, songs, and fiction. This work has
appeared in anthologies and journals. He is now at work on a
novel, *Red Blood*. Forbes's autobiography proceeds by alternating
poetry and narrative in such a way as to describe his attitudes
and his life: California childhood, his attraction during his college
years to American Indian history and culture, and his metamor-
phosis into poet and fiction writer.

181-E   FREDSON, JOHN. Edward Sapir. *Stories Told by John Fredson to
Edward Sapir*, retranscribed by Katherine Peter, ed. and trans.,
Jane McGary. Fairbanks: Alaska Native Language Center, Univ.
of Alaska, 1982. 113 pp.
1891–1945; narrated, 1923. Gwich'in Athabaskan. These
stories have a complicated history. In 1922 Fredson left Alaska to

enroll at the University of the South at Sewanee. While in the South he met Sapir, who found him to be a fine informant. Sapir recorded (some by dictation, some by phonograph) many hours of Fredson's Gwich'in-language narratives. Sapir transcribed these narratives and worked up word-for-word translations, with Fredson's assistance. But Sapir never published this manuscript. In 1973 Peter began the work of retranscribing this material into

> the modern Gwich'in practical writing system. The resulting retranscriptions, in Gwich'in only, were published as a series of six booklets under the title *Sapir John Haa Googwandak*. The booklets were intended for use in bi-lingual programs, which were then just beginning in Alaskan schools. (5)

In 1981 Peter and McGary decided to issue the narratives with a translation. (See no. 390-M for Peter's own autobiography.) Fredson's narratives appear here, then, in Gwich'in and English on facing pages. There is no continuous autobiographical narrative here; rather there are autobiographical stories—all having to do with his youth in the North—served up without connections. There are mythic narratives here as well, and a few stories of family history. This is to say that we have here just the kinds of stories that it later occurred to Momaday and Silko to put together to frame their own autobiographies.

181-G   Freeman, Minnie Aodla. *Life among the Qallunaat*. Edmunton: Hurtig, 1978. 217 pp.

Born, 1936; wrote, c. 1977. James Bay Eskimo. Freeman came south when she was twenty. She eventually became a nurses' aide and an interpreter and translator for hospitalized Eskimos. By the time of her writing, she had come to work for the Medical Social Services Program in Ottawa. Her autobiography, however, has mainly to do with her childhood and adolescence in the North and her experience of culture shock in the South, among the *Qallunaat*, the whites. Freeman's artless style is nicely in keeping with her life as she remembers it. She seems always to have been surprised by life, whether it was her first menstruation (for which she was utterly unprepared) or her first hot dog or her first automobile ride.

184-M   George, Sally. WILLIAM APESS (variant spelling of Apes, nos. 14, 14-M). "Experience of Sally George," in the book cited in no. 14-M, pp. 41–43.

Born, 1779; wrote, c. 1833. Pequod. See no. 14-M for other autobiographies in this little book. This has to do almost entirely with George's conversion to the sect of the Free-Will Baptists. Much of her spiritual experience, she writes, took place while she wandered in the forest.

186   Geronimo. BARRETT, S.M. *Geronimo's Story of His Life*. New York: Duffield, 1906. xxvii + 216 pp.
       1829–1909; collaborated, 1905–1906. Apache.

188-M Glancy, Diane. BRIAN SWANN and ARNOLD KRUPAT. "Two Dresses," in the book cited in no. 8-M.
       Born, 1941; wrote, 1984. Cherokee. For information about the collaboration and a list of the other Indian authors whose auto- biographies are collected in this book, see no. 8-M. Glancy is a poet, playwright, and fiction writer. Her method here is to alter- nate poems with commentary and autobiographical musings. Mostly this piece has to do, then, with her poetry and her sense of herself as a poet, particularly as an Indian poet. Her Indianness is important to her sense of herself and her sense of her work, even though she is just one-eighth Cherokee.

204   Greene, Alma. *Forbidden Voice: Reflections of a Mohawk Indian*. Lon- don: Hamlyn, n.d. [c. 1971]. 157 pp.
       Born, c. 1895; wrote, c. 1968. Mohawk.

205   Gregorio (pseudonym). ALEXANDER and DOROTHEA LEIGHTON. "The Life Story," in *Gregorio, The Hand-Trembler: A Psychobiological Personality Study of a Navaho Indian. Papers of the Peabody Museum of American Archaeology and Ethnology*, 40, no. 1 (1949):45–81. An abridgement of this narrative (with Gregorio's name changed to another pseudonym, Jaime) may be found in Leighton and Leighton, *The Navaho Door*, Cambridge: Harvard Univ. Press, 1944:95–109.
       Born, 1902; narrated, 1940. Navajo.

208   Griffis, Joseph K. *Tahan: Out of Savagery, into Civilization*. New York: George H. Doran, Co., 1915. 263 pp.
       Born, c. 1854; wrote, c. 1915. Griffis's parentage is not entirely certain, but it is likely that his mother was Osage.

214   Hanna, Mark. RICHARD G. EMERICK. "Man of the Canyon: Excerpts from a Life in a Time—in a Place—in a Culture,"in

Emerick, *Readings in Introductory Anthropology,* Vol. II, Berkeley, California: McCutchan Pub. Co., 1970:267–292.

Born, 1882; interviewed, 1953. Havasupai.

214-M Hansen, Anne. WICK R. MILLER. Texts nos. 3, 8, 9, 10, 12, 14–18, in *Acoma Grammar and Texts, University of California Publications in Linguistics,* 40 (1965).

Born, c. 1922; narrated, 1956–1959. Acoma Pueblo. Miller asked for native-language material, and some of what Hansen provided him was autobiographical if unremarkable: snow play, work as a tourist guide, going for salt, and more. The native-language texts are printed on facing pages with English translations.

214-S Harjo, Joy. BRIAN SWANN and ARNOLD KRUPAT. "Autobiography," in the book cited in no. 8-M.

Born, 1951; wrote, 1985. Creek. For more information about the collaboration and a list of the other Indian authors whose autobiographies are collected in this book, see no. 8-M. Harjo is a poet (e.g., *She Had Some Horses* [New York: Thunder's Mouth Press, 1983]) and English professor. Harjo proceeds here by alternating selections from her poetry with autobiographical commentary. See Harjo (1985) for more of her thoughts about her work as a poet.

217-M HASTIIN BIYO' (The Son of Former Many Beads). Robert W. Young. *The Ramah Navahos.* Navaho Historical Series, No. 1, n.p. (probably Phoenix: Phoenix Indian School Print Shop), n.d. (c. 1950). vii + 17 pp.

Born, c. 1866;[3] wrote, c. 1947. Navajo. The Navajo text appears on facing pages with Young's English translation. Young elicited, translated, and edited this narrative in the hope that this historical work by a Navajo might stimulate interest among white readers in the Navajos' problems. Hastiin Biyo' is mainly concerned here with land disputes; as we might expect, his is not a happy tale. Those interested in the relationship that so often pertains in Indian autobiography between personal and tribal history will be interested to note that this is yet another example of such linkage, and, according to his introduction, Young tried in his work of translation and editing to stay very close to the original.

219 Heavy Eyes (M). JAMES WILLARD SCHULTZ. Narratives are to be found in *Friends of My Life as an Indian.* Boston: Houghton Mifflin, 1923:18–23, 58–75, 190–202.

Born, probably c. 1835; narrated, 1922. Piegan mother, white
father.

220-F   HENRY, CHIEF. Eliza Jones. *The Stories that Chief Henry Told.*
Fairbanks: Alaska Native Language Center, Univ. of Alaska, 1982
[1979]. vii + 120 pp.

C. 1883–1976; narrated, c. 1975. Athabaskan. Henry was, Jones
assures us, a well-known storyteller. We may take it that the
stories published here are quite close to the versions Henry was
wont to tell, for Jones, who tape recorded, translated, and edited
the stories, was Henry's niece; and she knew her uncle well. The
stories appear in Koyukon Athabaskan and English on facing
pages. In editing her material, Jones tried to retain as much of
the flavor of an oral performance as possible. In this she was
influenced by her conversations with the linguists Ron and
Suzanne Scollon. (See Scollon and Scollon, 1979, 1981, for their
ideas about oral narrative and its representation.) The Scollons,
in turn, were influenced by the kind of work for which Tedlock
(1972, 1977, 1983) and Hymes (1977, 1981) are well known.
Momaday (see chapter 8)—by writing down native, oral materials
in ways that preserved a sense of oral performance—was also an
influence.[4]

As Jones, Henry's niece, editor, transcriber, and translator,
puts it,

> These stories are . . . about what life was like when he was young and
> people lived in the old way, when people stayed in fish camps in the
> summer putting up fish for the winter, and in trapping camp in the
> fall until December. Then after January all the families would go on
> nomadic hunts in the hills for caribou and moose. They moved around
> hunting until April when it gets too warm during the day to travel,
> because the snow gets wet and slushy. Then they would move to
> spring camp where they would stay for the spring breakup. (v)

220-J   Hensley, Albert. Two brief autobiographies may be found in chapter 6, above.

Born, c. 1875; narrated a brief autobiography in 1908; wrote a
brief autobiography in 1916. Winnebago.

220-M HENZIE, MOSES. Kurt Madison and Yvonne Yarber. *Moses
Henzie.* Surrey, B.C.: Hancock House, 1980. 80 pp.

Born, 1901; narrated, 1978. Athabaskan. For the other volumes
in this series and the details of the collaboration, see no. 31-R.
Henzie remembers his life in the North.

220-S HERBERT, BELLE. Bill Pfisterer, Alice Moses, Katherine Peter, and Jane McGary. *Shandaa: In My Lifetime.* Anchorage: Univ. of Alaska, Native Language Center, 1982. 207 pp.

Born before 1875, perhaps as early as 1860; narrated, 1979. Athabaskan. Pfisterer's interpreter, Alice Moses, was Herbert's granddaughter, and so the storytelling here is much more like the storytelling sessions Herbert was used to than an interview. Herbert frequently addresses Moses as "my grandchild" in her stories. (For the influences at work on Pfisterer and his colleagues, see no. 220-F, and for Peter's own autobiography, see no. 390-M.) Pfisterer describes their editorial method in his introduction:

> The accounts appear here with a minimum of editing, in the order Belle told them. The text is set up with the idea that there is more to telling a story than just the words and sentences. For instance, the places where a storyteller pauses while speaking are important in adding meaning and feeling. They set the pace of the story. The stories, in either language [Athabaskan and English appear on facing pages] should be read aloud. The reader should pause at the end of each line briefly, as if for breath; where there is a wider break between the lines, the pause should be longer. . . . When one reads the text in this manner, one should be able to give an impression of a storyteller rather than a writer. (5)

The result should be read by anyone interested in Indian autobiography or oral literature. The editorial style allows Herbert to speak to us in an ancient way. And then, white contact came so late in the North, and Herbert is so full of years, that we are able to read here one Athabaskan's sense of the whole history of her people's relations with the whites. She remembers a time before preachers, she remembers the Alaska gold rush, and she remembers arrows with bone points. I do not mean to suggest that Herbert is anything like a tribal historian; but her story and her point of view are quite remarkable—especially for 1979.

222-M HIGHWALKING, BELLE. Katherine M. Weist, *Belle Highwalking: The Narrative of a Northern Cheyenne Woman.* Billings, Montana: Montana Council for Indian Education, 1979. vii + 66 pp.

1892–1971; narrated, 1970–1971. Cheyenne. Highwalking tape recorded her reminiscences in Cheyene, with Weist doing little to direct the course of the narrative beyond occasionally suggesting that this or that might be expanded upon. Most of the narration was in Cheyenne, translated by Helen Highwalker, Highwalking's daughter-in-law. Weist did some cutting and rearranging, but the book very much retains the feel of a series of oral performances, mixing stories and personal, tribal, and family history, all quite unselfconsciously. (For other autobiographers who mix tribal, personal, and mythic history, see nos. 204, 344, 346, 385, 386, 452-M.) Highwalking is the sister of John Stands in Timber, and she sees herself as working on her book for the same reasons as motivated her brother in his work on *Cheyenne Memories* (no. 472).

226-M Hogan, Linda. BRIAN SWANN and ARNOLD KRUPAT. "The Two Lives," in the book cited in no. 8-M.
      Born, 1947; wrote, 1984. Chickasaw. For information about the collaboration and a list of the other Indian authors whose autobiographies are collected in this book, see no. 8-M. A poet and novelist, Hogan teaches in the American Studies/American Indian Studies program at the University of Minnesota. This narrative has mainly to do with Hogan's gradual coming to awareness that the poverty which she was born into was not her fault, that classism and racism were at work, that she could educate herself, and that she could escape from some of the conditions into which she was born.

228   Hollow Horn (M). JAMES WILLARD SCHULTZ. "To Old Mexico," in Schultz, *Why Gone Those Times*, ed. E. L. Silliman. Norman: Univ. of Oklahoma Press, 1974:53–59.
      Born, late 18th century; narrated, c. 1870. Blackfeet.

228-M HONEA, JOHN. Kurt Madison and Yvonne Yarber. *John Honea*. Surrey, B.C.: Hancock House, 1981. 86 pp.
      Born, 1911; narrated, 1979. Athabaskan. For the other volumes in this series and the details of the collaboration, see no. 31-R. Honea was born in the year that gold was discovered near the little town of Ruby, where he was born. One of the most interesting aspects of this book has to do with Honea's remembered sense of the differences between white and Indian. There was a time, he recalls, when he assumed that white people were, quite simply, incapable of learning—because they were white people—how to survive out in the woods. And throughout the book we find Honea moving back and forth between the two worlds, insofar as this was possible for him: he also remembers the prejudice he encountered as a "half-breed" from Indians and whites, especially in the early years. Honea, then, was quite self-conscious about the choices he faced, as we may see in the following passage:

About 1945 was the last time we hunt muskrats. . . . I used to like
it. Camping out how the old people used to do and I want to do the
same thing. I was getting quite a kick out of it. Hunting and get ducks
and live off whatever we kill. Cook it for ourself over the campfire. I
thought that was great. (57)

For the rest, he remembers the mining years fondly, as a time
when there were many people around (5,000 in Ruby) and many
ways to earn a living. He also recalls his work herding reindeer,
and many years of fishing and hunting in the far North. He also
tells about his and his people's troubles with the Bureau of Land
Management about fishing rights and logging rights. This volume
also includes a brief autobiographical narrative by Honea's
Athabaskan wife, Lorraine (61–69).

228-O Honea, Lorraine. See no. 228-M.

230   HOPKINS, SARAH WINNEMUCCA. Mrs. Horace Mann. *Life
among the Piutes: Their Wrongs and Claims*. Bishop, Cal.: Sierra
Media, Inc., 1969 [1883]. 268 pp.
        C. 1844 (or 1848)–1891; wrote, 1882. Paiute.

232-M Huff, Sam. WILLIAM C. STURTEVANT. "A Seminole Personal Document," *Tequesta: The Journal of the Historical Association
of Southern Florida*, 16 (1956):55–75.
        Born, c. 1883; narrated, 1950, 1952. Seminole. Huff knew but
a few words of English; these reminiscences were taken down in
Seminole, then, on a wire recorder. Sturtevant's Seminole assistant
asked Huff, "the most noticeable old man on the Dania Reservation" near Miami, to record whatever he wanted on the recorder.
Sturtevant was after samples for linguistic analysis, not a life
history. What Huff chose to record, however, was an anecdotal
life history. And so Sturtevant came to find Huff's narrative interesting "as a rare type of document: an American Indian's nondirected, spontaneous life-history" (70).

234   Hungry Wolf, Beverly. *The Ways of My Grandmothers*. New York:
William Morrow and Co., 1980. 256 pp.
        Born, 1950; wrote, beginning c. 1975. Blood.

234-M Hunt, George (Quesalid, Giving-Potlatches-in-the-World).
FRANZ BOAS. "Shamanism," in *The Religion of the Kwakiutl In-*

dians. New York: Columbia Univ. Contributions to Anthropology, 10, pt. 2 (1930),1–41.

Born, c. 1850; wrote, between 1895–1900. Tlingit mother, Scots father; but grew up among the Kwakiutl, with Kwakiutl as his mother tongue. Boas was in search of Kwakiutl texts for linguistic purposes, but he was also interested in Kwakiutl religion. He tapped into a wellspring when he taught Hunt to write in Kwakiutl. This whole book is a collection of Hunt's writings in Kwakiutl (Hunt's Kwakiutl texts appear in pt. 1, Boas's translations in pt. 2.). Hunt's narrative of the acquisition and practice of his shamanic powers is the most elaborate such account in the literature, and this is all the more remarkable for being published along with Hunt's descriptions of Kwakiutl ceremonies, rituals, medical practices, power songs, medicinal plants, and charms.

Those interested in the history of American Indian autobiography will be particularly intrigued by the comparison this book makes possible between Hunt's own narrative and the How-I-Came-by-My-Shamanic-Powers narrative he collected from Nenolo (Fool), his teacher (41–45). (This narrative is to be found, complete, above in the Appendix.)

237   Igjugarjuk (M). KNUD J. V. RASMUSSEN. Narrative to be found in *Intellectual Culture of the Caribou Eskimos. Report of the Fifth Thule Expedition, 1921–24,* 7, no. 2. Copenhagen: Glydendalske Boghandel, 1930:51–55.

Born, probably before 1870; narrated, c. 1922. Caribou Eskimo.

242   Jaime (pseudonym). See no. 205.

234-M James, George (Hattain Gelashmin). JAMES WALCOT. *The New Pilgrim's Progress; or, the Pious Indian Convert. Containing a Faithful Account of Hattain Gelashmin, a Heathen, who was baptis'd into the Christian Faith by the Name of George James . . . Together with a Narrative of his Laborious and dangerous Travels among the Savage Indians for their Conversion; his many Sufferings and Miraculous Deliverances, and the wonderful Things which he saw in a Vision.* London: M. Cooper, 1748. 316 pp. This has been reprinted: New York: Garland Publishing, Inc., 1974.

Despite the title's fulsome promise, this book is fiction. Those who need to be convinced that this is the case have only to read the account of James's vision, which is entirely in keeping with the conventions of the Medieval and Renaissance Dream Vision genre, complete with such allegorical figures as Shame, Remorse, Temperance, and Fortitude.

247-M Johnson, John. See no. 165.

251 JONES, REV. PETER. Wesleyan Missionary Committee. *Life and Journals of Kah-ke-wa-quo-na-by: (Rev. Peter Jones), Wesleyan Missionary.* Toronto: Anton Green, 1860. xi + 424 pp.
    1802–1856. Jones wrote the brief autobiography that constitutes the first chapter of this book shortly before his death; the journal that makes up the bulk of the book covers the years 1825–1856. Ojibwa mother; Welsh father.

253 Joseph, Chief. "An Indian's View of Indian Affairs," with an introduction by William H. Hare. *North American Review*, 128 (April, 1879):412–433. Reprinted numerous times, most recently as *Chief Joseph's Own Story*, with a foreword by Donald MacRae. Seattle: Shorey, 1975. 31 pp.
    1832–1904; narrated, 1879. Nez Perce.

255-M Kabotie, Fred. See no. 31-P.

261-M Kayrahoo, John. MARIUS BARBEAU. "The Deer Charm" and "An Old Hunter's Reminiscences," in *Huron-Wyandot Traditional Narratives, in Translations and Native Texts, National Museum of Canada*, Bulletin 165, Anthropological Series, No. 47 (1960):50–51, 289–291.
    C. 1840–1913; narrated, 1912. Wyandot (western branch of the Huron). Kayrahoo spoke only Wyandot, and Barbeau worked through an interpreter. Barbeau prints here the native-language text, literal translation, and free translation. Kayrahoo recalls his hunting and draws a sad comparison between the new and the old ways.

265 KENNEDY, DAN (OCHANKUGAHE). James R. Stevens. Toronto: McClelland and Stewart, 1972. 160 pp.
    Born, 1870; wrote, 1920s and 1930s. Assiniboine.

265-H Kenny, Maurice. "Wild Strawberry." *Wicazo Sa*. 1 (1985):40–44.
    Born, 1929; wrote, 1985. Mohawk. Kenny explains the composition of his poem, "Wild Strawberry," in autobiographical terms.

265-M ———. BRIAN SWANN and ARNOLD KRUPAT. "Waiting at the Edge: Words toward a Life," in the book cited in no. 8-M.

Wrote, 1984. For information about the collaboration and a list of the other Indian authors whose autobiographies are collected in this book, see no. 8-M. Kenny is a poet, author of numerous collections of poems, one of which, *The Mama Poems* (Buffalo, N.Y.: White Pine Press, 1984), won the American Book Award. Sometimes Kenny's method here is to alternate selections from his poetry with more explicitly autobiographical passages. One poem calls up wistful recollections of an Adirondack boyhood, first poetic stirrings, father's hunting. Sometimes the narrative is straightforwardly autobiographical: his education as a poet, his travels, and more.

273   LAME DEER, JOHN (FIRE). Richard Erdoes. *Lame Deer: Seeker of Visions*. New York: Simon and Schuster, 1972. 288 pp.

Born, c. 1900; collaborated, c. 1966–1970. Sioux.

279-M Le Claire, Peter. JAMES HOWARD. "Peter Le Claire—Northern Ponca." *American Indian Tradition*, 8 (1961):17–20.

1883–1968; wrote, 1949–1950. Ponca. Howard asked Le Claire (who had worked as an informant for Howard) to write his autobiography, and the result is printed here without alteration. There is a good deal of detail in these few pages. Le Claire remembers the wagon trains moving westward in Knox County, Nebraska; and he remembers visiting Indian graves at Wounded Knee just a few years after the massacre. For the rest we read of a succession of occupations and of his dancing. Le Claire was, in 1961, "one of the very few Northern Ponca who still own[ed] a dancing costume and participat[ed] in the Indian dances."

280   LEE, BOBBI. Don Barnett and Rick Sterling. *Bobbi Lee, Indian Rebel: Struggles of a Native Canadian Woman*, Vol. I. Richmond, B.C.: Liberation Support Movement Information Center, 1975. 120 pp.

Born, 1950; narrated, 1972. Métis.

283   Left Handed (M). WALTER DYK. *Son of Old Man Hat. A Navaho Autobiography*. Lincoln: Univ. of Nebraska Press, 1967 [1938]. xiv + 378 pp.

Born, 1868; interviewed, 1934. Navajo.

283-M ———. WALTER and RUTH DYK. *Left Handed: A Navajo Auto-*

biography, with a foreword by Fred Eggan. New York: Columbia Univ. Press, 1980. xxv + 578 pp.

Narrated, 1934–1935, except for the last chapter, which was done in 1947–1948. Navajo. For an account of the collaboration, see no. 283. Dyk began editing this volume himself; but because of a long illness, he was unable to finish the work. After his death in 1972, Ruth Dyk "continued the editing using the guidelines he had started: add nothing and leave out only minor experiences and repetitious episodes . . . so that the edited version differs in no essential way from the first telling" (xviii).

This volume is the second part of Left Handed's autobiography. The first part, *Son of Old Man Hat* (no. 283), takes us from his birth to about his twentieth year, the time of his marriage. This second part—all 571 pages—treats of just three years in the late 1880s. The narrative is, then, remarkably detailed. We hear about his feelings toward members of his family; we hear about his relations with his wife, about his preparations for the hunt, his "affairs," his hogan building, his gaming. Finally, Left Handed tells about his wife's unfaithfulness and their separation.

284-M Lindsey, Lilah Denton. "Memories of the Indian Territory Mission Field," *Chronicles of Oklahoma,* 36 (1958):181–198.

Born, c. 1864; wrote, 1938. One-fourth Creek. These are detailed and happy memories: schooling at Oklahoma's Tullahassee Manual Labor Boarding School, work in the Tullahassee Mission, and teaching at the Tulsa Indian School. A Biography of Lindsey has also been published (J. O. Misch, 1955).

302-M MacDONALD, RANALD. William S. Lewis and Naojiro Murakami. *Ranald MacDonald: The Narrative of His Early Life on the Columbia under the Hudson's Bay Company's Regime; of His Experiences in the Pacific Whale Fishery; and of His Great Adventure to Japan; with a Sketch of His Later Life on the Western Frontier, 1824–1894.* Spokane: Eastern Washington State Historical Society, 1923. 333 pp. Long sections of MacDonald's narrative are included, in Eva Emery Dye, *MacDonald of Oregon: A Tale of Two Shores,* Chicago: McClurg, 1906.

1824–1894; wrote c. 1856—but see below. Chinook mother, white father. The following is a brief paraphrase of the editors' account of the complicated history of this book (17–21). MacDonald prepared his original manuscript in 1856 and gave this to his friend Malcolm McLeod, who promptly began to edit it. Mac-

Donald then left for the northwest coast, and so lost contact with his friend for some twenty-five years. In 1890, then, McLeod prepared what was his third draft of the manuscript and sent this to MacDonald for final corrections. However, no publisher could be found, MacDonald and McLeod having missed the period of American interest in Japan by some forty years or so. Finally Williams and Murakami brought the book to press, with a minimum of editing and a maximum of detailed, explanatory footnotes. While little of MacDonald's original manuscript had survived, Williams and Murakami did see enough of MacDonald's correspondence to conclude that McLeod allowed the book to remain MacDonald's own "though evidences of McLeod's composition are apparent" (18).

MacDonald's mother died when he was just three months old, but he did enjoy occasional sojourns among his mother's people. He is able, then, to relate certain aspects of Chinook history and recall various Chinook traditions. It is clear, however, that he is the son of his father, the chief trader and chief factor of the Hudson's Bay Company.

After a brief account of his early years and of the ways of the Chinook, this narrative settles down to the telling of MacDonald's great adventure, his voyage to and his life in Japan (1848–1849), where, among other things, he taught English to the men who later served as the chief interpreters in Japan's negotiations with Commodore Perry.

313-M Marsden, Edward. "Myself Since 1869." *The Indian Helper: A Weekly Letter from the Indian Industrial School, Carlisle, Pa.*, 8, no. 12 (December 2, 1892):1,4.

Born, 1869; wrote, 1892. Tsimshian. This is a good, brief example of what I have called (chapter 6) the Carlisle Success Story. He began life in a very poor family in British Columbia, but by steadily applying himself to work and to learning practical trades, and by virtue of what he learned at Carlisle, he is able to conclude as follows:

> My first wages was three dollars and a few potatoes for the summer's work in 1880; but since that time, in 1890, I received three dollars a day.
>
> These are a few of the many facts that will help us to understand that, to reach the top of the hill, we must begin at the foot, and with patience and courage, struggle onward and upward, till the summit of the hill is reached.
>
> Be a *Man-Of-The-Best-Specimen!*

313-N ———. "An Experience with the Wild West Show," *The Indian Helper: A Weekly Letter from the Indian Industrial School, Carlisle, Pa.,* 11, no. 16 (January 24, 1896):1.

Marsden tells about seeing a Wild West Show, in order to make the point that such shows are "making money by upholding a bad relic of heathenism." He goes on to make the Carlisle Indian School's point that the Indian must leave off the old ways and win an education in order eventually to "find his way into the pulpit, the legislative hall, the commercial house and the scientist's laboratory."

318 Mathews, John Joseph. *Talking to the Moon.* Chicago: Chicago Univ. Press, 1945. 244 pp.

Born, 1895; wrote c. 1944. Osage.

319 Maxidiwiac. GILBERT L. WILSON. *Agriculture of the Hidatsa Culture: An Indian Interpretation. University of Minnesota Studies in the Social Sciences,* 9 (1917). viii + 129 pp.

Born, 1839; interviewed, 1912. Hidatsa.

320 ——— (pseudonym: Wa-Hee-Nee). ———. *Waheenee: An Indian Girl's Story, Told by Herself,* with an introduction by Jeffrey R. Hanson. Lincoln: Univ. of Nebraska, 1981 [1921]. 189 pp.

Interviewd, 1908–1918.

321 ———. ———. "Hidatsa Horse and Dog Culture." *Anthropological Papers of the American Museum of Natural History* 15, no. 2 (1924):125–311.

322-K McCARTHY, JAMES. John G. Westover. *A Papago Traveler: The Memories of James McCarthy.* Tucson: Univ. of Arizona Press, 1985. xxiv + 200 pp.

Born, 1895; wrote, 1973. Papago. Westover met McCarthy in 1983; soon he was so fascinated by McCarthy's stories that he began writing them down. After some months McCarthy confided that he had written a book about his life. *Papago Traveler,* then, is the edited version of an autobiography McCarthy wrote without prompting. Westover asserts that he strove "to retain absolutely the integrity of McCarthy's story" (xxi); but he understands this broadly enough to allow the deletion of sentences, for example, and all the changes necessary to conform McCarthy's prose to the dictates of Standard English—if we may judge by a comparison of the photocopy of a manuscript page (xii) with the edited version.

McCarthy recalls a remarkably eventful life. At the age of eleven, he decided to leave the Phoenix Indian School, without permission. He proceeded to walk back to his home outside Tucson, a trek of over a hundred miles, following the railroad tracks to find the way. And he remained a traveler throughout his life. He joined the army during World War I to see something of the world; he sailed in a windjammer to Alaska, where he worked in the canneries. He seems to have found fulfillment in travel, in meeting people. Perhaps this breadth of experience is partly responsible for the remarkable lack of bitterness we find in the book. He recounts no incident of racial prejudice. Even the leather strap and the ball and chain which were used for disciplinary purposes at the Phoenix school he seems to remember as simply a few among the many curiosities he has witnessed.

322-M McCarty, Jim. LESLIE SPIER. Narratives are to be found in "Southern Diegueño Customs," *Univ. of California Publications in American Archaeology and Ethnology,* 20 (1932):312–314, 316–321, 323–324, 336–337, 356. Some of this material is reprinted in Malcolm Margolin, *The Way We Lived: California Indian Reminiscences, Stories and Songs,* Berkeley: Heyday Books, 1981, pp. 13–14, 106.

Born, c. 1840; narrated, 1920. Diegueño. Spier worked here through an interpreter. McCarty talks about his shamanic powers (although he does not consider himself to be a shaman), about rituals in which he was a participant, about his training as a hunter, and more.

Margolin's book reprints a wide range of California Indian narratives and songs, most of which are otherwise available only in long-out-of-print anthropological journals; Margolin excerpts from materials cited in nos. 2, 250, 360, 365, 413, and 555. He also provides helpful commentary.

330-M MESTOKOSHO, MATHIEU. Serge Bouchard. *Chroniques de chasse d'un Montagnais de Mingan,* trans. Georges Mestokosho. Quebec: Ministere des affaires culturelles, Serie Cultures amerindiennes, 1977. 130 pp.

Born, c. 1887; narrated, 1970–1971. Montagnais. Bouchard edited a translation of Mestokosho's oral narrative. Bouchard writes that "le manuscrit est fidèle aux relations de Mathieu. La traduction française est presque littérale et l'adaption littéraire est voluntairemont modeste. Dans l'édition du texte, j'ai voulu respecter l'événementialité et la chronologie des commentaires. Il y a doné la minimum de manipulation" (9). Mestokosho does recall his childhood, but this narrative has mainly to do with his long life as a hunter, trapper, and woodsman.

343-M Momaday, N. Scott. *The Journey of Tai-me.* Santa Barbara: privately printed, 1967.
Born, 1934; wrote, 1966. Kiowa.

344 ———. *The Way to Rainy Mountain.* New York: Ballantine, 1973 [1969]. 119 pp.
Wrote, 1966–1969.

345 ———. *The Names.* New York: Harper and Row, 1976. 170 pp.
Wrote, c. 1974–1975.

349 Mountain Wolf Woman. NANCY OESTREICH LURIE. *Mountain Wolf Woman, Sister of Crashing Thunder: The Autobiography of a Winnebago Indian.* Ann Arbor: Univ. of Michigan Press, 1961. xx + 142 pp.
1884–1960; collaborated, 1958. Winnebago.

358-M Nenolo. See 234-M.

363-G Niatum, Duane. BRIAN SWANN and ARNOLD KRUPAT. "Auto-biographical Sketch of Duane Niatum," in the book cited in no. 8-M.
Born, 1938; wrote, 1985. Kallum. For information about the collaboration and a list of the other Indian authors whose autobiographies are collected in this book, see no. 8-M. Niatum has published numerous books, both as a poet (e.g., *Ascending Red Cedar Moon* [New York: Harper and Row, 1974]) and as an editor (e.g., *Harper's Book of Twentieth Century Native American Poetry* [New York: Harper and Row, 1986]). His poems are often anthologized and translated. He begins here with his memories of the Northwest, his mother's Kallum people, and the promise he made his grandfather "never to lose touch with his Coast Salish traditions." The rest of this autobiographical essay has mostly to do with his art—how he came to be a poet, what were early influences upon his work, his later artistic associations, and how he has striven in his art always to remember the promise to his grandfather.

363-M NICTUNE, OSCAR, SR. Kurt Madison and Yvonne Yarber. *Oscar Nictune, Sr.* Surrey, B.C.: Hancock House, 1980. 80 pp.

Born, 1901; narrated, 1978. Eskimo. For the other volumes in this series and the details of the collaboration, see no. 31-R. Nictune remembers his training for life in the North, his desire for schooling, his hunting, his journey to the South for treatment in a T.B. sanitorium, his various jobs, and more.

368   Nowell, Charles. CLELLAN S. FORD. *Smoke from their Fires: The Life of a Kwakiutl Chief.* Hamden, Conn.: Archon, 1968 [1941]. xiv + 248 pp.
       Born, 1870; interviewed, 1940. Kwakiutl.

370-M Occom, Samson. "A Short Narrative of my life." In Bernd Peyer, ed., *The Elders Wrote: An Anthology of Early Prose by North American Indians, 1768–1931.* Berlin: Dietrich Reimer Verlag, 1982:12–18.
       1723–1792; wrote, 1762. Mohegan. This is the oldest Indian autobiographical narrative I know of. Occom was "Born a Heathen and brought up in Heathenism" (12). There were no Christians among the Mohegans during these years, Occom tells us, "Neither did we Cultivate our Land, nor kept any Sort of Creatures except Dogs . . . and Dwelt in Wigwams" (13). But then Occom was inspired by a missionary to learn to read, and eventually he won his way to Eleazar Wheelock's school (see no. 18); later he became a teacher and missionary himself. His narrative ends with a reluctant complaint that he has not been paid for his missionary labors nearly as much as are white missionaries. (For more information on Occom, see Peyer, 1982. For a closely related document, see the journal [1765–1776] of the Puritan missionary Joseph Fish [1982]; Fish labored among the Narragansett, and he mentions Occom with admiration [82].)

379-M Ortiz, Simon J. BRIAN SWANN and ARNOLD KRUPAT. "The Language We Know: An Autobiographical Sketch," in the book cited in no. 8-M.
       Born, 1941; wrote, 1985. Acoma Pueblo. For information about the collaboration and a list of the other Indian authors whose autobiographies are collected in this book, see no. 8-M. Ortiz is a poet, scholar, and a writer of short stories. This autobiographical essay concentrates on his relation to his Acoma people and their language, and how these relations along with his educational experiences made him the writer he is. See Ortiz (1985) for more of his thoughts on his work as a poet.

383-K Parker, General Ely S. "Writings of General Parker: Extracts from His Letters, and an Autobiographical Memoir of Historical Interest," *Publications of the Buffalo Historical Society,* 8 (1905):520–536.

1828–1895; wrote, c. 1878. Seneca. The letters printed here include a good deal of autobiographical material, but the real attraction is "General Parker's Autobiography," (527–536). The narrative breaks off, incomplete, but it seems to be very nearly complete. Autobiography here is mingled with Indian and Seneca history and with Parker's ideas on the best ways to civilize and bring religion to the Indian. He tells about his decision to seek education, about his years of service in the army. Parker served as Grant's secretary during the Civil War, and it was Parker, then, who wrote up the final copy of the terms of surrender that Lee signed. He went on to become the Commissioner of Indian Affairs during Grant's first term as President, and he writes here of that period with some pride. These pages are, by the bye, closely printed; there is more here than the page numbers seem to indicate.

For biographies of Parker, see Arthur C. Parker (1919) and Tooker (1978).

383-M Parrish, Essie. ROBERT L. OSWALT. Autobiographical narratives are to be found in *Kashaya Texts, University of California Publications in Linguistics,* 36 (1964), texts nos. 40, 42, 43, 49, 69, 78.

Born, 1902; narrated, 1957–1958. Kashaya. Oswalt collected these texts largely for purposes of linguistic analysis, but Parrish is, as Oswalt says, an "accomplished" storyteller, and this material is quite interesting. Parrish is a mystic and a prophet. She recalls her childhood, but her most detailed remembrances have to do with her work as a sucking doctor. The assumptions of her doctoring are partly Christian, partly Kashaya.

385 PATENSIO, CHIEF FRANCISCO. Margaret Boynton and Kate Collins. *Stories and Legends of the Palm Springs Indians.* Palm Springs, California: Palm Springs Desert Museum, 1969 [1943]. xvi + 132 pp.

Born, c. 1860; narrated, 1939. Cahuilla.

386 ———. Kate Collins. *Desert Hours with Chief Patensio, as Told to Kate Collins by Chief Francisco Patensio,* ed., Roy F. Hudson. Palm Springs, California: Palm Springs Desert Museum, 1971. 38 pp.

387   Paytiamo, James. *Flaming Arrow's People: By An Acoma Indian.* New
       York: Duffield and Green, 1932. 158 pp.
           Born, probably before 1870; wrote, c. 1931. Acoma Pueblo.

390-M PETER, KATHERINE. Jane McGary. *Neets'aii Gwiindaii: Living
       in Chandalar.* Fairbanks: Alaska Native Language Center, Univ.
       of Alaska, 1981. xii + 147 pp.
           Born, c. 1920; wrote, c. 1980. Athabaskan. Peter learned to
       write in English as a child. She went on to become an elementary
       school teacher; but in 1973 she learned to write, in a newly devel-
       oped syllabary, in her native Gwich'in. Soon she began writing
       materials for use in Gwich'in language bilingual education pro-
       grams. (She also served as transcriber for no. 220-S.) Her auto-
       biography is the longest Gwich'in language text yet published.
       Her Gwich'in original appears here on facing pages with her own
       English translation, as edited by McGary.
           Peter describes here her young womanhood (1936–1947), her
       years of living in a way that was not very far from the old ways
       of her people: moving—usually by dog sled—from one camp to
       another according to the dictates of the food supply, camping here
       for the caribou hunt, there for the bearberries, then on the move
       again for the fishing. Others have described this way of life among
       the Athabaskans (see, e.g., nos. 220-F, 228-M), but Peter's narra-
       tive is distinctive, for example, for her description of what is
       involved in dog sledding in killing cold with a baby there under
       the furs.

392-M PIERCE, Rev. WILLIAM HENRY. Rev. J.P. Hicks. *From Pot-
       latch to Pulpit, Being the Autobiography of the Rev. William Henry Pierce,
       Native Missionary to the Indian Tribes of the Northwest Coast of British
       Columbia.* Vancouver: Vancouver Bindery, 1933. 176 pp.
           Born, 1856; wrote, 1910. Scots father, Tsimshian mother. Hicks
       tells us that Pierce wrote his autobiography at the urging of "the
       missionary authorities in Toronto, who hoped to arrange for its
       publication" (86). Pierce's manuscript was not published, how-
       ever, until the Vancouver Bindery arranged to have Hicks edit it.
       Hicks arranged the material into two parts: the autobiography
       proper (7–85) and Pierce's accounts of tribal history, "supersti-
       tions," warfare, totem poles, potlatches, law, and other Tsimshian
       lore (108–176). He also added a brief, biographical "Editor's
       Note" (86–107) covering the period from 1910–1933.
           Pierce was raised by his mother's Tsimshian family, and so he
       remembers the coming of the missionaries to his people and the

strife in his village between those who were willing to accept the missionaries and the schools and those who opposed the white man's innovations. Pierce was himself a bit of flotsam on these tides, first being sent to school by his grandfather, then being ordered home by the chief, beginning to learn the Dog-dance, but never actually dancing it. But soon he is converted to Methodism, becomes a missionary interpreter, and then goes on to his own missionary career.

397   Plenty-coups. FRANK B. LINDERMAN. *Plenty-coups, Chief of the Crows*. Lincoln: Univ. of Nebraska Press, 1962 [1930]. ix + 324 pp.
      1847–1932; collaborated, c. 1928. Crow.

398-M   Pokagon, Chief Simon. "Indian Superstitions and Legends." *The Forum*, 35 (July, 1898):618–629. Reprinted in William Clements, *Native American Folklore in Nineteenth-Century Periodicals*, Athens, OH.: Swallow, 1986:237–252.
      1830–1899; wrote, 1898. Potawatomi. Pokagon wrote first in Potawatomi, then translated into English. His written English required the help of an editor but for little beyond grammar and spelling (Dickason, 1961). Pokagon here tells about his own life and his changing attitudes toward tribal legends and beliefs as a framework for his recounting of those legends and beliefs.

399   ———. *O-Gi-Maw-Kwe Mit-I-Gwa-Ki (Queene of the Woods), Also Brief Sketch of the Algaic Language*. Hartford: MI.: C. H. Engle, 1899. vii + 255 pp.
      Wrote, c. 1898. For a discussion of this book see Larson (1978:37–46).

404   Pretty-shield (F). FRANK B. LINDERMAN. *Pretty-shield: Medicine Woman of the Crows*. Lincoln: Univ. of Nebraska Press, 1974 [1932]. 256 pp.
      Born, c. 1857; interviewed, shortly before 1932. Crow.

406   Price, Anna (Her Eyes Grey). GRENVILLE GOODWIN. Narratives are to be found in the book cited in no. 85:19–20, 54, 76–79, 84, 89–91, 233–234, 244–245, 252, 330–332, 355, 380, 385–386, 389, 406–409, 470, 472, 482–485, 530, 560–561, 564, 670–690.
      C. 1837–1937; interviewed, 1931. White Mountain Apache.

409-M   Quesalid. See no. 234-M.

409-M Rain-in-the-Face (M). CHARLES ALEXANDER EASTMAN. "Rain-in-the-Face: The Story of a Sioux Warrior." *Outlook* 84 (October 27, 1906):507–512. An abridgement appeared with the same title, *The Teepee Book*, 2 (June, 1916):31, 32, 99–101.

C. 1835–1905; narrated, 1905. Sioux. With the passage of the Dawes Severalty Act in 1887 it became increasingly important that Indians have first and second names, names that would remain with them throughout their lives. Consequently the government instituted a program to establish legal names for individual Indians. Eastman, who was himself convinced of the importance of this project, worked on this program from 1903 to 1909 (see Wilson, 1983:120). Eastman was ideal for the work, because of his native familiarity with Sioux customs and language. This meant that he spent a great deal of time out on the reservations, meeting a great many people. One of those he met was the great warrior Rain-in-the-Face, and he took down this life story from the old man. For the most part, Rain-in-the-Face limits himself to his war deeds, and about half the narrative is devoted to the Custer battle.

412 Rave, John. PAUL RADIN. "John Rave's Account of the Peyote Cult and of His Conversion," in *The Winnebago Tribe*, Lincoln: Univ. of Nebraska Press, 1970 [1923]:341–346.
Born, c. 1855; narrated, 1910. Winnebago.

416 Red Crow (M). ROBERT N. WILSON. "The Life History and Adventures of Red Crow, Late Head Chief of the Bloods (Blackfoot Confederacy)," as found in Samuel H. Middleton, *Kainai Chieftainship: History, Evolution and Culture of the Blood Indians*, Lethbridge, Alberta: Lethbridge Herald, 1953: 113–164. Excerpts are to be found in Adolph Hungry Wolf, *The Blood People: A Division of the Blackfoot Confederacy*, New York: Harper and Row, 1977:239–254.
C. 1830–1900; narrated, 1881. Blood.

417 Red Eagle (M). JAMES WILLARD SCHULTZ. "Laugher, the Story of a Tame Wolf" and "The End of Laugher," in the book cited in no. 228:175–202.
Born, c. 1810; narrated, c. 1877. Blackfeet.

420 RED FOX (M). Cash Asher. *The Memoirs of Chief Red Fox*. New York: McGraw Hill Book Co., 1971. xii + 209 pp.

Born, 1870 (according to Red Fox); Asher claims that Red Fox did his writing in 1968. Sioux.

424-M Revard, Carter. BRIAN SWANN and ARNOLD KRUPAT. "Walking among the Stars," in the book cited in no. 8-M.

Born, 1931; wrote, 1984. Osage. For information about the collaboration and a list of the other Indian authors whose autobiographies are collected in this book, see no. 8-M. Rhodes Scholar, medievalist, and English professor, Revard is also a widely published poet (e.g., *Ponca War Dancers* [Norman, Ok.: Point Riders Press, 1980]). Revard's narrative has mainly to do with his childhood, during the hard years in Oklahoma during the Great Depression, of the uncles shot while bootlegging and bank robbing, and of the warm sense of family that has inspired much of his poetry over the years.

430 Rope, John. GRENVILLE GOODWIN. Narratives are to be found in the book cited in no. 85:52, 79–80, 82–83, 95, 124, 396–397, 462, 464, 465, 468, 475–476, 485–486.

Born, c. 1850; interviewed, 1932. White Mountain Apache.

431-M Rose, Wendy. BRIAN SWANN and ARNOLD KRUPAT. "Autobiographical Essay," in the book cited in no. 8-M.

Born, 1948; wrote, 1984. Hopi father, Anglo/Miwok mother. For information about the collaboration and a list of the other Indian authors whose autobiographies are collected in this book, see no. 8-M. Rose is a poet (e.g., *Hopi Roadrunner Dancing* [Greenfield Center, N.Y.: Greenfield Press, 1973]) and scholar teaching in the American Indian Studies program at Fresno City College. Rose's is the most powerful narrative in the volume. She makes explicit here much of the pain that is implicit in her poetry—the physical and the emotional bruises she suffered at the hands of stepfather, husband, school nuns, and others who ought to have done better by her.

436-H Saayaachapis, Tom (I give the spelling here that appears in later collections of narratives; the name is actually spelled *Sayachapis* in this early publication). EDWARD SAPIR and MORRIS SWADESH. The "Tom" narratives in Sapir and Swadesh, *Nootka Texts*. Philadelphia: Linguistic Society of America, 1939:128–209.

Born, probably c. 1860; interviewed, 1910–1914. Nootka.

436-M ———. "The Yearly Round," "Beliefs," "Tom's Big Wolf Ritual,"
"Dance Teams," "Alex Thomas' Marriage," "Puberty Potlatch
for William Tutuutsch's Daughter," "Gift Visit to the Ucluelets,"
"Potlatch Trip," "Mourning Potlatch for a Child," "Kwiistuh's
Big Potlatch," "Becomes-Ten Gives a Potlatch," "A Contest be-
tween Orators," "Uchucklesitis Exterminate Kiihin," and
"Ahousets Threaten Tsishaa," as found in Sapir and Swadesh,
Native Accounts of Nootka Ethnography, New York: AMS, 1978 [1955],
passim.

Narrated, 1913–1924. Nootka. While there was undoubtedly
some questioning along the way, especially in "The Yearly
Round," internal evidence suggests that Saayaachapis needed little prompting. Indeed, some of these narratives seem obviously to
be stories that he has told many times, complete down to formulaic
endings. And since the man who recorded most of these narratives,
Alex Thomas, was his grandson, and since Saayaachapis was
speaking in his native language, we can be fairly confident that
many of these narratives are nearly as authentic in their patterns
as in their content. The native-language texts are printed along
with Sapir's translations. The titles given above suggest the con-
tents.

For a biographical account of Saayaachapis, see Sapir's
"Sayach'apis, a Nootka Trader," in Parsons (1967 [1922]:297–
324).

436-S Salisbury, Ralph. BRIAN SWANN and ARNOLD KRUPAT.
"The Quiet Between Lightning and Thunder," in the book cited
in no. 8-M.

Born, 1926; wrote, 1985. Cherokee. For information about the
collaboration and a list of the other Indian authors whose autobiographies are collected in this book, see no. 8-M. Salisbury is a
poet, essayist, novelist, and English Professor. Salisbury proceeds
here by elaborating on the autobiographical elements of his poems
and fiction, alternating poems with the autobiographical remembrances they suggest, remembrances of his family, his own apprenticeship under the poet Robert Lowell at the University of Iowa,
and family stories, stories about his father, a "travelling minstrel"
and part-time bootlegger, his family's life in Iowa and the clay
hills of Kentucky, and his own passage from "primitive existence"
to a post-World War II "world that was far from primitive."

437 Sanapia. DAVID JONES. Narratives in *Sanapia, Comanche Medicine Woman.* New York: Holt, 1972. xvii + 107 pp.
    Born, 1895; collaborated, interviewed, 1968. Comanche.

441 SAVALA, REFUGIO. Kathleen Sands. *The Autobiography of a Yaqui Poet.* Tucson: Univ. of Arizona Press, 1980. xxiii + 228 pp.
    Born, 1904; wrote, 1964– c. 1969. Yaqui.

441-D Sayachapis, Tom. See nos. 436-H and 436-M.

441-K Scholder, Fritz. See no. 31-P.

441-M Sconchin, Peter. VERNE RAY. Narratives are to be found in *Primitive Pragmatists,* Seattle: Univ. of Washington, 1963, pp. 67–68, 107–109, 111–112. Some of this material is reprinted in the second book cited in no. 322-M, pp. 173–175.
    Born, c. 1850; narrated, 1930. Modoc. The narratives cited above are the edited results of English language interviews with fieldworkers' questions edited out. (Ray himself was not the fieldworker.) Sconchin was the last living Modoc participant in the 1872–1873 war. Here he recalls his childhood games, childhood fighting, and, most interestingly, the war-related experiences that led him to lose faith in the Modoc shamans.

452-M Silko, Leslie Marmon (F). *Storyteller.* New York: Seaver Books, 1981. 278 pp.
    Born, 1948; wrote this material during the 1970s. Laguna and white. Silko is working here along the lines established by N. Scott Momaday in his *Way to Rainy Mountain* (no. 344) and *The Names* (no. 345). This is to say that she wants to give us an idea of who she is by telling brief stories about herself, her people, and her family and by telling traditional stories as well. And, again like Momaday, she provides very few connections between stories; and so we are left to piece together traditions in *something* like the way participants in an oral culture might piece together their sense of their culture by hearing a lifetime of stories.

453-M SIMON, EDWIN. Kurt Madison and Yvonne Yarber. *Edwin Simon.* Surrey, B.C.: Hancock House, 1980. 120 pp.
    1898–1979; narrated, 1978. Athabaskan. For the other volumes

in this series and the details of the collaboration, see no. 31-R. Simon tells stories here about life in the far North, stories about hunting, fishing, and making do. He also tells about the devastation of the tuberculosis epidemic and other family stories.

455   Sinyella (M). LESLIE SPIER. "Historical Tales," in *Havasupai Ethnography, Anthropological Papers of the American Museum of Natural History* 29, pt. 3 (1928), 111–112, 222–223, 226–227, 238–241, 246–248, 251–253, 279–281, 322–323, 333–334, 356–380.
       Born c. 1845; interviewed, c. 1920. Havasupai.

463-M SOLOMON, MADELINE. Kurt Madison and Yvonne Yarber. *Madeline Solomon*. Surrey, B.C.: Hancock House, 1981. 98 pp.
       Born, 1905; narrated, 1978. Athabaskan. For the other volumes in this series and the details of the collaboration, see no. 31-R. Solomon recalls a full and various life. She tells about hunting— bear, caribou, moose, muskrats—and about the fishing which is such an important part of the rural economy for these northern Indians. Like the other autobiographers in this series, she also has a good deal to say about native crafts. But she talks about human relations as well, her two husbands, her doctoring, and her children.

463-T The Son of Former Many Beads. See no. 217-M.

469   STANDING BEAR, LUTHER. E. A. Brinninstool. *My People the Sioux*, with an introduction by Richard N. Ellis. Lincoln: Univ. of Nebraska Press, 1975 [1928]. xx + 288 pp.
       1863 (1868?)–1939; wrote, c. 1928. Oglala Sioux.

471   ———. *My Indian Boyhood*. New York: Houghton Mifflin, 1931. 190 pp.

472   STANDS IN TIMBER, JOHN. Margot Liberty. *Cheyenne Memories*. Lincoln: Univ. of Nebraska Press.
       1884–1967; collaborated, 1956–1967. Cheyenne. Autobiographical passages are scattered throughout this book, but there is a brief autobiography proper, pp. 286–301.

480   Sword. J. R. WALKER. An unfinished autobiography is to be found in Walker, *The Sun Dance and Other Ceremonies of the Oglala*

Division of the Teton Sioux. Anthropological Papers of the American Museum of Natural History, 17, pt. 2 (1917):159.

Born, probably before 1865; wrote, probably before 1910. Oglala Sioux.

483   Talayesva, Don. LEO W. SIMMONS. *Sun Chief: The Autobiography of a Hopi Indian*. New Haven: Yale Univ. Press, 1974 [1942]. xx + 460 pp.

Born, 1890; collaborated, 1938–1941. Hopi.

483-M Tallmountain, Mary. BRIAN SWANN and ARNOLD KRUPAT. "Yes You Can Go Home: A Sequence," in the book cited in no. 8-M.

Born, 1918; wrote, 1985. Koyukon Athabaskan. For information about the collaboration and a list of the other Indian authors whose autobiographies are collected in this book, see n. 8-M. Tallmountain is a poet, author of a book of poems entitled *There Is No Word for Goodbye* (Marvin, S. D.: Blue Cloud Quarterly Press, 1982). This is autobiography after the fashion of Momaday and Silko: discontinuous narrative, mixing personal reminiscences with tribal history. Tallmountain links her own past—with her moves to Alaska, Arizona, New Mexico, California—to the nomadic past of her own people.

Tens, Isaac. MARIUS BARBEAU. "The Career of a Medicine Man, According to Isaac Tens, a Gitksan," as found in Barbeau, *Medicine Men of the Pacific Coast, National Museums of Canada*, Bul. 152, Anthropological Series, no. 42 (1958):39–55. Excerpts reprinted in Joan Halifax, *Shamanic Voices*, New York: Dutton, 1979:183–191.

Born, probably c. 1880. Interviewed, probably 1954. Gitksan.

490-M Thlaamahuus, Dick. EDWARD SAPIR and MORRIS SWADESH. "Gift Visit to the Nitinats," "Puberty Potlatch for Dick Thlaamahuus's Daughter," as found in the first book cited in no. 436–M, pp. 131–219, 230–253.

Born, probably c. 1870; narrated, 1922. Nootka. For the details of the collaboration, see no. 436-M. Both of these narratives are quite interesting. In the former Thlaamahuus describes praying naked in the snow and surf for four nights that he might prevail in the *Slahal* (a gambling guessing game) during the visit. The visit, and the extraordinary tensions of the game, are described in some detail.

492   THRASHER, ANTHONY APAKARK. Gerard Deagle and Alan
         Mettrick. *Thrasher . . . Skid Row Eskimo.* Toronto: Griffin House,
         1976. xii + 164 pp.
              Born, 1937; wrote, c. 1970–1975. Eskimo.

493   Three Suns (Big Nose [M]). JAMES WILLARD SCHULTZ.
         "Battle on Sun River" and "Three Suns' War Record," in the
         book cited in no. 31:252–270.
              C. 1823–1896; narrated, probably in the 1880s. Piegan.

497-M   TOBUK, FRANK. Kurt Madison and Yvonne Yarber. *Frank
         Tobuk.* Surrey, B.C.: Hancock House, 1980. 64 pp.
              Born, 1900; narrated, 1978. Athabaskan. For the other volumes
         in this series and for the details of the collaboration, see no. 31-R.
         Like all of the autobiographers in this series, Tobuk grew up with
         an awareness of cultural differences. Tobuk's parents were
         Athabaskan, but he also learned a good deal from his Eskimo
         neighbors, and then there were the whites as well, represented in
         his youth by the people at the nearby mission. His life, as he
         remembers it for us, has been full of hunting, trapping, family,
         and hard work.

504   Tubbee, Okah. Daniel Littlefield is preparing a new edition of
         Tubbee's *A Thrilling Sketch of the Life of the Distinguished Chief Okah
         Tubbee.* I cite two editions in the *Bibliography;* Littlefield (personal
         communication) assures me that there are others as well.
         Littlefield has also determined that Tubbee was not really, as he
         claimed, a Choctaw. He was, evidently, "passing" as an Indian
         in order to escape slavery.

506   Two Leggings. PETER NABOKOV. *Two Leggings: The Making of
         a Crow Warrior.* New York: Crowell, 1967. xxv + 226 pp.
              C. 1847–1923; interviewed, beginning in 1919. Crow.

512-M   Vizenor, Gerald. BRIAN SWANN and ARNOLD KRUPAT.
         "Crows Written on the Poplars: Autocritical Autobiographies," in
         the book cited in no. 8-M.
              Born, 1934; wrote, 1985. Ojibwa mixedblood. For information
         about the collaboration and a list of the other Indian authors
         whose autobiographies are collected in this book, see no. 8-M.
         Vizenor has written poems, essays, short fiction, a novel, and a
         screenplay. (For a bibliography of his work, see Ruoff, 1985.) This

is very self-conscious autobiography indeed. Vizenor begins, for example, as follows:

> This is a mixedblood autobiographical causerie and a narrative on the slow death of a common red squirrel. The first and third person personas are me.
>
> Gerald Vizenor believes that autobiographies are imaginative histories . . . , wild pastimes over the pronouns.

And this autobiographical essay is even complete with references to Gertrude Stein and such theoreticians on matters autobiographical as Georges Gusdorf (1980), Avrom Fleishman (1983), and James Olney (1980).

513-M Wa-Hee-Nee. See nos. 319–321.

522 WHITE BULL, CHIEF JOSEPH. James H. Howard. *The Warrior Who Killed Custer: The Personal Narrative of Chief Joseph White Bull,* trans. and ed., James H. Howard. Lincoln: Univ. of Nebraska Press, 1968. xix + 84 pp.
Born, 1850; wrote 1931. Teton Sioux.

524 White Calf (M). RICHARD LANCASTER. *Piegan: A Look from Within at the Life, Times, and Legacy of an American Indian.* Garden City: Doubleday. 359 pp.
Born, 1857 [according to White Calf]; narrated, 1962. Piegan.

527 White Horse Eagle (M). EDGAR VON SCHMIDT-PAULI. *We Indians: The Passing of a Great Race.* New York: Dutton, 1931. 256 pp.
Born 1822 (according to White Horse Eagle's claim); collaborated, 1922. Osage.

531-M Whitewolf, Howard. "A Short Story of My Life," *American Indian Magazine,* 5 (January–March, 1917):29–31.
Born, c. 1866; wrote, c. 1917. Comanche. Whitewolf tells about his youth: "I can remember as a dream, that White Eagle said he had received a revelation from the Great Spirit that the white men's guns would have nothing but powder in them, and no bullets" (29). But for the most part this narrative has to do with his conversion to Christianity and his three years at Carlisle. He tells his story in such a way as to urge the importance of education and religion.

532   WHITEWOLF, JIM (pseudonym). Charles S. Brant. *Jim Whitewolf: The Life of a Kiowa-Apache Indian*. New York: Dover, 1969. xii + 144.
     C. 1878– c. 1955; narrated 1948–1949. Kiowa-Apache.

538-M Winnemucca, Sarah. See no. 230.

540   Wolf-chief (M). ROBERT H. LOWIE. A narrative is to be found in Lowie, "Sun Dance of the Shoshoni, Ute, and Hidatsa," *Anthropological Papers of the American Museum of Natural History*, 16, pt. 5 (1919):421–427.
     Born, 1849; interviewed, c. 1910. Hidatsa.

541   ———. GILBERT L. WILSON. *Hidatsa Horse and Dog Culture, Anthropological Papers of the American Museum of Natural History*, 15, no. 2 (1924):125–311.
     Interviewed, beginning in 1908.

542   ———. ———. *Hidatsa Eagle Trapping, Anthropological Papers of the American Museum of Natural History*, 30, no. 4 (1928):99–245.

542-M ———. See no. 31-M.

543-M Wolf Killer. WILLIAM JUSTIN HARSHA. *Ploughed Under: The Story of an Indian Chief, Told by Himself*. New York: 1881. 268 pp.
     The Bibliography cites this book because it has elsewhere been listed as autobiography, while in fact it is fiction. But since Harsha's name does not appear on the title page, and since the book can so easily be mistaken for autobiography, I should have included a reference to the (fictional) narrator's name, Wolf Killer.

547   YAVA, ALBERT. Harold Courlander. *Big Falling Snow: A Tewa-Hopi Indian's Life and Times and the History of His People*. New York: Crown, 1978. xiv + 178 pp.
     Born, 1888; interviewed, 1969–1971. Tewa-Hopi.

554   Yellow Wolf. LUCULLUS VIRGIL McWHORTER. *Yellow Wolf: His Own Story*. Caldwell, Idaho: Caxton, 1983 [1940]. 324 pp.
     Born, 1855; collaborated, 1908–1935. Nez Perce.

562   Zitkala-Sa (Gertrude Bonnin). *American Indian Stories*. Glorieta,
        New Mexico: Rio Grande Press, 1976 [1921]. 107 pp.
            1875–1938; wrote, c. 1899–1902. Sioux.

563-M   Unknown (M). RUTH BENEDICT. "Buffalo Hunting on the
        Plains," as found in *Tales of the Cochiti Indians, Smithsonian Institution
        Bureau of American Ethnography*, Bul. 98 (1931):197–200.
            Born, probably c. 1865; narrated, late 1920s. Cochiti Pueblo.
        This is one of the eight informants Boas and Benedict worked with
        at Cochiti. Benedict here publishes a translation of an oral narra-
        tive. It turns out to be one of the very good hunting stories.

569   Unknown (F). TRUMAN MICHELSON. "The Autobiography
        of a Fox Indian Woman." *40th Annual Report of the Bureau of American
        Ethnology to the Secretary of the Smithsonian Institution, 1918–1919*,
        Washington, D.C., 1905:291–349.
            Born, probably before 1870; narrated, 1918. Fox.

577   Unknown (M). LESLIE WHITE. "Autobiography of an Acoma
        Indian," in White, *New Material from Acoma, Smithsonian Institution,
        Bureau of Anthropology*, Bul. no. 32 (1943), 326–337.
            Born, 1868; interviewed, 1941. Acoma Pueblo.

Notes to the Autobiographies

1. William Sturtevant (personal communication) assures me that the *Journal* was written in 1792, and not 1791, as Coates asserts.

2. This birth date comes from Gilbert L. Wilson (1924:131); Bowers provides a c. 1858 birth date, but this is almost certainly wrong.

3. "I am told that I was born . . . at the time when some of the Navahos went to live among the Chiricahuas. . . . When I was two years old, The People started moving back from Fort Sumner" (2).

4. My sense of the lines of influence here comes from personal communication with Bill Pfisterer, Ron Scollen, and Ray Barnhardt, all of whom are active (along with Yarber and Madison) in setting down native-Alaskan oral traditions, especially for use in the schools.

Bibliography
of Other Sources Cited

Adams, Henry (1961 [1918]). *The Education of Henry Adams*. New York: Scribner.

Bataille, Gretchen, and Kathleen Sands (1984). *American Indian Women: Telling their Lives*. Lincoln: Univ. of Nebraska Press.

Bedford, Denton R. (1974). "Lone Walker, the Small Robe Chief." *The Indian Historian*, 7:41–54.

Benton, J. F. (1982). "Consciousness of the Self and Perceptions of Individuality." In R. L. Benton et al., *Renaissance and Renewal in the 12th Century*. Cambridge: Harvard Univ. Press.

Berthoff, Warner (1971). "Witness and Testament: Two Contemporary Classics." *New Literary History*, 2:311–327.

Bierhorst, John (1971). *In the Trail of the Wind: American Indian Poems and Ritual Orations*. New York: Farrar, Straus and Giroux.

Boas, Franz (1930). *The Religion of the Kwakiutl Indians*, pt. 2, translations. Columbia University Contributions to Anthropology, 10. New York: Columbia Univ. Press.

———— (1943). "Recent Anthropology." *Science* 98:311–314, 334–337.

Brumble, H. David, III (1981). *An Annotated Bibliography of American Indian and Eskimo Autobiographies*. Lincoln: Univ. of Nebraska Press.

———— (1981b). "Reasoning Together." *Canadian Review of American Studies*, 12:260–270; reprinted in Swann (1983):353–364.

———— (1983). "Indian Sacred Materials: Kroeber, Kroeber, Waters, and Momaday." In Swann (1983):283–300.

———— (1985a). "Sam Blowsnake's Confessions: *Crashing Thunder* and the History of American Indian Autobiography." *Canadian Review of American Studies*, 16:271–282; reprinted in Swann and Krupat (1987).

———— (1985b). "The Two Albert Hensley Autobiographies and the History of American Indian Autobiography." *American Quarterly*, 37:702–718.

———— (1986), "*Sun Chief* and Gregorio's 'Life Story': Social Scientists and American Indian Autobiographers." *Journal of American Studies*, 20:273–289.

Bruss, Elizabeth (1976). *Autobiographical Acts: The Changing Situation of a Literary Genre*. Baltimore: Johns Hopkins Univ. Press.

Budge, E. A. Wallis (1914). *The Literature of the Ancient Egyptians.* London: Dent.

Burgos-Debray, Elizabeth (1984). See Rigoberta Menchu.

Butterfield, Herbert (1981). *The Origins of History.* New York: Basic Books.

Canfield, Gae Whitney (1983). *Sarah Winnemucca of the Northern Paiutes.* Norman: Univ. of Oklahoma.

Carnegie, Andrew (1889). "Wealth." *North American Review* 148:653–664.

Carrithers, Michael, Steven Collins, and Steven Lukes (1985). *The Category of the Person: Anthropology, Philosophy, History.* Cambridge: Cambridge Univ. Press.

Castro, Michael (1979). "Poetic License in Neihardt's *Black Elk Speaks.*" A paper presented at a special session of the Modern Language Association devoted to American Indian autobiography. This material was later incorporated into the following:

———— (1983). *Interpreting the Indian: Twentieth-Century Poets and the Native American.* Albuquerque: Univ. of New Mexico Press.

Clements, William (1986). *Native American Folklore in Nineteenth-Century Periodicals.* Athens, Ohio: Swallow.

Cook-Lynn, Elizabeth (1985). "Survival, in Hexasyllables." *Wicazo Sa,* 1: 49–52.

Crapanzano, Vincent (1969). *The Fifth World of Enoch Maloney: Portrait of a Navaho.* New York: Random.

———— (1972). *The Fifth World of Forster Bennett: A Portrait of a Navaho.* New York: Viking.

———— (1977). "The Life History in Anthropological Field Work." *Anthropology and Humanism Quarterly,* 2:3–7.

———— (1980). *Tuhami: Portrait of a Moroccan.* Chicago: Univ. of Chicago Press.

———— (1987). "Editorial." *Cultural Anthropology,* 2:179–189.

Crews, Frederick (1986). *Skeptical Engagements.* New York: Oxford.

Deloria, Vine, Jr. (1979). Introduction to John G. Neihardt, *Black Elk Speaks.* Lincoln: Univ. of Nebraska Press.

DeMallie, Raymond (1984a). *The Sixth Grandfather: Black Elk's Teachings Given to John G. Neihardt.* Lincoln: Univ. of Nebraska Press.

———— (1984b). Foreword to Stanley Vestal, *Warpath: The True Story of the Fighting Sioux Told in a Biography of Chief White Bull.* Lincoln: Univ. of Nebraska Press.

Denig, E. T. (1928). *Indian Tribes of the Upper Missouri. Annual Report of the Bureau of American Ethnology,* 46.

Dickason, David H. (1961). "Chief Simon Pokagon: 'The Indian Longfellow.'" *Indiana Magazine of History,* 52:127–140.

Dixon, Joseph Kossuth (1913). *The Vanishing Race: The Last Great Indian Council*, with photographs by Rodman Wanamaker. Garden City: Doubleday.

Dollard, John (1935). *Criteria for the Life History*. New Haven: Yale Univ. Press.

Dorsey, George A., and H. R. Voth (1901). *The Oraibi Soyal Ceremony. Field Museum of Natural History Publication 55, Anthropological Series* 3, no. 1.

Du Bois, Cora (1960 [1944]). *The People of Alor: A Social-Psychological Study of an East Indian Island*. Cambridge: Harvard Univ. Press.

Dumont, Louis (1985). "A Modified View of Our Origins: The Christian Beginnings of Modern Individualism." In Carrithers et al. (1985):93–122.

Dundes, Alan (1964). *The Morphology of North American Folktales*. Helsinki: Suomalainen Tiedeakatemia.

Eakin, Paul John (1980). "Malcolm X and the Limits of Autobiography." In Olney (1980), pp. 181–194.

Eastman, Elaine Goodale (1978). *Sister to the Sioux: The Memoirs of Elaine Goodale Eastman, 1885–91*, ed. Kay Graber. Lincoln: Univ. of Nebraska Press.

Eliade, Mircea (1974 [1964]). *Shamanism*, trans. Willard Trask. Princeton: Bollingen Series.

Ellis, John M. (1974). *The Theory of Literary Criticism: A Logical Analysis*. Berkeley, Los Angeles, London: Univ. of California Press.

Evers, Lawrence J. (1977). "Words and Place: A Reading of *House Made of Dawn*." *Western American Literature,* 11:297–320.

Fabrega, Horacio, Jr., and Juan Mezzich (1987). "Adjustment Disorder and Psychiatric Practice: Cultural and Historical Aspects." *Psychiatry,* 50:31–49.

Fish, Joseph (1982). *Old Light on Separate Ways: The Narragansett Diary of Joseph Fish 1765–1776*, eds. William S. Simmons and Cheryl L. Simmons. Hanover: New England Univ. Press.

Fleishman, Avrom (1983). *Figures of Autobiography*. Berkeley, Los Angeles, London: Univ. of California Press.

Fowler, Catherine S. (1978). "Sarah Winnemucca, Northern Paiute, ca. 1844–1891." In Liberty (1978):33–44.

Frake, Charles O. (1983). "Did Literacy Cause the Great Divide?" *American Ethnologist,* 10:368–371.

Fredrickson, George M. (1971). *The Black Image in the White Mind: The Debate on Afro-American Character and Destiny: 1817–1914*. New York: Harper & Row.

Geertz, Clifford (1984). "From the Native's Point of View: On the Nature of Anthropological Understanding." In Richard Shweder and Robert Levine, *Culture Theory: Essays in Mind, Self, and Emotion*. Cambridge: Cambridge Univ. Press.

Goddard, Pliny Earle (1915). *Sarsi Texts. University of California Publications in American Archeology and Ethnology*, 11, no. 3.

———— (1919*a*). "Notes on the Sun Dance of the Sarsi." *Anthropological Papers of the American Museum of Natural History*, 16:271–282.

———— (1919*b*). "Notes on the Sun Dance of the Cree in Alberta." *Anthropological Papers of the American Museum of Natural History*, 16:295–310.

Goodwin, Grenville (1969 [1942]). *The Social Organization of the Western Apache*. Tucson: Univ. of Arizona Press.

Goody, Jack (1977). *The Domestication of the Savage Mind*. Cambridge: Cambridge Univ. Press.

————, and Ian Watt (1963). "The Consequences of Literacy." *Comparative Studies in History and Society*, 5:304–345.

Gould, Steven J. (1980). *The Panda's Thumb: More Reflections in Natural History*. New York: Norton.

Grinnell, George Bird (1960 [1910]). "Coup and Scalp Among the Plains Indians." In Frederica de Laguna, *Selected Papers From the American Anthropologist 1888–1920*. Evanston: Univ. of Illinois Press, 650–664.

———— (1960). *Blackfoot Lodge Tales: The Story of a Prairie People*. Lincoln: Univ. of Nebraska Press.

———— (1962 [1926]). *By Cheyenne Campfires*. Lincoln: Univ. of Nebraska Press.

Haley, Alex (1973). *The Autobiography of Malcolm X*. New York.

Halifax, Joan (1979). *Shamanic Voices*. New York: Dutton.

Harjo, Joy (1985). "The Woman Hanging from the Thirteenth Floor Window." *Wicazo Sa*. 1:38–40.

Harris, Marvin (1969). *The Rise of Anthropological Theory*. New York: Crowell.

Heller, T. C., et al. (1986). *Reconstructing Individualism*. Palo Alto: Stanford Univ. Press.

Hertzberg, Hazel (1981 [1971]). *The Search for an American Indian Identity: Modern Pan-Indian Movements*. Syracuse: Syracuse Univ. Press.

Hirschfelder, Arlene (1973). *American Indian and Eskimo Authors*. New York: Association on American Indian Affairs.

Hodge, William (1976). *A Bibliography of Contemporary North American Indians*. New York: Interland, Inc.

Hoebel, E. Adamson (1940). *The Political Organization and Law Ways of the Commanche Indians. American Anthropological Memoir*, 54.

———— (1978 [1960]). *The Cheyennes: Indians of the Great Plains*. New York: Holt.

Hofstadter, Richard (1969). *Social Darwinism in American Thought.* New York: Braziller.

Holler, Clyde (1984). "Lakota Religion and Tragedy: The Theology of *Black Elk Speaks.*" *Journal of the Academy of Religion,* 52:19–45.

Holly, Carol T. (1979). "*Black Elk Speaks* and the Making of Indian Autobiography." *Genre,* 12:117–136.

Horse Capture, George (1980). *The Seven Visions of Bull Lodge, as Told by His Daughter, Garter Snake.* Ann Arbor: Bear Claw Press.

Horton, Robin (1982). "Tradition and Modernity Revisited." In Martin Hollis and Steven Lukes, *Rationality and Relativism,* Cambridge: MIT Press, 201–260.

Hountondji, Paulin (1983 [1976]). *African Philosophy.* Paris: Bloomington: Univ. of Indiana Press.

Hultkrantz, Ake (1979). *The Religions of the American Indians,* trans. Monica Setterwall. Berkeley, Los Angeles, London: Univ. of California Press.

Hymes, Dell (1977). "Discovering Oral Performance and Measured Verse in American Indian Narrative." *New Literary History,* 8:431–457.

——— (1981). *In Vain I Tried to Tell You.* Philadelphia: Univ. of Pennsylvania.

Johnson, Broderick (1977). *Stories of Traditional Navajo Life and Culture, by Twenty-Two Navajo Men and Women.* Tsaile, Arizona: Navajo Community College Press.

Kluckhohn, Clyde (1943). Review of *Sun Chief. American Anthropologist,* 45: 267–270.

——— (1944). "The Influence of Psychiatry upon Anthropology in America During the Last One Hundred Years." In *Centennial History of American Psychiatry,* New York: Columbia Univ. Press.

——— (1945). "The Personal Document in Anthropological Science." In Louis Gottschalk et al., *The Use of Personal Documents in History, Anthropology, and Sociology.* Social Science Research Bulletin, no. 54:77–173.

Kroeber, Theodora (1970). *Alfred Kroeber: A Personal Configuration.* Berkeley, Los Angeles, London: Univ. of California Press.

——— (1971 [1961]). *Ishi in Two Worlds.* Berkeley and Los Angeles: Univ. of California Press.

——— (1973 [1964]). *Ishi, Last of His Tribe.* New York: Bantam.

Krupat, Arnold (1983). Introduction and afterword to Paul Radin, *Crashing Thunder.* Lincoln: Univ. of Nebraska Press.

——— (1985). *For Those Who Come After: A Study of American Indian Autobiography.* Berkeley, Los Angeles, London: Univ. of California Press.

——— (1987*a*). See Swann (1987*a*).

——— (1987*b*). See Swann (1987*b*).

La Barre, Weston (1971 [1959]). *The Peyote Cult.* New York: Schocken.

Laird, Carobeth (1975). *Encounter with an Angry God: Recollections of My Life with John Peabody Harrington*. Banning, Cal.: Malki Museum Press.

Lakoff, G., and M. Johnson (1980). *Metaphors We Live By*. Chicago: Univ. of Chicago Press.

Lancaster, Richard (1966). *Piegan: A Look from within at the Life, Times, and Legacy of an American Indian*. Garden City: Doubleday.

Langness, L. L. (1965). *The Life History in Anthropological Science*. New York: Holt.

———, and Gelya Frank (1981). *Lives: An Anthropological Approach to Biography*. Novato, Cal.: Chandler and Sharp.

Larson, Charles R. (1978). *American Indian Fiction*. Albuquerque: Univ. of New Mexico Press.

Leighton, Alexander H. and Dorothea Leighton (1944). *The Navaho Door: An Introduction to Navaho Life*. Cambridge: Harvard Univ. Press.

——— (1949). *Gregorio, The Hand-Trembler: A Psychobiological Personality Study of a Navaho Indian*. Papers of the Peabody Museum of American Archaeology and Ethnology, 40, no. 1.

Lejeune, Philippe (1975). *Le pacte autobiographique*. Paris: Editions du Seuil.

Lévi-Strauss, Claude (1943). Review of *Sun Chief*. *Social Research* 10:515–516.

——— (1963). *Structural Anthropology*. New York: Basic Books.

——— (1982). *The Way of the Masks*. Seattle: Univ. of Washington Press.

Libby, O. G. (1973 [1920]). *The Arikara Narrative of the Campaign against the Hostile Dakotas, June 1876*. New York: Sol Lewis.

Liberty, Margot (1978). *American Indian Intellectuals*. St. Paul: West Publishing Co.

Lincoln, Kenneth (1983). *Native American Renaissance*. Berkeley, Los Angeles, London: Univ. of California Press.

Llewellyn, K. N., and E. Adamson Hoebel (1967 [1941]). *The Cheyenne Way: Conflict and Case Law in Primitive Jurisprudence*. Norman: Univ. of Oklahoma Press.

Lord, Albert B. (1981 [1960]). *The Singer of Tales*. Cambridge: Harvard Univ. Press.

Louch, Alfred (1986). "Critical Discussion": a review of Michael Fischer, *Does Deconstruction Make a Difference? Post-structuralism and the Defense of Poetry in Modern Criticism*. Bloomington: Indiana Univ. Press (1985). In *Philosophy and Literature*, 10:325–333.

Lowie, Robert H. (1915). "The Sun Dance of the Crow Indians." *Anthropological Papers of the American Museum of Natural History*, 16:1–50.

——— (1959). *Robert H. Lowie, Ethnologist: A Personal Record*. Berkeley and Los Angeles: Univ. of California Press.

Lurie, Nancy Oestreich (1966). "Women in Early American Anthropology." In June Helm, *Pioneers of American Anthropology: The Uses of Biography,* Seattle: Univ. of Washington: 31–81.

Mandel, Barrett J. (1968). "The Autobiographer's Art." *Journal of Aesthetics and Art Criticism* 27:215–226.

——— (1972). "The Didactic Achievement of Malcolm X's Autobiography." *Afro-American Studies,* 2:269–274.

Mandelbaum, David G. (1934). *The Plains Cree. Anthropological Papers of the American Museum of Natural History,* 37, pt. 2.

——— (1973). "The Study of Life History: Gandhi." *Current Anthropology,* 14:177–196.

Mauss, Marcel (1938). "A Category of the Human Mind: The Notion of Person; the Notion of Self," trans. W. D. Halls. In Carrithers et al., 1985:1–25.

McCallister, Mick (1978). "The Topology of Remembrance in *The Way to Rainy Mountain.*" *Denver Quarterly,* 12:19–31.

McClusky, Sally (1972). "*Black Elk Speaks,* and So Does John Neihardt." *Western American Literature* 6:231–242.

Melody, Michael Edwards (1977). *The Apaches: A Critical Bibliography.* Bloomington: Indiana Univ. Press.

Menchu, Rigoberta (1984). *I . . . Rigoberta Menchu: An Indian Woman in Guatemala,* ed. Elizabeth Burgos-Debray, trans. Ann Wright. London: Verso.

Miller, David Reed (1978). "Charles Alexander Eastman, The 'Winner,' From Deep Woods to Civilization." In Liberty (1978):61–74.

Miller, J. Hillis (1975). "Deconstructing the Deconstructors." *Diacritics,* 5:24–31.

Miller, Ross (1972). "Autobiography as Fact and Fiction: Franklin, Adams, Malcolm X." *Centennial Review,* 16:221–232.

Misch, Georg (1911). "Von den Gestaltungen der Persönlichkeit." *Weltanschauung: Philosophie und Religion in Darstellungen,* ed. Max Frischeisen-Köhler. Berlin: Reichl, pp. 79–126.

——— (1951). *A History of Autobiography in Antiquity,* 2 vols. Cambridge: Harvard Univ. Press.

Mischel, Theodore (1977). *The Self: Psychological and Philosophical Issues.* Oxford: Basil Blackwell.

Mishkin, Bernard (1940). *Rank and Warfare among the Plains Indians. Monographs of the American Ethnological Society,* vol. 3.

Momaday, N. Scott (1966). *House Made of Dawn.* New York: Harper and Row.

——— (1970). "The Man Made of Words." Rpt. in Abraham Chapman, ed., *Literature of the American Indians*. New York: NAL, 1975:96–110.

———— (1976*a*). "Kiowa Legends from *The Journey of Tai-me.*" *Sun Tracks: An American Indian Literary Magazine*, 3, no. 1:6–8.

———— (1976*b*), "Oral Tradition and the American Indian." In John R. Maestas, ed., *Contemporary Native American Address*. Provo, Utah: Brigham Young Univ. Press.

Mooney, James (1979 [1898]). *Calendar History of the Kiowa Indians,* with an introduction by John C. Ewers. Washington: Smithsonian.

Morgan, Lewis Henry (1964 [1877]). *Ancient Society,* ed. and introduction by Leslie White. Cambridge: Harvard Univ. Press.

Naipaul, V. S. (1981). *Among the Believers: An Islamic Journey*. New York: Knopf.

Nash, Dennison, and Ronald Wintrob (1972). "The Emergence of Self-consciousness in Ethnography." *Current Anthropology*, 13:527–542.

Nichols, William (1983). "Black Elk's Truth." In Swann (1983):334–343.

O'Brien, Lynn Woods (1973). *Plains Indian Autobiographies*. Boise, Idaho: Western Writers Series, no. 10.

Ohmann, Carol (1970). "*The Autobiography of Malcolm X:* A Revolutionary Use of the Franklin Tradition." *American Quarterly*, 22:131–149.

Olney, James (1980). *Autobiography: Essays Theoretical and Critical*. Princeton: Princeton Univ. Press.

Olson, Paul A. (1982). "*Black Elk Speaks* as Epic and Ritual Attempt to Reverse History." In Virginia Faulkner and Frederick C. Luebke, *Vision and Refuge: Essays on the Literature of the Great Plains,* Lincoln: Univ. of Nebraska Press, 3–30.

Ortiz, Simon J. (1985). "That's the Place Indians Talk about." *Wicazo Sa*, 1:45–49.

Overholt, Thomas W. (1978). "Short Bull, Black Elk, Sword, and 'The Meaning' of the Ghost Dance." *Religion*, 8:171–195.

Parker, Arthur C. (1919). *The Life of General Ely S. Parker*. Buffalo: Buffalo Historical Society.

Parsons, Elsie Clews (1967 [1922]). *American Indian Life*. Lincoln: Univ. of Nebraska Press.

Pascal, Roy (1960). *Design and Truth in Autobiography*. Cambridge: Harvard Univ. Press.

Pearce, Roy Harvey (1965). *Savagism and Civilization: A Study of the Indian and the American Mind*. Baltimore: Johns Hopkins Univ. Press.

Peyer, Bernd (1982). "Samson Occom: Mohegan Missionary and Writer of the 18th Century." *American Indian Quarterly*, 6:208–217.

Radin, Paul (1970 [1923]). *The Winnebago Tribe*. Lincoln: Univ. of Nebraska Press.

———— (1983 [1926]). *Crashing Thunder,* with a foreword and appendix by Arnold Krupat. Lincoln: Univ. of Nebraska Press.

———— (1948). *Winnebago Hero Cycles*. Baltimore: Waverly Press.

———— (1949). *The Culture of the Winnebago: As Described by Themselves*. Indiana Univ. *Publications in Anthropology and Linguistics*, no. 2.

Raju, P. T., and A. Castell (1968). *East-West Studies on the Problem of the Self*. The Hague: Martinus Nijhoff.

Rasmussen, Knud (1930). *The Intellectual Culture of the Iglulik Eskimos*, vol. 7, no. 2, of *The Report of the Fifth Thule Expedition, 1921–24*. Copenhagen: Gyldendalske Boghandel.

Reichard, Gladys (1974 [1950]). *Navajo Religion: A Study of Symbolism*. Princeton: Princeton Univ. Press.

Revard, Carter (1980). "History, Myth, and Identity Among Osages and Other Peoples." *Denver Quarterly*, 14:84–97.

Rice, Julian (1985). "*Akicita* of the Thunder: Horses in Black Elk's Vision." *Melus*, 12:5–24.

Rohner, Ronald P. (1969). *The Ethnography of Franz Boas: Letters and Diaries of Franz Boas, Written on the Northwest Coast from 1886 to 1931*. Chicago: Univ. of Chicago Press.

Rosen, L. (1985). "Intentionality and the Concept of the Person." In J. R. Pennock and J. W. Chapman, *Criminal Justice*, New York: New York Univ. Press.

Ruoff, A. LaVonne (1985). "Gerald Vizenor: A Selected Bibliography." *American Indian Quarterly*, 9:75–78.

———— (forthcoming). "Nineteenth-Century American Indian Autobiographers: William Apes, George Copway, and Sarah Winnemucca." In Jerry Ward, ed., *The New American Literary History*, New York: MLA.

Sanchez, Thomas (1972). *Rabbit Boss*. New York: Knopf.

Saturday Review of Literature (May 16, 1942). Review of *Sun Chief*.

Sayre, Robert F. (1971). "Vision and Experience in *Black Elk Speaks*." *College English*, 32:509–535.

Schubnell, Matthias (1985). *N. Scott Momaday: The Cultural and Literary Background*. Norman: Univ. of Oklahoma Press.

Schultz, James Willard (n.d. [1907]). *My Life as an Indian*. Greenwich, Conn.: Fawcett.

———— (1923). *Friends of My Life as an Indian*. Boston: Houghton Mifflin.

———— (1962). *Blackfeet and Buffalo: Memories of Life among the Indians*, ed. Keith Seele. Norman: Univ. of Oklahoma.

———— (1974). *Why Gone Those Time? Blackfoot Tales by James Willard Schultz*, ed., Eugene Lee Silliman. Norman: Univ. of Oklahoma Press.

Schultz, Jessie Donaldson (1960). "Adventuresome, Amazing Apikuni." *Montana: The Magazine of Western History*, 10:2–18.

Scollon, Ronald, and Suzanne Scollon (1979). *Linguistic Convergence: An Ethnography of Speaking at Fort Chipewyan, Alberta*. New York: Academic Press.

——— (1981). *Narrative, Literacy and Face in Interethnic Communication.* Norwood, N.J.: ABLEX.

Scribner, Sylvia, and Michael Cole (1981). *The Psychology of Literacy.* Cambridge: Cambridge Univ. Press.

Seele, Keith (1962). See Schultz (1962).

Shea, Daniel B., Jr. (1968). *Spiritual Autobiography in Early America.* Princeton: Princeton Univ. Press.

Simmons, William S., and Cheryl L. Simmons (1982). See Joseph Fish.

Skinner, Alanson (1919). "Notes on the Sun Dance of the Sisseton Dakota." *Anthropological Papers of the American Museum of Natural History,* 16, pt. 4:381–385.

Smith, Marian W. (1938). "The War Complex of the Plains Indians." *Proceedings of the American Philosophical Society,* 78, no. 3:425–464.

——— (1951). "American Indian Warfare." *Transactions of the New York Academy of Sciences,* 13:348–365.

Smith, William F. (1975). "American Indian Autobiographies." *American Indian Quarterly,* 2:237–245.

Spencer, Herbert (1897 [1876–1896]). *Principles of Sociology,* 3 vols. New York: Appleton.

Spier, Leslie (1928). *Havasupai Ethnography, Anthropological Papers of the American Museum of Natural History,* 29, pt. 3.

Stanton, William (1960). *The Leopard's Spots: Scientific Attitudes Toward Race in the United States.* Chicago: Univ. of Chicago Press.

Stevenson, Matilda Coxe (1904). *The Zuni Indians. Twenty-third Annual Report of the Bureau of American Ethnography, 1901–1902.* Washington, D.C.

Steward, Julian (1973). *Alfred L. Kroeber.* New York: Columbia Univ. Press.

Stone, Albert (1972). "Autobiography and American Culture." *American Studies: An International Newsletter,* 11:22–36.

Swann, Brian (1983). *Smoothing the Ground: Essays on Native American Oral Literature.* Berkeley, Los Angeles, London: Univ. of California Press.

——— and Arnold Krupat (1987*a*). *Recovering the Word: Essays on Native American Literature.* Berkeley, Los Angeles, London: Univ. of California Press.

——— (1987*b*). *I Tell You Now: Autobiographical Essays by Native American Writers.* Lincoln: Univ. of Nebraska Press.

Tedlock, Dennis (1972). *Finding the Center: Narrative Poetry of the Zuni Indians.* New York: Dial.

——— (1977). "Toward an Oral Poetics." *New Literary History,* 8:507–519.

——— (1983). *The Spoken Word and the Work of Interpretation.* Philadelphia: Univ. of Pennsylvania Press.

Theisz, R. D. (1981). "The Critical Collaboration: An Approach to the

Study of Native American Bi-autobiography." *American Indian Research and Culture,* 5:65–80.

Tooker, Elisabeth (1978). "Ely S. Parker, Seneca, ca. 1828–1895." In Liberty (1978):14–30.

Ullman, W. (1967). *The Individual and Society in the Middle Ages.* Baltimore: Johns Hopkins Univ. Press.

Underhill, Ruth (1971). Foreword to Nancy O. Lurie, *Mountain Wolf Woman, Sister of Crashing Thunder.* Ann Arbor: Univ. of Michigan Press.

Velie, Alan (1982). *Four American Indian Literary Masters: N. Scott Momaday, James Welch, Leslie Marmon Silko, and Gerald Vizenor.* Norman: Univ. of Oklahoma Press.

Vestal, Stanley (1984 [1934]). *Warpath: The True Story of the Fighting Sioux Told in a Biography of Chief White Bull,* with a foreword by Raymond J. DeMallie. Lincoln: Univ. of Nebraska Press.

———— (1957). "The Man Who Killed Custer." *American Heritage,* 8:4–9, 90–91.

von Schmidt-Pauli, Edgar (1933*a*). *Hitlers Kampf um die Macht.* Berlin: Georg Stilke.

———— (1933*b*). *Adolf Hitler: Ein Weg aus eigner Kraft.* Berlin: Verlag Deutsches Volksbuch.

Walker, J. R. (1917). *The Sun Dance and Other Ceremonies of the Oglala Division of the Teton Sioux. Anthropological Papers of the American Museum of Natural History,* 17, pt. 2:53–221.

Wallis, W. D. (1919). *The Sun Dance of the Canadian Dakota. Anthropological Papers of the American Museum of Natural History,* 16:318–380.

Waters, Frank (1970 [1942]). *The Man Who Killed the Deer.* Chicago: Swallow.

Watson, Lawrence C., and Maria-Barbara Watson-Franke (1985). *Interpreting Life Histories: An Anthropological Inquiry.* New Brunswick: Rutgers Univ. Press.

Weintraub, Karl J. (1975) "Autobiography and Historical Consciousness." *Critical Inquiry,* 1:821–848.

———— (1978). *The Value of the Individual: Self and Circumstance in Autobiography.* Chicago: Univ. of Chicago Press.

White, Leslie (1943). "Autobiography of an Acoma Indian." In *New Material from Acoma, Smithsonian Institution, Bureau of Anthropology,* Bull. no. 32 (1943), 326–337.

Wildschut, William (1959). *Crow Indian Bead Work,* ed. John C. Ewers. New York: Museum of the American Indian, Heye Foundation.

———— (1960). *Crow Indian Medicine Bundles,* ed. John C. Ewers. New York: Museum of the American Indian, Heye Foundation.

Wilson, Gilbert L. (1924). *Hidatsa Horse and Dog Culture. Anthropological*

Papers of the American Museum of Natural History, 15, no. 2:125–311.
Wilson, Raymond (1983). *Ohiyesa: Charles Eastman, Santee Sioux.* Urbana: Univ. of Illinois Press.
Wissler, Clark (1918). *The Sun Dance of the Blackfoot Indians. Anthropological Papers of the American Museum of Natural History,* 16, pt. 3:225–270.
Wong, David B. (1985). "Anthropology and the Identity of the Person." A paper presented at the Divisional Meeting of the American Philosophical Association, Washington, D.C.
Yoors, Jan (1983 [1967]). *The Gypsies.* New York: Simon and Schuster.

Index

INDEX OF INDIANS AND ESKIMOS

GENERAL INDEX

Designer: U.C. Press Staff
Compositor: Janet Sheila Brown
Text: 11/13 Baskerville
Display: Baskerville
Printer: Braun-Brumfield, Inc.
Binder: Braun-Brumfield, Inc.